MR. BOSTON
OFFICIAL
BARTENDER'S
GUIDE

EDITED BY Anthony Giglio with Jim Meehan

PHOTOGRAPHY BY Ben Fink

JOHN WILEY & SONS, INC.

This book is printed on acid-free paper. ⊗

Copyright © 2009 by Barton Incorporated. All rights reserved
Color insert photography © 2009 by Ben Fink.

Design of a man's head and Boston are registered trademarks, and
Mr. Boston is a trademark of Barton Incorporated.

Published by John Wiley & Sons, Inc., Hoboken, New Jersey
Published simultaneously in Canada

No part of this publication may be reproduced, stored in a retrieval
system, or transmitted in any form or by any means, electronic, me-
chanical, photocopying, recording, scanning, or otherwise, except as
permitted under Section 107 or 108 of the 1976 United States Copyright
Act, without either the prior written permission of the Publisher, or
authorization through payment of the appropriate per-copy fee to the
Copyright Clearance Center, 222 Rosewood Drive, Danvers, MA 01923,
(978) 750–8400, fax (978) 750–4470, or on the web at www.copyright.
com. Requests to the Publisher for permission should be addressed to
the Permissions Department, John Wiley & Sons, Inc., 111 River Street,
Hoboken, NJ 07030, (201) 748–6011, fax (201) 748–6008, or on the web
at: http://www.wiley.com/go/permissions.

Limit of Liability/Disclaimer of Warranty: While the publisher and the
author have used their best efforts in preparing this book, they make no
representations or warranties with respect to the accuracy or complete-
ness of the contents of this book and specifically disclaim any implied
warranties of merchantability or fitness for a particular purpose. No
warranty may be created or extended by sales representatives or written
sales materials. The advice and strategies contained herein may not be
suitable for your situation. You should consult with a professional where
appropriate. Neither the publisher nor the author shall be liable for
any loss of profit or any other commercial damages, including but not
limited to special, incidental, consequential, or other damages.

For general information about our other products and services, please
contact our Customer Care Department within the United States at
(800) 762–2974, outside the United States at (317) 572–3993 or fax (317)
572–4002.

Wiley also publishes its books in a variety of electronic formats.
Some content that appears in print may not be available in electronic
books. For more information about Wiley products, visit our website
at www.wiley.com.

Cover design by Paul DiNovo
Interior design by Vertigo Design NYC
Composition by North Market Street Graphics

Library of Congress Cataloging-in-Publication Data
Mr. Boston : official bartender's guide / edited by Anthony Giglio with
Jim Meehan ; photography by Ben Fink. — [67th ed.]
      p.   cm.
  Includes index.
  ISBN 978-0-470-39065-8 (cloth : alk. paper)
  1. Bartending. 2. Cocktails. I. Giglio, Anthony. II. Meehan,
Jim. III. Title: Mister Boston : official bartender's guide.
  TX951.M7 2008
  641.8'74—dc22

                                        2008036191

Printed in China

10 9 8 7 6 5 4 3 2 1

CONTENTS

INTRODUCTION

Welcome!

YOU ARE HOLDING IN YOUR HANDS the 67th edition of the definitive guide to mixing perfect drinks. *Mr. Boston Official Bartender's Guide* has been the go-to manual of bartenders and spirits professionals since it was first published in 1935. It has been endorsed, consulted, and considered a basic tool for bartenders for decades. In fact, over 11 million copies have been printed since it first appeared shortly after the repeal of Prohibition.

This edition comes 73 years after the very first printing of what was then called the *Old Mr. Boston Deluxe Official Bartenders Guide*. That rare, hard-to-find first edition was compiled and edited by Leo Cotton, a purchasing agent for the Mr. Boston® liquor brand, who was as meticulous about his work as he was passionate about cocktails. His foreword in the original book remains timeless:

> *With repeal came the inevitable avalanche of cocktail books, most of them published without regard to accuracy or completeness. A survey proved the need for a cocktail book that would be authentic and accurate. The task of compiling this* Official Bartenders Guide *was thereupon undertaken and now after almost one year of tedious work it is presented to the thousands of bartenders throughout the country and to that portion of the American public who desire a truly official source of information for home mixing.*

> *The* Official Bartenders Guide *was compiled and edited in collaboration with four old time Boston Bartenders whose background and experience make them authorities on the correct ingredients to be used and the proper manner of serving cocktails. This experience plus the fact that every cocktail has been* actually tested *makes this truly an* Official Bartenders Guide.

Leo Cotton's enthusiasm was such that his editing side-job became a near-full-time vocation; he updated the *Official Bartenders Guide* through its 49th edition, until he retired in 1970.

Though Leo Cotton died in 1990, his spirit lives on in this latest edition. The current cocktail renaissance, which began in the early 1990s, has brought with it a return to classicism in the art of cocktail making. The popularity of cocktails has increased dramatically since we last updated this book in 2005; it's been heralded as the "cocktail revolution," bringing with it a whole new "cocktail culture." In fact, soon after the 66th edition debuted, *Food & Wine* magazine declared 2006 "The Year of the Cocktail" and noted that the "radical change in restaurant and bar culture has transformed entertaining."

All of which amounts to the enjoyment of a heck of a lot of spirits. According to the Distilled Spirits Council of the United States, distilled spirits grew in 2007 for the eighth straight year, with sales up 5.6 percent to $18.2 billion and volume rising 2.4 percent to 181.5 million cases. The council also reported that, despite a weakening economy, growth is expected to continue this year, forecasting sales growth of 4.6 percent to $19 billion, with volume expected to rise 1.9 percent to 185 million cases.

What on earth is in all those bottles that we're drinking? Just about everything. Spirits distributors have responded to our enthusiasm with flavors old and new, bringing out explosively exciting products like St. Germain Elderflower liqueur and organic spirits, and, at the same time, bolstering lost categories like rye, pisco, cachaça, and Old Tom Gin.

Categorically, vodka is still the most popular spirit for the masses, representing around 30 percent of the market, but other spirits like gin and rum are finally giving it serious competition. Gin, in fact, is in a dynamic state of flux. In addition to the traditional London dry style, with its hallmark (read: heavy) juniper berry aromas and flavors, a new style has evolved that's lighter and more balanced, called New Western dry, intended for sipping solo as much as for mixing into cocktails. Historical styles of gin are making a comeback, too, such as Old Tom (a sweeter version of London dry) and the lower-proof Dutch original genièvre, which is distilled from malted grain mash similar to whiskey.

Rum, too, has taken off in a new direction that's positively old in origin—thanks to a renaissance in using sugar cane instead of molasses. If you see the words "rhum agricole" on a bottle or menu, it refers to how pure-cane rum is known on the French island of Martinique, while Brazilians call their pure-cane spirit "cachaça."

On the whiskey front, rye has returned from its post-Prohibition banishment with such a vengeance producers can't make enough of it. And new small-batch whiskies seem to debut every year now, with distilleries offering an array of boutique finishes. Blended Scotch has been reborn by emphasizing the quality of the grain whiskey being blended with malt whiskey. And bourbon, while not as popular as rye, is still going strong.

How we're mixing these spirits into cocktails today is also remarkable. Mixology has returned to its culinary roots, embracing the zeitgeist and techniques of today's chefs, including taking farm to glass—as opposed to table. Once bartenders start working with someone who understands flavor combinations, like a chef, the drinks become more flavor driven than spirit driven. And that means mixers are more important than ever. With the introduction of high-quality, all-natural tonics from Fever Tree and Q Tonic, and GuS (Grown-up Soda) and Izze sparkling juices, bartenders have abandoned their soda guns—and all of the high-fructose corn syrup concoctions they spout—for "cleaner" mixers sweetened with cane sugar and agave nectar. This can change how drinks are made *and* how they taste. For example, the Paloma can be made with Izze grapefruit soda or GuS grapefruit soda (instead of Fresca), and the Cuba Libre with Boylan's Sugar Cane Cola (instead of Coke).

All of which means that you won't find pre-fabricated mixers in this edition that didn't exist when this book was first published. In other words, you won't find references to "sour mix," "daiquiri mix," or "Collins mix." We also got rid of all mentions to powdered sugar—which actually were in the original—because today's powdered sugar contains corn starch to keep it soft. Instead, many recipes call for Simple Syrup (sugar water) and citrus juices to achieve a superior substitute to the quick-fix mixes that invaded this book through its many incarnations.

What you will find in this 67th edition are nearly 200 completely new recipes reflecting the most popular spirits, liqueurs, and juices of the moment. Nearly 100 of the best bartenders, bar chefs, and mixologists from across the United States and beyond conributed recipes, tips, and advice for nothing more than a mention on the contributors' page (see pages xiii–xiv). We'd like to think their contributions were an homage to the book that first inspired many of them to start mixing drinks at the beginning of their careers.

In addition to the new recipes, the myriad details of the overall subtle changes that went into rebuilding this book might be lost on the novice or first-time reader of this guide. But our hope is that professional or veteran *Mr. Boston* readers will be pleasantly surprised by this latest incarnation. We'd like to think that Leo Cotton would be pleased to see how much of this book reflects the spirit of his original edition (which, by the way, didn't contain a single vodka cocktail).

By the time Cotton wrote the first edition of this book, the great-granddaddy of American cocktails, Jerry Thomas, was long gone—and with him many of the techniques that set his service apart from lesser-mortal barmen back in the late nineteenth century. Indeed, ask any serious bartender or mixologist today who inspires their showmanship and creativity, and the answer will probably be "Jerry Thomas." Or perhaps it will be Thomas's twentieth-century incarnation, Dale DeGroff, who may not have single-handedly revived the cocktail classicism movement of the 1990s, but certainly was and continues to be one of the most passionate, dynamic bartenders alive today.

Because DeGroff has spent more than twenty years traveling around the country educating generations of modern mixologists—when not mixing drinks behind the bar—it seems appropriate to cite his "Five Commandments for Bartenders," which are universal to all cocktail professionals and those passionate about being a good host:

I: SET THE TONE

The rapport between a bartender and guest is set by the bartender. If a guest is short or less than cordial, you, the bartender—according to the social contract he or she upholds—cannot respond in kind. This is a one-sided contract weighted in favor of the guest, but in practice it is an opportunity for the bartender to do what he or she was hired to do best: turn difficult guests into friends, make great drinks, and even, on occasion, teach people how to have a good time.

II: BE OBSERVANT

Good bartenders need to sharpen their powers of observation and develop their ability to listen. In the first encounter with a guest the bartender will determine not only the drink but the mood of the guest, if conversation is welcome or not, and generally why the guest has come. This is your opportunity to make the visit to your bar a success.

III: KNOW YOUR RECIPES

You're the chef of the bar and have the same responsibility to guests as the chef de cuisine has to diners. Are you putting the dash of Angostura bitters in your Manhattan? Do you use fresh lime juice in your Mojito? It took me a couple of years to get over the arrogance I developed in the first six months of bartending, then it took me several years after that to research the correct recipes for the 150 or so classic and popular drinks that are 90 percent of a bartender's regular repertoire.

IV: PERFECT YOUR CRAFT

The skill a bartender possesses in the handling of tools and the small theatrical elements he or she demonstrates, such as the flaming of citrus peels, can return huge dividends in both esteem and gratuity—not to mention return business. This is not a circus act but rather exuding a sense of confidence that impresses your guests. A bartender is most definitely on stage, so expect to be scrutinized down to your fingernails.

V: EXUDE GRAVITAS

A bartender's skill and cleverness in being many things to many people is one of the most compelling and challenging aspects of the job. The bartender is a source of information on the day's news and sporting events, as well as a glossary of where to dine, drink, see, and be seen. You have the ability to keep peace in a light-handed way between customers. Rudeness to a bar guest is never acceptable; there are myriad ways of reacting coolly to a difficult guest. And even the most difficult of guests can be handled with a professional demeanor, though sometimes help is required.

Before you continue reading, please take a moment to think about both the responsible use and serving of alcoholic drinks. The consumption of alcohol dates back many centuries, and in many cultures throughout the world is part of social rituals associated with significant occasions and celebrations. The majority of adults who choose to drink do not abuse alcohol and are aware that responsible drinking is key to their own enjoyment, health, and safety, as well as that of others, particularly when driving. Be a responsible drinker, and if you're under the legal drinking age, our nonalchoholic drinks chapter is the only one for you.

So, congratulations! You're well on your way to enhancing your expertise as a professional bartender or a properly prepared host. Let's raise a proverbial glass in honor of Mr. Boston, as he was introduced in his 1935 debut:

Sirs—May we now present to you Old Mr. Boston in permanent form. We know you are going to like him. He is a jolly fellow, one of those rare individuals, everlastingly young, a distinct personality and famous throughout the land for his sterling qualities and genuine good fellowship. His friends number in the millions those who are great and those who are near great even as you and I. He is jovial and ever ready to accept the difficult role of "Life of the Party," a sympathetic friend who may be relied upon in any emergency. Follow his advice and there will be many pleasant times in store for you.

Gentlemen, Old Mr. Boston

ACKNOWLEDGMENTS

THE EDITOR WOULD LIKE TO OFFICIALLY ACKNOWLEDGE the following people behind the 67th edition of the *Mr. Boston Official Bartender's Guide*:

Editor extraordinaire Pamela Chirls, and her team at John Wiley & Sons, Inc., including Christine DiComo, Rebecca Scherm, Ava Wilder, and Michael Olivo, for grace under fire;

Fabulous photographer Ben Fink for his keen eye, and stylists Susan Sugarman and Roy Finamore for making the drinks look sexy and beautiful;

Lori Logan at Barton Brands for her steadfast vision and for keeping us on message;

Historian Robert Hess, founder of drinkboy.com, for his tireless research and resources;

Rock-star mixologist Jim Meehan for creating, collecting, and testing this edition's cocktail additions;

My "brother from another mother," journalist and drinks authority Jeffery Lindenmuth, for reporting on trends;

Cocktail professionals David Wondrich, Audrey Saunders, Julie Reiner, Tony Abou Ganim, Gary Regan, Jonathan Pogash, and Dale DeGroff for their brilliant resourcefulness and generous spirit;

The thoughtful Bonnie Berman, Leo Cotton's daughter, for reminding us how passionate her dad was about editing the first forty-nine editions of this book—and never receiving a penny in royalties;

And my wife, Antonia LoPresti Giglio, and our two greatest cocktails, Sofia and Marco, for their patience during my absence while editing this book.

Jonny Raglin

Gary Regan

Julie Reiner

Patricia Richards

Holly Roberts

Sam Ross

Steve Schneider

Joseph Schwartz

Andy Seymour

Aisha Sharpe

Daniel Shoemaker

Willy Shine

T.J. Siegal

Joaquin Simo

David Slape

LeNell Smothers

Chad Solomon

Kelley Swenson

Marcos Tellos

Todd Thrasher

Stanislav Vadrna

Charles Vexenat

Charlotte Voisey

Phil Ward

Thomas Waugh

Neyah White

Angus Winchester

Damian Windsor

David Wondrich

Naren Young

Dushan Zaric

CONTRIBUTORS TO THIS EDITION

Tony Abou Ganim

Erik Adkins

Bridget Albert

Eric Alperin

Stephan Berg

Jeff Berry

Greg Best

Jacques Bezuidenhout

Richard Boccato

Jamie Boudreau

Jacob Briar

Jackson Cannon

Tad Carducci

Tony Conigliaro

Gerry Corcoran

Jason Crawley

Jane Danger

Alex Day

Brian Dayton

Dale DeGroff

Leo DeGroff

John Deragon

Philip Duff

Damon Dyer

H. Joseph Ehrmann

Tobin Ellis

Vincenzo Errico

Daniel Eun

Molly Finnegan

Eben Freeman

St. John Frizell

Matt Gee

John Gertsen

Giuseppe Gonzales

Kenta Goto

Ted Haigh

Charles Hardwick

Reed Hayes

Nick Hearin

Charles Joly

Misty Kalkofen

Ted Kilgore

Eben Klemm

Jason Kosmas

Francesco Lafranconi

Don Lee

James Lee

Kevin Ludwig

Michael Madrusan

Ryan Magarian

Toby Maloney

Vincenzo Marianella

Lynnette Marrero

Duggan McDonnell

Becky McFalls

Michael McIlroy

Junior Merino

Jorg Meyer

Brian Miller

Steve Olson

Sasha Petraske

Christy Pope

BAR BASICS

Equipment

THE RIGHT TOOLS make mixing drinks easier, but some tasks simply can't be done without the right gizmo.

BOSTON SHAKER: Two-piece set comprised of a mixing glass and a slightly larger metal container that acts as a cover for the mixing glass for shaking cocktails. The mixing glass can be used alone for stirring drinks that aren't shaken.

BARSPOON: Long-handled, shallow spoon with a twisted handle, used for stirring drinks.

HAWTHORNE STRAINER: Perforated metal top for the metal half of a Boston shaker, held in place by a wire coil. Serves as a strainer.

JULEP STRAINER: Perforated, spoon-shaped strainer used in conjunction with a mixing glass.

COCKTAIL SHAKER: Metal pitcher with a tight-fitting lid, under which sits a strainer. While styles vary widely, the popular retro-style pitcher has a handle as well as a spout that's sealed with a twist-off cap.

ELECTRIC BLENDER: Absolutely necessary to make frozen drinks, puree fruit, and even crush ice for certain recipes.

CUTTING BOARD: Either wood or plastic, it is used to cut fruit upon for garnishes.

PARING KNIFE: Small, sharp knife to prepare fruit for garnishes.

MUDDLER: Looks like a wooden pestle, the flat end of which is used to crush and combine ingredients in a serving glass or mixing glass.

GRATER: Useful for zesting fruit or grating nutmeg.

BOTTLE OPENER: Essential for opening bottles that aren't twist-off.

CHURCH KEY: Usually metal, it is pointed at one end to punch holes in the tops of cans, while the other end is used to open bottles.

CORKSCREW: There are a myriad of styles from which to choose. Professionals use the "waiter's corkscrew," which looks like a pen-knife, the "screw-pull," or the "rabbit corkscrew." The "winged corkscrew," found in most homes, is considered easiest to use but often destroys the cork.

CITRUS REAMER: Essential for juicing fruit, it comes in two styles. The strainer bowl style has the pointed cone on top, or there is the wooden handle style with the cone attached, which must be used with a strainer.

JIGGER: Essential for precise measuring, it typically has two cone-shaped metal cups conjoined at the narrow end—each side representing a quantity of ounces (quarter, half, whole, etc.), fractionalized by lines etched in the metal.

ICE BUCKET WITH SCOOP AND TONGS: A bar without ice is like a car without gas. Use the scoop—never the glass—to gather ice in a mixing glass or shaker and tongs to add single cubes to a prepared drink.

MISCELLANEOUS ACCOUTREMENTS: Sipsticks or stirrers, straws, cocktail napkins, coasters, and cocktail picks.

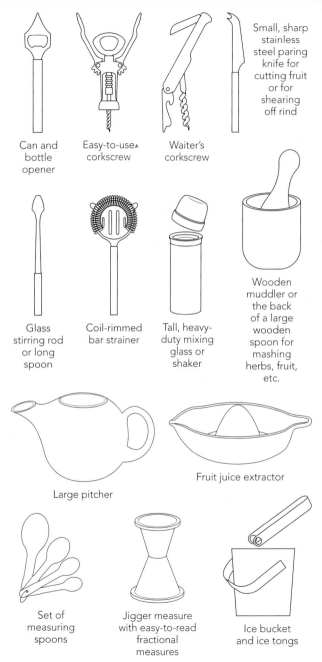

Can and bottle opener

Easy-to-use corkscrew

Waiter's corkscrew

Small, sharp stainless steel paring knife for cutting fruit or for shearing off rind

Glass stirring rod or long spoon

Coil-rimmed bar strainer

Tall, heavy-duty mixing glass or shaker

Wooden muddler or the back of a large wooden spoon for mashing herbs, fruit, etc.

Large pitcher

Fruit juice extractor

Set of measuring spoons

Jigger measure with easy-to-read fractional measures

Ice bucket and ice tongs

Glassware

CLEAN, POLISHED GLASSES show off good drinks to great advantage. The best glasses should be thin-lipped, transparent, and sound off in high registers when "pinged." In practice, these five glasses could be used to make most of the mixed drinks and cocktails found in this book:

COCKTAIL GLASS (also known as martini glass): Typically 4 to 8 ounces, but lately much larger.

COLLINS GLASS: Tall and narrow, typically 8 to 12 ounces.

HIGHBALL GLASS: Shorter Collins glass, typically 8 to 10 ounces.

HURRICANE GLASS: Short-stem, hourglass-shaped, typically 14 to 20 ounces.

OLD-FASHIONED GLASS: Wide and squat, typically 6 to 8 ounces.

A complete inventory of glassware, however, would include the following:

BEER MUG

BEER/PILSNER GLASS

BRANDY SNIFTER

CHAMPAGNE COUPE

CHAMPAGNE FLUTE

CORDIAL OR PONY GLASS

IRISH COFFEE GLASS

PARFAIT GLASS

POUSSE CAFÉ GLASS

RED WINE GLASS

SHERRY GLASS

SHOT GLASS

SOUR GLASS

WHITE WINE GLASS

Taking Stock

NOBODY EVER SAID stocking a home bar is easy or inexpensive, which is probably why so few people bother to do it. However, if you're above the fray, feeling inspired by this book, and make the reasonable rationalization about the money you'll spend stocking your bar versus the money you'll save on buying drinks at bars, here's what you'll need to do it right:

BITTERS

Angostura Bitters

Peychaud's Bitters

Orange Bitters

FRUIT JUICES

Lime Juice

Lemon Juice

Cranberry Juice

Pineapple Juice

Other Juices and Nectars

SAVORY INGREDIENTS

Tomato Juice

Clam Juice

Horseradish

Hot Sauces

Worcestershire Sauce

SWEETENING INGREDIENTS

Simple Syrup (Equal parts water and granulated sugar, heated over a flame, and then cooled and stored in refrigerator until needed. Keeps indefinitely refrigerated in a scrupulously clean container.)

Superfine Sugar

Granulated Sugar

Coconut Cream

Various Fruit Syrups (Orgeat, Elderflower)

Grenadine

DAIRY/EGG INGREDIENTS

Milk

Cream (Heavy, Half-and-Half)

Butter

Eggs

SODAS

Seltzer/Club Soda

Quinine/Tonic Water

Various: Cola, Lemon-lime, etc.

GARNISHES

Lemon Wedges

Lime Wedges

Assorted Fruit Wheels

Pineapple Chunks

Maraschino Cherries

Olives

Celery

Fresh Herbs (Mint, Basil, etc.)

Techniques

CHILLING GLASSWARE

Always chill before you fill—even your cocktail shaker before mixing the drink. There are two ways to make a cocktail glass cold:

1. Put the glasses in the refrigerator or freezer a couple of hours before using them.

2. Fill the glasses with ice and water, stir, then discard when drink is ready.

FLAMING LIQUORS

The secret of setting brandy (or other high-alcohol spirits) aflame is first to warm it and its glass until almost hot. You can warm a glass by holding it by its stem above the flame or electric coil on your stove until the glass feels warm. (Avoid touching the glass to the flame or coil, which could char or crack it.)

Next, heat some brandy in a saucepan above the flame (or in a cooking pan). When the brandy is hot, ignite it with a match. If it's hot enough, it will flame instantly. Pour the flaming liquid carefully into the other brandy you want flamed. If all the liquid is warm enough, it will ignite.

Warning: Flames can shoot high suddenly. Look up and be sure there's nothing "en route" that can ignite. That includes your hair. Have an open box of baking soda handy in case of accidents. Pour it over flames to extinguish them. Use pot holders to protect your hands from the hot glass, spoon, or pan.

FLOATING LIQUEURS

Creating a rainbow effect in a glass with different colored cordials requires a special pouring technique. Simply pour each liqueur slowly over an inverted teaspoon (rounded side up) into a glass: Start with the heaviest liqueur first. (Recipes will give proper order.) Pour slowly. The rounded surface of the spoon will spread each liqueur over the one beneath without mixing them. You can accomplish the same trick using a glass rod. Pour slowly down the rod.

CHOOSING FRUIT AND FRUIT JUICES

Whenever possible, use only *fresh* fruit. Wash the outside peel before using. Fruit can be cut in wedges or in slices. If slices are used, they should be cut about one-quarter-inch thick and slit toward the center to fix the slice on the rim of the glass. Make sure garnishes are fresh and cold.

When mixing drinks containing fruit juices, always pour the liquor last. Squeeze and strain fruit juices just before using to ensure freshness and good taste. Avoid artificial, concentrated substitutes.

When recipes call for a twist of lemon peel, rub a narrow strip or peel around the rim of the glass to deposit the oil on it. Then twist the peel so that the oil (usually one small drop) drops into the drink. Then drop in the peel. The lemon oil gives added character to the cocktail, which many prefer.

MUDDLING FRUIT AND HERBS

Muddling is a simple mashing technique for grinding fruit and herbs, such as mint, smooth in the bottom of a glass. You can buy a wooden muddler in a bar supply store; they typically range from six to ten inches long, flattened on one end (the muddling end) and rounded on the other (the handle). When muddling pulpy or fibrous fruit, you might want to pass the liquid through a julep strainer before serving.

RIMMING A GLASS

This technique separates the pros from the amateurs. Into a saucer or a small bowl pour kosher salt—never use iodized salt—or sugar, depending on the drink. Using a wedge of fresh lemon or lime, carefully wet only the outside rim of the cocktail glass. Then, holding the glass sideways, dab the rim into the salt while slowly turning the glass, until the entire rim is covered. Finally, hold the glass over the sink and tap the glass gently against your free hand to knock off any excess salt. The effect is a delicately salted rim that looks almost frosted.

ROLLING DRINKS

To prevent drinks that call for thick juices or fruit purees from foaming, roll them instead of shaking. Rolling is the act of pouring the drink—a Bloody Mary, for example—back and forth between two shaker glasses. After rolling the drink a half-dozen times, it should be completely incorporated and ready to be strained.

SHAKING

As a rule of thumb, shake any drink made with juices, sugar, or cream.

Assemble

Assemble the ingredients in the glass part of the Boston shaker, adding the fresh juice first *before* the ice, then the dashes, modifiers, and the base spirit, followed by the ice. On the other hand, with drinks using only spirits, add the ice first, then the spirits.

Seal

Place the metal half of the Boston shaker over the glass while it's sitting on the bar. Holding the glass firmly, clap the upturned end of the metal half twice with the heel of your free hand to form a seal. (To test the seal, lift the shaker by the metal top slightly off the bar to see if it holds; if not, do it again or replace one of the parts.)

Flip, Then Shake

Turn the conjoined shakers over so that the glass is on top and the metal half rests on the bar. Grasp the shakers with the metal half sitting securely in the palm of one hand and the other hand wrapped securely over the top of the glass half, then shake hard with the glass half of the set on top. (In case the seal breaks, the liquid stays in the bigger metal half.) Shake vigorously, rendering the drink effervescent.

HOW MANY DRINKS TO PLAN

Whether you're hosting an intimate dinner party or throwing a bash for a crowd, the buying guide charts in this section can make it easy for you to determine how much liquor and wine you'll need.

	FOR FOUR PEOPLE	FOR SIX PEOPLE	FOR TEN PEOPLE
LUNCH	6 cocktails/wine	10 cocktails/wine	15 cocktails/wine
	6 glasses wine with lunch	10 glasses wine with lunch	15 glasses wine with lunch
	4 liqueurs	6 liqueurs	10 liqueurs
COCKTAILS	8 cocktails *or*	12 cocktails *or*	20 cocktails *or*
	8 glasses wine first 2 hours	12 glasses wine first 2 hours	20 glasses wine first 2 hours
	6 drinks an hour thereafter	9 drinks an hour thereafter	15 drinks an hour thereafter
DINNER	8 cocktails/wine	12 cocktails/wine	20 cocktails/wine
	8 glasses wine with dinner	12 glasses wine with dinner	20 glasses wine with dinner
	4 liqueurs	6 liqueurs	10 liqueurs
	4 drinks an hour after dinner	6 drinks an hour after dinner	10 drinks an hour after dinner
EVENING	16 cocktails/wine	24 cocktails/wine	40 cocktails/wine

HOW MANY BOTTLES OF WINE FOR DINNER

Table Wines, Champagnes, Sparkling Wines
average 2 servings, 5 ounces each, per person

PEOPLE	4	6	8	10	12	20
750-ml	2	2+	3+	4	5	8
1.5-liter	1	1+	2	2	2+	4

Generally, bottle quantities recommended provide some small overages of wine from 10-ounces-per-guest formula; "+" indicates somewhat less formula and you may desire to have an additional bottle on hand.

HOW MANY DRINKS PER BOTTLE

Cocktails, Mixed Drinks
1.5-ounce liquor servings

Bottles	1	2	4	6	8	10	12
750-ml	16	33	67	101	135	169	203
Liter	22	45	90	135	180	225	270
1.5-liter	39	78	157	236	315	394	473

TABLE WINES, CHAMPAGNES, SPARKLING WINES

5-ounce wine servings

Bottles	1	2	4	6	8	10	12
750-ml	5	10	20	30	40	50	60
Liter	6	13	27	40	54	67	81
1.5-liter	10	20	40	60	81	101	121
3-liter	20	40	80	121	161	202	242
4-liter	27	54	108	162	216	270	324

Measures

Here are conversions for unusual measures typically found in nineteenth-century recipes:

Pony/Cordial	= 1 ounce
Pousse Café Glass	= 1.5 ounces
Cocktail Glass	= 2 ounces
Gill	= 4 ounces
Wine Glass	= 4 ounces
Small Tumbler	= 8 ounces
Large Tumbler	= 16 ounces

STANDARD BAR MEASUREMENTS (U.S.)

Pony	= 1 ounce
1 ounce	= 3 centiliters
Jigger, shot	= 1.5 ounces
Mixing Glass	= 16 ounces
Splash	= ½ ounce
6 drops	= 1 dash = ⅙ teaspoon

OTHER MEASURES

6 drops	= 1 dash
12 dashes	= 1 teaspoon
1 teaspoon	= ⅛ ounce
2 teaspoons	= ¼ ounce
1 tablespoon	= ½ ounce
2 tablespoons	= 1 ounce
¼ cup	= 2 ounces
½ cup	= 4 ounces
1 cup or ½ pint	= 8 ounces
2 cups or 1 pint	= 16 ounces
4 cups, 2 pints, or 1 quart	= 32 ounces

BOTTLE SIZE MEASURES

Split = 187 ml = 6.4 ounces
Half-Bottle = 375 ml = 12.7 ounces
Fifth = 750 ml = 25.4 ounces
Liter =1000 ml = 33.8 ounces
Magnum = 1.5 liters = 2 wine bottles
Jeroboam = 3 liters = 4 wine bottles
Rehoboam = 6 wine bottles
Methuselah = 8 wine bottles
Salmanazar = 12 wine bottles
Balthazar = 16 wine bottles
Nebuchadnezzar = 20 wine bottles
Sovereign = 34 wine bottles

FRESH FRUIT EQUIVALENTS

APRICOTS
8–12 fresh = 1 lb. or 3 cups of sliced

BANANAS
3 medium = 1 lb. fresh = 1½ cups of mashed

CANTALOUPES
1 whole 3-lb. cantaloupe yields 5 cups of cubed

CHERRIES
1 lb. fresh = 2⅓ cups pitted

GRAPEFRUITS
1 medium = 1 lb. fresh

JUNIPER BERRIES
4 berries = ½ tsp. crushed

KIWIS
5 medium = 2⅓ cups sliced

LEMONS
1 lb. = 4–6 medium lemons, yields 1 cup for juice
1 medium = 3 tbsps. juice
1 medium = 2–3 tsps. grated peel

MANGOES

1 large = 1 lb. = 1¾ cups diced

PASSION FRUITS

Approximately 3 = 2 ounces; 5–6 whole yields ½ cup of
   pulp

PEACHES

3–4 medium yields 1 lb. or 2 cups pureed; 7–8 medium
   yields 1 quart or 4 cups pureed

RASPBERRIES

1 pint = ¾ lb.

STRAWBERRIES

12 large or 36 small = 1 pint or ⅔ cups pureed

1 cup of whole = 1 cup pureed

20 oz. frozen = 2¼ cups pureed

COCKTAIL CLASSICS

BEING A BARTENDER REQUIRES far more than memorizing a few recipes and learning to use some basic tools. Sure, you might be able to mix a drink, but that is no guarantee you will consistently produce truly great drinks.

A bartender is in many ways like a chef—taking individual ingredients and mixing them together to create an artful blending of flavors. The best cocktails are a form of cuisine in their own right.

Just as a great chef must have a command of the foundations of cooking, like a mastery of classic French sauces, the bartender must understand the basic techniques, processes, methods, and products involved in the craft. And this includes an understanding and appreciation of the classic cocktails. These recipes are the foundation for nearly every existing drink and provide the basis for creating new and distinctive drinks.

The following ten cocktails form the basis for most modern cocktails. Understand their histories, variations, and processes, and you'll be well on your way to a better appreciation of your craft as well as being able to create original cocktails that may someday take their place among the greats.

The Old-Fashioned Whiskey Cocktail

Unlike other cuisines of the world, the cocktail is only a few hundred years old. While we don't know precisely when or where the cocktail made its official first appearance, we can trace it back as far as 1806. There, in a popular New York publication called *The Balance, and Columbian Repository*, we find the cocktail defined.

In the May 13th edition, an editor responded to a letter from a devoted reader about the term "cock-tail" as it appeared in the previous week's edition, saying:

> *As I make it a point, never to publish anything (under my editorial head) but which I can explain, I shall not hesitate to gratify the curiosity of my inquisitive correspondent: Cocktail, then is a stimulating liquor, composed of spirits of any kind, sugar, water and bitters—it is vulgarly called a bittered sling.*

At the core of this, you see the definition of the cocktail: "spirits of any kind, sugar, water, and bitters." While the term "cocktail" has since been broadened to include far more drinks, and with a far less distinct definition, this original definition is one of which all bartenders should be aware. As the cocktail evolved, this earliest of cocktails became known simply as the Old-Fashioned.

There are many who claim the Old-Fashioned was invented at the Pendennis Club in Louisville, Kentucky. One of the oldest records of a recipe going by the name of Old-Fashioned is from *Modern American Drinks* by George J. Kappeler, published in 1895:

☐ THE OLD-FASHIONED WHISKEY COCKTAIL

Dissolve a small lump of sugar with a little water in a whiskey-glass; add two dashes Angostura bitters, a small piece ice, a piece lemon-peel, one jigger whiskey. Mix with small bar-spoon and serve, leaving spoon in glass.

Remembering the earlier stated definition of a cocktail, what is an Old-Fashioned but "spirits of any kind [whiskey], sugar, water and bitters"? To draw an even closer connection, many recipes of that time would also indicate that other spirits could be used in an Old-Fashioned in order to make an Old-Fashioned Brandy Cocktail, or an Old-Fashioned Rum Cocktail.

In the first known bartender's guide, *How to Mix Drinks* (Dick & Fitzgerald, 1862), Jerry Thomas writes:

🍸 WHISKEY COCKTAIL

Use a small bar glass.

> 3 or 4 dashes of gum syrup
> 2 do. Bitters (Bogart's)
> 1 wine-glass of whiskey, and a piece of lemon peel.
>
> Fill one-third full of fine ice; shake and strain in a fancy red-wine glass.

Editor's note: "do." was an abbreviation for "ditto," which referred to the word "dashes" in the line above.

This is the same cocktail as the Old-Fashioned (gum syrup is essentially just sugar and water with the addition of gum arabic for extra body) and leads to the conclusion that the Pendennis Club didn't actually invent the Old-Fashioned, but simply provided their customers with a whiskey cocktail made the old-fashioned way. Many cocktails have far more stories attempting to describe their origins. After all, drinking and storytelling go hand in hand, so treat any tale of cocktail invention with a bit of skepticism.

Our favorite Old-Fashioned cocktail:

☐ OLD-FASHIONED WHISKEY COCKTAIL

> 1 tsp. Simple Syrup
> 2 dashes Angostura Bitters
> 1½ oz. Bourbon or Rye Whiskey
>
> Fill a 5-oz. old-fashioned glass with cracked ice. Stir to mix the syrup, bitters, and the water, which will melt off the ice. Add the whiskey.

Stir to mix and chill. Garnish with a lemon twist, serve with straws or small swizzle stick.

This Old-Fashioned reflects the way this cocktail should taste. Simple syrup is used because it's easier than dissolving the sugar in the glass and also provides a more consistent sweetening. Unlike modern renditions, there is no cherry or orange muddled in with the bitters and sweetener at the beginning and there is no soda or water at the end.

The beauty of this recipe lies in its simplicity and authenticity. Hundreds of years ago, spirits were so rough that sweeteners were needed to mask their flavors. Today, spirits are of much higher quality and don't need to be masked; instead the sweetener is being used to counterbalance the alcoholic bite, as well as fill out the flavor profile in areas where the spirit doesn't touch.

Bitters, as we have seen, are at the very heart of the definition of a cocktail. Prior to around 1900 it was almost unthinkable to have a cocktail that didn't include bitters in some form. Bitters, when added in small amounts, offer complexity to the overall flavor of the drink.

Finally, the water that is added to the Old-Fashioned and other cocktails through the ice serves to tone down and mellow the overall flavors as well as soften the bite typical of a straight spirit. Topping the drink off with additional water, as is often done, only results in a very diluted drink.

But what about that cherry and orange? They were not part of the original drink and are in fact relative newcomers to the old-fashioned glass. You'll find an orange slice being used instead of a lemon twist in the 1930 printing of The Savoy Cocktail Book by Harry Craddock. For the next several decades you'll see lemon, pineapple, orange, and cherry all make an appearance, either separately or in various combinations, but always as a garnish. Exactly when the practice of muddling the fruit came into fashion is hard to determine, but it doesn't appear to be referenced in print much before the 1990s.

The modern maraschino cherry didn't come onto the scene until the early 1900s, just before Prohibition. It was intended as a "temperance" replacement for the brandy-soaked marasca cherries, which had been previously in common use. Prohibition made the original version impossible to obtain in the United States, and so maraschino cherries quickly replaced them in baking and garnishing. Muddling them into the drink does little to improve the flavor or the aesthetics of this drink.

The orange is a slightly different story. If you glance over many of the historical recipes, you will occasionally see a dash of orange curaçao added. Muddling a slice of orange into the Old-Fashioned extracts similar essential oils to those found in orange liqueurs. Another way to obtain these oils is to slice off a small disk of orange peel, about the size of a half-dollar, point the orange side toward the ice in the glass, and squeeze the peel to release its oils over the ice before adding the whiskey. This will provide an excellent essence of orange to the drink. Garnish the drink with a half orange-wheel and cherry, permitting the fresh fruits to play the ornamental role for which they were intended.

By playing with these techniques and various spirits you will rediscover this seminal cocktail as it was crafted over two hundred years ago.

The Manhattan Cocktail

A hundred years after the Old-Fashioned, near the end of the 1800s, we find the Manhattan. In the second half of the 1800s cocktails began to really catch on, and bartenders were expanding both their repertoire of drinks and the palette of products at their disposal for making them. Simplicity of design, however, was still very much at the core of all drinks.

The Manhattan appears to have come onto the scene about 1882, at which time it was mentioned that a cocktail made from just whiskey, sweet vermouth, and bitters was coming into vogue. It went by not only "Manhattan," but also "Turf Club Cocktail" and "Jockey Club Cocktail." The "Manhattan" moniker almost certainly comes from the Manhattan Club of New York, with the other clubs eager to have their names attached to the drink as well.

Like the Old-Fashioned, the recipe for the Manhattan is deceptively simple—just whiskey, sweet vermouth, and bitters. And likewise, the art of making a great one is in the details.

Our favorite Manhattan recipe:

￼ MANHATTAN
1½ oz. Rye Whiskey
½ oz. Sweet Vermouth
1 dash Angostura Bitters

Stir with ice and strain into a chilled cocktail glass. Garnish with a cherry or lemon twist.

You'll note two peculiarities in this recipe. The first is the use of rye whiskey; the second is that it is stirred.

As indicated earlier, this drink originated in New York, and in those days the rye whiskey distillers were located in the East, making rye whiskey the spirit of choice. Bourbon, from Kentucky and the surrounding area, was far less common here. Today, Bourbon is the default spirit of the Manhattan, but rye has been making a comeback and is worth seeking out. Many people substitute Canadian whisky for rye, but the two are actually quite a bit different. For one thing, rye whiskey must be made from at least 51 percent rye, while Canadian whisky contains far less. This doesn't mean that you can't make a Manhattan with Canadian whisky, or Bourbon for that matter, but they will yield vastly different results.

Stirring versus shaking is an age-old debate, and it plays a big role in getting the proper results in many cocktails, specifically a Manhattan. Both shaking and stirring are intended to chill the drink. In addition, as the ice chills the drink it also is melting and therefore contributing water to the drink, an important addition to every cocktail.

Whether you choose to shake or stir your drink, you'll find that both do an excellent job. There are, however, differences: Stirring takes slightly longer to chill the drink. And shaking will result in a cloudy, aerated drink, while stirring creates one that remains crystal clear. From a presentation standpoint, it is often better to stir, while from a speed standpoint it is always better to shake. When a drink contains a citrus juice or other cloudy ingredient, then you might as well shake. However, if it contains only clear ingredients, as in the case of a Manhattan, then stirring is preferred.

Just as the Old-Fashioned could be made with different spirits to create slightly different variations on a theme, there are also variations of the Manhattan. Initially, the Manhattan was designed to use sweet vermouth. But if a customer wanted it made with dry vermouth instead, they would ask for a "dry" Manhattan. And asking for a "perfect" Manhattan indicates a 50/50 mixture of sweet and dry vermouth.

Like its progenitor the Old-Fashioned, this recipe contains bitters. And while the vogue for the past decade was to provide bitters on a "by request" basis, this vital ingredient has staged a deserved return to the Manhattan and should be provided as a standard ingredient.

The Martini Cocktail

Making its appearance only a few years after the Manhattan, the Martini is a cocktail that has come to be the icon of this genre, so much so that almost any drink in a stemmed cocktail glass is now dubbed a Martini by the drinking public.

There are many stories surrounding the origins of the Martini, but its true origins appear to lie with its forgotten sibling, the Martinez. In *The Bar-Tender's Guide* (1887), Jerry Thomas writes:

☐ MARTINEZ COCKTAIL

Use a small wine-glass.

Take:

    1 dash of Boker's bitters
    2 dashes of Maraschino
    1 pony of Old Tom gin
    1 wine-glass of vermouth
    2 small lumps of ice

Shake up thoroughly, and strain into a large cocktail glass. Put a quarter of a slice of lemon in the glass and serve. If the guest prefers it very sweet, add two dashes of gum syrup.

Editor's note: Boker's bitters was an aromatic bitters similar to angostura, Old Tom gin was a sweetened gin that is no longer available, and "wine-glass" was a term usually used to refer to a 2-ounce pour.

In the same book, a recipe for a Manhattan was listed that was essentially the same, except that it used rye whiskey instead of gin. As we previously saw, the Manhattan had also been described five years earlier as being simply whiskey, sweet vermouth, and bitters, so clearly there were some significant variations making the rounds, and it would take a few years for a consensus to settle in on what the proper recipe was. In those days, the art of bartending was in its golden age, with a great deal of competition, experimentation, and advancement of the craft.

By the 1890s recipes for a drink now known as the Martini were appearing. In *Modern American Drinks: How to Mix and Serve All Kinds of Cups and Drinks* (1895), George J. Kappeler writes:

☐ MARTINI COCKTAIL

Half a mixing-glass full of fine ice, three dashes orange bitters, one-half jigger Tom gin, one-half jigger Italian vermouth, a piece lemon peel. Mix, strain into cocktail-glass. Add a maraschino cherry, if desired by customer.

From this we can see that the Martini, containing just gin, sweet vermouth, and bitters, was really a gin version of the Manhattan. And like the Manhattan, when ordered normally it would be made with sweet vermouth, and when ordered "dry" with dry vermouth.

While the Manhattan has pretty much survived to the modern day with its recipe intact, the Martini has not fared so well. It was following Prohibition, when untrained amateurs took to the bar, that the concept of "dry" when applied to the Martini came to mean using less dry vermouth. Today some bartenders use none at all. Orange bitters, once a required component of the Martini, were forgotten, to the point of near extinction.

One could hardly consider a glass of cold gin a cocktail deserving of the name Martini. To rediscover the sophisticated balance and complexity that is possible with the Martini, it is necessary to return to its roots.

Y MARTINI COCKTAIL (SWEET)

1 oz. Gin
1 oz. Sweet Vermouth
1 dash Orange Bitters

Stir with ice, strain into a chilled cocktail glass. Garnish with a lemon twist.

Y MARTINI COCKTAIL (DRY)

1 oz. Gin
1 oz. Dry Vermouth
1 dash Orange Bitters

Stir with ice, strain into a chilled cocktail glass. Garnish with a lemon twist.

Try each of the above exactly as indicated. As with any culinary product, the quality of the ingredients that go into it will greatly affect the outcome, so be sure to use a good gin and good vermouth.

There are several aspects of these recipes that you will notice as being significantly different from what you might be used to. For one thing, there are only 2 ounces of total liquid being used here; this obviously will result in a drink that will look rather lost in today's 5- to 8-ounce cocktail glasses. In the days before Prohibition, the typical cocktail glass was about 4 ounces in size, so the recipes above, with the addition of water from mixing, resulted in a perfectly sized drink.

Another difference you'll see is what appears to be a massive amount of vermouth being used. The result is a drink that bears little resemblance to today's Martini. Push your prejudices aside and instead focus simply on the overall taste of the drink itself, and you'll find the vermouth is not only enjoyable but in perfect balance with the gin.

You'll also notice that we have reintroduced orange bitters to the recipe. Prior to Prohibition, orange bitters were more commonly used in cocktails than the ubiquitous angostura. Currently there are two brands being sold in America: The Sazerac Company of New Orleans manufactures "Reagan's Orange Bitters #6," and Fee Brothers of Rochester, New York, also produces a full line of bitters, which includes their own orange bitters.

As noted, the Martini should be stirred, like the Manhattan, to retain its clarity.

And while the olive is the more popular modern garnish, the olive brine affects the delicate balance of the drink. We prefer, at least initially, to get to know this drink with this more understated lemon twist.

Perhaps more than with any other cocktail, the ratios of the ingredients in a martini require precise balance. No one ingredient should outshine the other, and all ingredients should be playing together in the final product.

The Martini recipes listed above would be inappropriate to serve to a random customer who simply asked for a "Martini." But through the careful understanding of not only the history of this drink but its blending of complex flavors, you'll gain new insights into the mystique of this cocktail.

Margarita, Daiquiri, and Sidecar

As we've seen through the Old-Fashioned, Manhattan, and even Martini, drinks in the mixed drink category known as "cocktail" always included bitters as one of their ingredients. In those days, there were many different categories of mixed drinks, with the category itself defining much of the recipe. Forgotten monikers like daisy, fizz, shrub, crusta, and the still-surviving sour, were each categories of their own.

The term "cocktail," which is actually the newcomer on the scene, grew to such popularity that it eventually came to encompass many of the drinks that were previously from other categories. The "sour" is one such category and it even has vestiges in many modern cocktail names, like the whiskey sour.

The traditional sour was made using a spirit of any kind, a sweetening ingredient, and a souring ingredient. The sweetener could be as simple as just sugar, or it could be a sweet liqueur or cordial. The souring ingredient was normally lemon juice, but it could also be lime juice or grapefruit juice, or some combination of these.

Today, the Margarita is the reigning sour. Like most cocktails, the history of the Margarita is often debated and never resolved. A commonly repeated story has it being invented in 1948 by Margarita Sames for a large party she was holding in Acapulco, Mexico. There is a competing story that claims it was created in 1942 by Francisco Morales, who called this drink a "Daisy," which in Spanish is "Margarita." Another tale insists it was created in the early 1930s at the Caliente Race Track in Tijuana. These and many other conflicting stories all claim to recount the origins of the most popular tequila-based cocktail. But one thing that all of them agree upon is that the original recipe consists of tequila, Cointreau, and lime juice, which clearly follows the classic recipe for a sour.

The Daiquiri is a rum version of the traditional sour, although these days many people will unfortunately confuse it with the blended ice "slushee" version, which is more reminiscent of drinks from childhood.

It is fairly certain that the name of this drink comes from the similarly named town on the east coast of Cuba. While the commonly told story says that it was an American by the name of Jennings Cox who was living in Daiquiri who invented the drink, it is more likely that this was just a commonly served drink, and that Americans who came to visit Mr. Cox and were served this drink began referring to it as "that Daiquiri drink." While the Margarita uses Cointreau as its sweetening ingredient, the Daiquiri uses just plain sugar or simple syrup for the task. However, it too is a sour.

The first appearance of the Sidecar recipe is found in *Cocktails: How to Mix Them*, by Robert Vermeire, published in 1922. Here, the recipe was listed as "⅙ gill of fresh Lemon Juice, ⅙ gill of Cointreau, ⅙ gill of Cognac Brandy." The use of "gill" here might be confusing, but the important thing to note is the equal proportions. It is debated whether this drink originated in Paris or London, but it is generally accepted that this drink was created in Europe at just about the same time that American Prohibition began.

For all of these cocktails it has become overly common for bars to use a "sour mix" to make them, often just combining a premade sour mix with the base spirit in order to quickly and efficiently churn out drinks. This approach, however, is not one that should be followed by a quality bar, any more than a quality restaurant would premake all of their meals and simply reheat them in the microwave.

In achieving balance, these drinks should be neither overly sour nor overly sweet. And the base spirit, while not dominant, should be present in flavor.

Our favorite recipes:

▽ MARGARITA
1½ oz. Tequila
1 oz. Cointreau
½ oz. Lime Juice

Shake with ice and strain into a salt-rimmed cocktail glass, or a salt-rimmed, ice-filled margarita glass. Garnish with a wedge of lime.

ℽ DAIQUIRI

2 oz. Light Rum
½ oz. Lime Juice
1 tsp. Bar Sugar

Shake with ice and strain into a chilled cocktail glass. Garnish with a slice of lime.

ℽ SIDECAR

2 oz. Cognac
1 oz. Cointreau
½ oz. Lemon Juice

Shake with ice and strain into a chilled cocktail glass. Garnish with a lemon twist.

While each of these cocktails follows the same basic approach of spirit plus sweet plus sour, the actual ratios being used for each of them is listed differently. Because of the variation among spirits brands and the even greater variation in things like natural citrus, you should be prepared to adjust your recipes for balance. These recipes are merely a starting point.

A mastery of these principles can help you to improve the way you make drinks like the Lemon Drop, Kamikaze, Cosmopolitan, Between the Sheets, and Aviation, all of which owe their origins to the sour.

The Mai-Tai

Just as America was coming out of Prohibition, Don Beach was setting up shop with his Polynesian-themed restaurants, which became known as "Don the Beachcomber." In the 1940s Victor Bergeron threw his hat in the ring and started the "Trader Vic's" chain. These two franchises specifically ushered in a new era, not only in restaurant culture but in the cocktails they produced as well. Rum was the prominent spirit, with various, often exotic, juices and syrups being used as flavoring agents. This was the time of the "tiki craze," and there were many similarly themed restaurants that sprang up during this time in order to provide the American public with a much-needed vacation, one sip at a time.

Competition between these restaurants was often fierce, with their various cocktail recipes being so closely guarded that even the bartenders themselves did not know how to make them. They would use custom-made flavored syrups and mixes labeled "Don's Mix #1," "Don's Mix #2", and so forth. The bartenders wouldn't know precisely what was in the mix, and therefore couldn't reveal the recipes even if they wanted to.

This caused a problem, however, for the customers. After having a particularly fine drink at one bar, they would innocently attempt to order it at some other bar and be faced with an apologetic bartender who had no idea how to make it. Often, these bartenders would attempt to come up with a close approximation. If they felt that their result was a fine-tasting drink, it would then become a new incarnation of the drink.

With the casual proliferation of such a variety of different recipes for a drink with a single name, it is difficult to identify which is the original drink. One of the most popular drinks during this time was the Mai-Tai, and because of this it probably ended up with the highest number of variations. Fortunately, the version that started its popularity, which is referred to as the original Mai-Tai, was recorded by Victor "Trader Vic" Bergeron in 1944. There was apparently a similarly named drink listed on an earlier "Don the Beachcomber" menu, but its recipe was so radically different (and unpopular) that the Trader Vic recipe is clearly a different drink entirely.

As recorded by Mr. Bergeron himself, the original recipe for the Mai-Tai was as follows:

☐ MAI-TAI (ORIGINAL FORMULA)
2 oz. 17-year-old J. Wray Nephew Jamaican Rum
½ oz. French Garnier Orgeat
½ oz. Holland DeKuyper Orange Curaçao
¼ oz. Rock Candy Syrup
Juice from one fresh lime

Hand shake and garnish with half of the lime shell inside the drink and float a sprig of fresh mint at the edge of the glass.

Over time, this recipe went through a number of changes, often to accommodate changes in product brands, with the final (and present-day) version being one that turns to a custom-made Mai-Tai mix to be added to rum and lime juice. Those in the know, however, will order their Mai-Tai's at Trader Vic's by requesting a "San Francisco Mai-Tai," a drink made from scratch, without the mix.

This drink is served at bars across the country with ingredients as far reaching as pineapple juice, grenadine, passion fruit syrup, orange juice, amaretto, and even cherry brandy. Sometimes, the resultant drink may be quite good indeed, but technically it is not a Mai-Tai and would be better to take an original name than to wear the guise of this classic.

A variation of the original Mai-Tai that holds up well without worrying about specific branded products is this one:

☐ MAI-TAI
1 oz. Light Rum
1 oz. Gold Rum
½ oz. Orange Curaçao
½ oz. Orgeat
½ oz. Lime Juice

Shake with ice. Strain into an ice-filled Old-Fashioned glass. Garnish with a speared pineapple chunk, cherry, and a sprig of mint.

Another variation is to include super-premium or exotic rums.

Bloody Mary

The Bloody Mary is an interesting cocktail, with ingredients more commonly found in the kitchen than behind the bar. The most credible story is that it was invented by Fernand Petiot of Harry's American Bar in Paris around 1920.

A vodka-based cocktail, the Bloody Mary owes its flavor to the other ingredients.

The basic Bloody Mary recipe:

☐ BLOODY MARY

1½ oz. Vodka
4 oz. Tomato Juice
¼ oz. Fresh Lemon Juice
2 dashes Worcestershire
4 dashes Tabasco
Pinch of Salt and Pepper

Combine all ingredients in mixing glass and roll back and forth to mix. Strain into an ice-filled pint glass or red-wine glass. Garnish with wedge of lemon and lime.

Something interesting has happened with the Bloody Mary that sets it apart from other drinks. While it is often easy to get into a debate over the "correctness" of one recipe or the other, the Bloody Mary has become a drink in which the differences between personal renditions are celebrated.

The above is essentially the "mother" recipe from which different offspring arise. The vodka and tomato juice are the core ingredients, but as for the rest, anything goes as long as you arrive at a spicy and savory drink with a rich and robust flavor.

Among the creative ingredients that have found their way into the Bloody Mary are celery salt, soy sauce, wasabi, horseradish, cumin, chili powder, curry powder, cayenne pepper, ginger, liquid smoke, steak sauce, angostura bitters, sherry, beef broth, clam juice, and countless others. The Bloody Mary has essentially become the "meat loaf" of cocktails. Almost anything goes as long as it's recognizable in the end.

And while originally the garnish of a wedge of lemon and lime was relatively unassuming, such a modest appointment is almost an insult today. The choices for garnishing a Bloody Mary can range from a simple selection of olives and different vegetables, to cooked appetizers that are specifically designed to be a value-added accompaniment. Bloody Marys have appeared with sautéed peppers, roasted baby onions, spicy shrimp, chicken satay, cubes of beef, and even whole raw oysters. It's the drink that drinks like a meal, where a little ostentation is welcome.

BRANDY

BRANDY TAKES ITS NAME from the Dutch word "brandewijn," or "burned wine," which refers to the process of heating the wine during distillation. Brandy as a category embodies a dizzying number of subcategories, including fruit brandy, grappa, marc, pomace, and eau de vie, to name only a few. The most generic definition for this spirit is that it is distilled from fermented fruit; it is sometimes aged in oak casks or barrels; and it usually clocks in at around 80 proof. While it is often considered an after-dinner sipping spirit, brandy is also widely used in cocktails.

Generally, fruit brandies and eau de vie can legally be made from practically any fruit, including apples, pears, apricots, blackberries, and cherries. At the high end of the brandy spectrum, you'll find Calvados from the north of France, Cognac and Armagnac from southwest France, and Solera Gran Reserva under the Brandy de Jerez—or sherry—imprimatur from the south of Spain. Artisanal brandies are also being made here in the United States, but not from any specific region, though the best hail from California and Oregon.

In cocktails, dry sherry is sometimes employed in place of vermouth, while Cognac plays a leading role in a number of recipes dating back to the birth of the cocktail in Antoine Peychaud's apothecary shop in New Orleans. Indeed, the original juleps were made with Cognac, as were many of the early Pousse Café recipes. Armagnac, Cognac's rustic cousin, has a distinctly stronger flavor than Cognac, and is employed as a substitute to enhance the brandy presence in a cocktail. Calvados, made with apples, is naturally used to ratchet up the quality of any cocktail calling for mere fruit or apple brandy.

� THE "23"

2½ oz. Armagnac
½ oz. Sweet Vermouth
½ oz. Lemon Juice
2 dashes Bitters

Shake with ice and strain into chilled, sugar-rimmed cocktail glass. Garnish with a twist of lemon peel.

� AFTER-DINNER COCKTAIL

1 oz. Apricot-flavored Brandy
1 oz. Triple Sec
1 oz. Lime Juice

Shake with ice and strain into chilled cocktail glass. Leave lime in glass.

☐ ALABAZAM

2 oz. Armagnac
¾ oz. Lemon Juice
½ oz. Orange Curaçao
½ oz. Superfine Sugar (or Simple Syrup)
2 dashes Angostura Bitters
2 dashes Peychaud's Bitters

Shake with ice and strain into ice-filled old-fashioned glass. Garnish with a flamed orange peel.

� ALEXANDER COCKTAIL NO. 2

1 oz. Crème de Cacao (White)
1 oz. Brandy
1 oz. Light Cream

Shake with ice and strain into chilled cocktail glass. Garnish with fresh-grated nutmeg on top.

Say Hello

Greet all guests as they arrive at the bar. If you are busy with a guest make eye contact with new arrivals. Eye contact and a quick smile or nod of awareness will put a new arrival at ease. It will give them the confidence to enjoy the friend they may be with or their surroundings without monitoring your every move to make that initial contact. If you are really slammed the guest will give you the few extra minutes you need if you just give them a smile and a nod.

—DALE DEGROFF (a.k.a. King Cocktail),
author of *The Craft of the Cocktail*

AMERICAN BEAUTY COCKTAIL

½ oz. Orange Juice

½ oz. Grenadine

½ oz. Dry Vermouth

½ oz. Brandy

¼ tsp. Crème de Menthe (White)

1 dash Port

Shake first five ingredients with ice and strain into chilled cocktail glass. Top with a dash of port.

APPLE BRANDY COCKTAIL

1½ oz. Apple Brandy

1 tsp. Grenadine

1 tsp. Lemon Juice

Shake with ice and strain into chilled cocktail glass.

APPLE BRANDY HIGHBALL

2 oz. Apple Brandy

Ginger Ale or Club Soda

Pour brandy into ice-filled highball glass. Fill with ginger ale or club soda. Add a twist of lemon peel, if desired, and stir.

APPLE BRANDY RICKEY

½ oz. Lime Juice

1½ oz. Apple Brandy

Club Soda

Pour lime juice and brandy into ice-filled highball glass. Fill with club soda and stir. Garnish with a wedge of lime.

APPLE BRANDY SOUR

1 oz. Lemon Juice

½ tsp. Superfine Sugar (or Simple Syrup)

2 oz. Apple Brandy

Shake with ice and strain into chilled sour glass. Garnish with a half-slice of lemon and a maraschino cherry.

APRICOT BRANDY RICKEY

½ oz. Lime Juice

2 oz. Apricot-flavored Brandy

Club Soda

Pour lime juice and brandy into ice-filled highball glass. Fill with club soda and stir. Garnish with a wedge of lime.

APRICOT COCKTAIL

½ oz. Lemon Juice

1 oz. Orange Juice

1½ oz. Apricot-flavored Brandy

1 tsp. Gin

Shake with ice and strain into chilled cocktail glass.

APRICOT COOLER

½ tsp. Superfine Sugar (or Simple Syrup)

Club Soda

2 oz. Apricot-flavored Brandy

Ginger Ale (optional)

In Collins glass, dissolve sugar/syrup and club soda. Stir and fill glass with ice and add brandy. Add club soda or ginger ale and stir again. Insert a spiral of orange or lemon peel (or both) and dangle end over rim of glass.

APRICOT FIZZ

1 oz. Lemon Juice

½ oz. Lime Juice

1 tsp. Superfine Sugar (or Simple Syrup)

2 oz. Apricot-flavored Brandy

Club Soda

Shake juices, sugar/syrup, and brandy with ice and strain into ice-filled high-ball glass. Fill with club soda and stir.

B & B

½ oz. Bénédictine

½ oz. Brandy

Use cordial glass and carefully float the brandy on top of the Bénédictine.

BABBIE'S SPECIAL COCKTAIL

½ oz. Light Cream

1½ oz. Apricot-flavored Brandy

¼ tsp. Gin

Shake with ice and strain into chilled cocktail glass.

BEE STINGER

½ oz. Crème de Menthe (White)

1½ oz. Blackberry Brandy

Shake with ice and strain into chilled cocktail glass.

BETSY ROSS

1½ oz. Brandy

1½ oz. Port

1 dash Triple Sec

Stir with ice and strain into chilled cocktail glass.

BISTRO SIDECAR

1½ oz. Brandy

½ oz. Tuaca

½ oz. Frangelico

¼ oz. Lemon Juice

¼ oz. Superfine Sugar (or Simple Syrup)

1 wedge Tangerine, squeezed

Shake with ice. Strain into chilled, sugar-rimmed cocktail glass. Garnish with a roasted hazelnut.

BLACK FEATHER

1 oz. Brandy

1 oz. Dry Vermouth

½ oz. Triple Sec

1 dash Angostura Bitters

Stir and strain into chilled cocktail glass. Garnish with a lemon twist.

BOMBAY COCKTAIL

½ oz. Dry Vermouth
½ oz. Sweet Vermouth
1 oz. Brandy
¼ tsp. Anisette
½ tsp. Triple Sec

Stir with ice and strain into chilled cocktail glass.

BOSOM CARESSER

1 oz. Brandy
1 oz. Madeira
½ oz. Triple Sec

Stir with ice and strain into chilled cocktail glass.

BRANDIED MADEIRA

1 oz. Brandy
1 oz. Madeira
½ oz. Dry Vermouth

Stir with ice and strain into ice-filled old-fashioned glass. Add a twist of lemon peel.

BRANDIED PORT

1 oz. Brandy
1 oz. Tawny Port
½ oz. Lemon Juice
1 tsp. Maraschino Liqueur

Shake all ingredients and strain into ice-filled old-fashioned glass. Add a slice of orange.

BRANDY ALEXANDER

½ oz. Crème de Cacao (Brown)
½ oz. Brandy
½ oz. Heavy Cream

Shake well with ice and strain into chilled cocktail glass.

BRANDY CASSIS

1½ oz. Brandy
1 oz. Lemon Juice
1 dash Crème de Cassis

Shake with ice and strain into chilled cocktail glass. Add a twist of lemon peel.

BRANDY COBBLER

1 tsp. Superfine Sugar (or Simple Syrup)
2 oz. Club Soda
2 oz. Brandy

Dissolve sugar/syrup in club soda. Fill red-wine glass with shaved ice. Add brandy. Stir well and garnish with fruits in season. Serve with straws.

BRANDY COCKTAIL

2 oz. Brandy
¼ tsp. Superfine Sugar (or Simple Syrup)
2 dashes Bitters

Stir ingredients with ice and strain into chilled cocktail glass. Add a twist of lemon peel.

BRANDY COLLINS

1 oz. Lemon Juice
1 tsp. Superfine Sugar (or Simple Syrup)
2 oz. Brandy
Club Soda

Shake lemon juice, sugar/syrup, and brandy with ice and strain into ice-filled Collins glass. Fill with club soda and stir. Garnish with a slice of orange or lemon and a maraschino cherry. Serve with straws.

BRANDY CURSTA COCKTAIL

1 tsp. Maraschino Liqueur
1 dash Bitters
1 tsp. Lemon Juice
½ oz. Triple Sec
2 oz. Brandy

Moisten the edge of a cocktail glass with lemon and dip into sugar. Cut the rind of half a lemon into a spiral and place in glass. Stir above ingredients with ice and strain into chilled, sugar-rimmed glass. Add a slice of orange.

BRANDY DAISY

1 oz. Lemon Juice
½ tsp. Superfine Sugar (or Simple Syrup)
1 tsp. Raspberry Syrup or Grenadine
2 oz. Brandy

Shake with ice and strain into beer mug or 8-oz. metal cup. Add cubes of ice and garnish with fruit.

BRANDY FIX

1 oz. Lemon Juice
1 tsp. Superfine Sugar (or Simple Syrup)
1 tsp. Water
2½ oz. Brandy

Mix lemon juice, sugar/syrup, and water in highball glass. Stir. Then fill glass with shaved ice and brandy. Stir, add a slice of lemon. Serve with straws.

BRANDY FIZZ

1 oz. Lemon Juice
1 tsp. Superfine Sugar (or Simple Syrup)
2 oz. Brandy
Club Soda

Shake lemon juice, sugar/syrup, and brandy with ice and strain into ice-filled highball glass. Fill with club soda and stir.

BRANDY GUMP COCKTAIL

1½ oz. Brandy
1 oz. Lemon Juice
½ tsp. Grenadine

Shake with ice and strain into chilled cocktail glass.

BRANDY HIGHBALL

2 oz. Brandy
Ginger Ale or Club Soda

Pour brandy into ice-filled highball glass. Fill with ginger ale or club soda. Add a twist of lemon peel and stir gently.

BRANDY JULEP

1 tsp. Superfine Sugar (or Simple Syrup)

5–6 Mint Leaves

2½ oz. Brandy

Put sugar/syrup, mint leaves, and brandy into Collins glass. Fill glass with finely shaved ice and stir until mint rises to top, being careful not to bruise leaves. (Do not hold glass while stirring.) Garnish with a slice of pineapple, orange, or lemon, and a maraschino cherry. Serve with straws.

BRANDY SANGAREE

½ tsp. Superfine Sugar (or Simple Syrup)

1 tsp. Water

2 oz. Brandy

Club Soda

½ oz. Port

Dissolve sugar/syrup in water and add brandy. Pour into ice-filled highball glass. Fill with club soda and stir. Float port on top and garnish with fresh-grated nutmeg.

BRANDY SLING

1 tsp. Superfine Sugar (or Simple Syrup)

1 tsp. Water

1 oz. Lemon Juice

2 oz. Brandy

Dissolve sugar/syrup in water and lemon juice in old-fashioned glass. Fill with ice, add brandy, and stir. Garnish with a twist of lemon peel.

BRANDY SMASH

1 cube Sugar

1 oz. Club Soda

4 sprigs Mint

2 oz. Brandy

Muddle cube of sugar with club soda and mint in old-fashioned glass. Add brandy and ice. Stir and garnish with a slice of orange and a maraschino cherry. Add a twist of lemon peel on top.

BRANDY AND SODA

2 oz. Brandy

Club Soda

Pour brandy into ice-filled Collins glass. Fill with club soda.

BRANDY SOUR

1 oz. Lemon Juice

½ tsp. Superfine Sugar (or Simple Syrup)

2 oz. Brandy

Shake with ice and strain into chilled sour glass. Garnish with a half-slice of lemon and a maraschino cherry.

BRANDY SQUIRT

1½ oz. Brandy
1 tbsp. Superfine Sugar
    (or Simple Syrup)
1 tsp. Grenadine
Club Soda

Shake first three ingredients with ice. Strain into chilled highball glass and fill with club soda. Garnish with a stick of pineapple and strawberries.

BRANDY SWIZZLE

1 tsp. Superfine Sugar (or
    Simple Syrup)
1 oz. Lime Juice
2 oz. Club Soda
2 dashes Bitters
2 oz. Brandy

Dissolve the sugar/syrup in lime juice and club soda in Collins glass. Fill glass with ice and stir. Add bitters and brandy. Add club soda and serve with a swizzle stick.

BRANDY TODDY

½ tsp. Superfine Sugar (or
    Simple Syrup)
1 tsp. Water
2 oz. Brandy
1 Ice Cube

Dissolve the sugar/syrup and water in old-fashioned glass. Add the brandy and the ice cube. Stir and add a twist of lemon peel on top.

BRANDY VERMOUTH COCKTAIL

½ oz. Sweet Vermouth
2 oz. Brandy
1 dash Bitters

Stir with ice and strain into chilled cocktail glass.

BRANTINI

1½ oz. Brandy
1 oz. Gin
1 dash Dry Vermouth

Stir with ice and strain into ice-filled old-fashioned glass. Add a twist of lemon peel.

BRUNSWICK STREET COCKTAIL

1½ oz. Cognac
1½ oz. Sherry (Pedro
    Ximenez)
1 Egg Yolk

Shake and strain into chilled cocktail glass. Garnish with fresh-grated nutmeg on top.

BULLDOG COCKTAIL

1½ oz. Cherry-flavored
    Brandy
¾ oz. Gin
½ oz. Lime Juice

Shake with ice and strain into chilled cocktail glass.

BULL'S EYE

1 oz. Brandy

2 oz. Hard Cider

Ginger Ale

Pour brandy and hard cider into ice-filled highball glass and fill with ginger ale. Stir.

BULL'S MILK

1 tsp. Superfine Sugar (or Simple Syrup)

1 oz. Light Rum

1½ oz. Brandy

1 cup Milk

Shake with ice and strain into chilled Collins glass. Garnish with fresh-grated nutmeg and a pinch of cinnamon on top.

BUTTON HOOK COCKTAIL

½ oz. Crème de Menthe (White)

½ oz. Apricot-flavored Brandy

½ oz. Anisette

½ oz. Brandy

Shake with ice and strain into chilled cocktail glass.

CADIZ

¼ oz. Dry Sherry

¼ oz. Blackberry-flavored Brandy

½ oz. Triple Sec

½ oz. Light Cream

Shake with ice and strain into ice-filled old-fashioned glass.

CALVADOS COCKTAIL

1½ oz. Calvados (Apple Brandy)

1½ oz. Orange Juice

¾ oz. Triple Sec

¾ oz. Orange Bitters

Shake with ice and strain into chilled cocktail glass.

CARA SPOSA

1 oz. Coffee-flavored Brandy

1 oz. Triple Sec

½ oz. Light Cream

Shake with ice and strain into chilled cocktail glass.

CARROL COCKTAIL

1½ oz. Brandy

¾ oz. Sweet Vermouth

Stir with ice and strain into chilled cocktail glass. Garnish with a maraschino cherry.

CHAMPS ÉLYSÉES COCKTAIL

1 oz. Brandy

½ oz. Chartreuse (Yellow)

½ oz. Lemon Juice

½ tsp. Superfine Sugar (or Simple Syrup)

1 dash Bitters

Shake with ice and strain into chilled cocktail glass.

CHARLES COCKTAIL

1½ oz. Sweet Vermouth

1½ oz. Brandy

1 dash Bitters

Stir with ice and strain into chilled cocktail glass.

❦ CHERRY BLOSSOM

1½ oz. Brandy
½ oz. Cherry-flavored Brandy
1½ tsps. Triple Sec
1½ tsps. Grenadine
2 tsps. Lemon Juice

Prepare chilled cocktail glass by dipping rim in cherry brandy and then superfine sugar. Shake ingredients with ice and strain into prepared glass. Add a maraschino cherry.

CHERRY FIZZ

1 oz. Lemon Juice
2 oz. Cherry-flavored Brandy
Club Soda

Shake with ice and strain into ice-filled highball glass. Fill with club soda and garnish with a maraschino cherry.

CHERRY SLING

2 oz. Cherry-flavored Brandy
1 oz. Lemon Juice

Combine in ice-filled old-fashioned glass and stir. Add a twist of lemon peel.

CHICAGO COCKTAIL

2 oz. Brandy
1 dash Bitters
¼ tsp. Triple Sec

Prepare chilled old-fashioned glass by rubbing slice of lemon around rim and then dipping into sugar. Stir ingredients with ice and strain into prepared glass.

CLASSIC COCKTAIL

½ oz. Lemon Juice
1½ tsps. Curaçao
1½ tsps. Maraschino Liqueur
1 oz. Brandy

Prepare rim of chilled old-fashioned glass by rubbing with lemon and dipping into superfine sugar. Shake ingredients with ice and strain into prepared glass.

COFFEE GRASSHOPPER

¾ oz. Coffee-flavored Brandy
¾ oz. Crème de Menthe (White)
¾ oz. Light Cream

Shake with ice and strain into ice-filled old-fashioned glass.

COGNAC HIGHBALL

2 oz. Cognac
Ginger Ale or Club Soda

Pour Cognac into ice-filled highball glass and fill with ginger ale or club soda. Add a twist of lemon peel, if desired, and stir.

❦ COLD DECK COCKTAIL

½ tsp. Crème de Menthe (White)
½ oz. Sweet Vermouth
1 oz. Brandy

Stir with ice and strain into chilled cocktail glass.

CRÈME DE CAFÉ

1 oz. Coffee-flavored Brandy

½ oz. Rum

½ oz. Anisette

1 oz. Light Cream

Shake with ice and strain into chilled old-fashioned glass.

THE CRUX

¾ oz. Dubonnet

¾ oz. Triple Sec

¾ oz. Brandy

¾ oz. Lemon Juice

Stir and serve in chilled cocktail glass with a twist of orange.

CUBAN COCKTAIL NO. 2

½ oz Lime Juice

½ oz. Apricot-flavored Brandy

1½ oz. Brandy

1 tsp. Light Rum

Shake with ice and strain into chilled cocktail glass.

D'ARTAGNAN

½ tsp. Armagnac

½ tsp. Grand Marnier

3 tsps. Orange Juice

½ tsp. Simple Syrup

3 oz. Champagne, Chilled

Orange Peel, cut into thin strips

Chill first four ingredients in mixing glass and strain into champagne flute. Top with Champagne and add strips of orange peel so they extend the length of the glass.

DEAUVILLE COCKTAIL

½ oz. Lemon Juice

½ oz. Brandy

½ oz. Apple Brandy

½ oz. Triple Sec

Shake with ice and strain into chilled cocktail glass.

DELORES

1 oz. Brandy (Spanish)

1 oz. Cherry Liqueur

1 oz. Crème de Cacao

1 Egg White

Shake and strain into a champagne flute. Garnish with fresh-grated nutmeg on top.

DEPTH BOMB

1 oz. Apple Brandy

1 oz. Brandy

1 dash Lemon Juice

1 dash Grenadine

Shake with ice and strain into ice-filled old-fashioned glass.

DREAM COCKTAIL

¾ oz. Triple Sec

1½ oz. Brandy

¼ tsp. Anisette

Shake with ice and strain into chilled cocktail glass.

Y EAST INDIA COCKTAIL NO. 1

1½ oz. Brandy
½ tsp. Pineapple Juice
½ tsp. Triple Sec
1 tsp. Jamaican Rum
1 dash Bitters

Shake with ice and strain into chilled cocktail glass. Add a twist of lemon peel and a maraschino cherry.

Y ETHEL DUFFY COCKTAIL

¾ oz. Apricot-flavored Brandy
¾ oz. Crème de Menthe (White)
¾ oz. Triple Sec

Shake with ice and strain into chilled cocktail glass.

Y FALLEN LEAVES

¾ oz. Calvados (Apple Brandy)
¾ oz. Sweet Vermouth
¼ oz. Dry Vermouth
1 dash Brandy
1 squeeze Lemon Peel

Stir with ice and strain into chilled cocktail glass. Squeeze lemon twist into drink, and use as garnish.

Y FANCY BRANDY

2 oz. Brandy
1 dash Bitters
¼ tsp. Triple Sec
¼ tsp. Superfine Sugar (or Simple Syrup)

Shake with ice and strain into chilled cocktail glass. Add a twist of lemon peel.

Y FANTASIO COCKTAIL

1 tsp. Crème de Menthe (White)
1 tsp. Maraschino Liqueur
1 oz. Brandy
¾ oz. Dry Vermouth

Stir with ice and strain into chilled cocktail glass.

Y FONTAINEBLEAU SPECIAL

1 oz. Brandy
1 oz. Anisette
½ oz. Dry Vermouth

Shake with ice and strain into chilled cocktail glass.

Y FRENCH QUARTER

2½ oz. Brandy
¾ oz. Lillet Blonde

Stir with ice and strain into chilled cocktail glass. Garnish with a thin quarter wheel of lemon.

Y FROUPE COCKTAIL

1½ oz. Sweet Vermouth
1½ oz. Brandy
1 tsp. Bénédictine

Stir with ice and strain into chilled cocktail glass.

▯ GEORGIA MINT JULEP

2 sprigs Mint
1 tsp. Superfine Sugar (or Simple Syrup)
1 splash Water
1½ oz. Brandy
1 oz. Peach-flavored Brandy

Put mint, sugar/syrup, and splash of water into Collins

glass and muddle. Fill with ice, and then add brandy and peach-flavored brandy. Garnish with mint leaves.

GILROY COCKTAIL

½ oz. Lemon Juice

½ oz. Dry Vermouth

¾ oz. Cherry-flavored Brandy

¾ oz. Gin

1 dash Orange Bitters

Shake with ice and strain into chilled cocktail glass.

GOAT'S DELIGHT

1¾ oz. Kirschwasser

1¾ oz. Brandy

¼ oz. Orgeat Syrup (Almond Syrup)

¼ oz. Cream

¼ oz. Pastis (Pernod or Other Absinthe Substitute)

Shake with ice and strain into chilled cocktail glass.

GOLDEN DAWN

1 oz. Apple Brandy

½ oz. Apricot-flavored Brandy

½ oz. Gin

1 oz. Orange Juice

1 tsp. Grenadine

Shake all ingredients except grenadine with ice and strain into ice-filled old-fashioned glass. Add grenadine.

GOTHAM

½ tsp. Pernod (or Absinthe Substitute)

3 dashes Peach Bitters

3 oz. Brandy

Coat a chilled old-fashioned glass with Pernod (or absinthe substitute), and then add the peach bitters and brandy. Garnish with a twist of lemon peel.

HARVARD COCKTAIL

1½ oz. Brandy

¾ oz. Sweet Vermouth

1 dash Bitters

1 tsp. Grenadine

2 tsps. Lemon Juice

Shake with ice and strain into chilled cocktail glass.

HARVARD COOLER

½ tsp. Superfine Sugar (or Simple Syrup)

Club Soda

2 oz. Apple Brandy

Ginger Ale (optional)

In Collins glass, stir sugar/syrup into club soda. Add ice cubes and apple brandy. Fill with club soda or ginger ale and stir again. Insert a spiral of orange or lemon peel (or both) and dangle end over rim of glass.

HONEYMOON COCKTAIL

¾ oz. Bénédictine

¾ oz. Apple Brandy

1 oz. Lemon Juice

1 tsp. Triple Sec

Shake with ice and strain into chilled cocktail glass.

JACK-IN-THE-BOX

1 oz. Apple Brandy

1 oz. Pineapple Juice

1 dash Bitters

Shake with ice and strain into chilled cocktail glass.

JACK MAPLES

2 oz. Applejack

1 tsp. Maple Syrup (Medium-Amber)

1 dash Fee's Aromatic Bitters

Stir and strain into cocktail glass. Garnish with a cinnamon stick.

JACK ROSE COCKTAIL

1½ oz. Apple Brandy

½ oz. Lime Juice

1 tsp. Grenadine

Shake with ice and strain into chilled cocktail glass.

JAMAICA GRANITO

1 small scoop Lemon or Orange Sherbet

1½ oz. Brandy

1 oz. Triple Sec

Club Soda

Combine in Collins glass and stir. Garnish with fresh-grated nutmeg on top.

JAMAICA HOP

1 oz. Coffee-flavored Brandy

1 oz. Crème de Cacao (White)

1 oz. Light Cream

Shake well with ice and strain into chilled cocktail glass.

JAPANESE

2 oz. Brandy

½ oz. Orgeat Syrup (Almond Syrup)

2 dashes Angostura Bitters

Stir with ice and strain into chilled cocktail glass. Garnish with a twist of lemon peel.

JERSEY LIGHTNING

1½ oz. Apple Brandy

½ oz. Sweet Vermouth

1 oz. Lime Juice

Shake with ice and strain into chilled cocktail glass.

LADY BE GOOD

1½ oz. Brandy

½ oz. Crème de Menthe (White)

½ oz. Sweet Vermouth

Shake with ice and strain into chilled cocktail glass.

LA JOLLA

1½ oz. Brandy

½ oz. Crème de Banana

1 tsp. Orange Juice

2 tsps. Lemon Juice

Shake with ice and strain into chilled cocktail glass.

LIBERTY COCKTAIL

¾ oz. Light Rum

1½ oz. Apple Brandy

¼ tsp. Superfine Sugar (or Simple Syrup)

Stir with ice and strain into chilled cocktail glass.

⅄ LUGGER

1 oz. Brandy

1 oz. Apple Brandy

1 dash Apricot-flavored Brandy

Shake with ice and strain into chilled cocktail glass.

⅃ LUXURY COCKTAIL

3 oz. Brandy

2 dashes Orange Bitters

3 oz. Well-chilled Champagne

Stir and pour into champagne flute.

⅄ MERRY WIDOW COCKTAIL NO. 2

1¼ oz. Maraschino Liqueur

1¼ oz. Cherry-flavored Brandy

Stir with ice and strain into chilled cocktail glass. Garnish with a maraschino cherry.

⅄ METROPOLE

1½ oz. Brandy

1½ oz. Dry Vermouth

2 dashes Orange Bitters

1 dash Peychaud's Bitters

Stir with ice and strain into chilled cocktail glass. Garnish with a maraschino cherry.

⅄ METROPOLITAN COCKTAIL

1¼ oz. Brandy

1¼ oz. Sweet Vermouth

½ tsp. Superfine Sugar (or Simple Syrup)

1 dash Bitters

Stir with ice and strain into chilled cocktail glass.

⅄ MIDNIGHT COCKTAIL

1 oz. Apricot-flavored Brandy

½ oz. Triple Sec

½ oz. Lemon Juice

Shake with ice and strain into chilled cocktail glass.

☐ MIKADO COCKTAIL

1 oz. Brandy

1 dash Triple Sec

1 dash Grenadine

1 dash Crème de Noyaux

1 dash Bitters

Stir in old-fashioned glass over ice cubes.

☐ MONTANA

1½ oz. Brandy

1 oz. Port

½ oz. Dry Vermouth

Stir in ice-filled old-fashioned glass.

⬜ MOONLIGHT

2 oz. Apple Brandy

1 oz. Lemon Juice

1 tsp. Superfine Sugar (or Simple Syrup)

Shake with ice and strain into ice-filled old-fashioned glass.

🍸 MORNING COCKTAIL

1 oz. Brandy

1 oz. Dry Vermouth

¼ tsp. Triple Sec

¼ tsp. Maraschino Liqueur

¼ tsp. Anisette

2 dashes Orange Bitters

Stir with ice and strain into chilled cocktail glass. Garnish with a maraschino cherry.

⬜ NETHERLAND

1 oz. Brandy

1 oz. Triple Sec

1 dash Orange Bitters

Stir in ice-filled old-fashioned glass.

🍸 NICKY FINN

1 oz. Brandy

1 oz. Triple Sec

1 oz. Lemon Juice

1 dash Pernod (or Absinthe Substitute)

Shake with ice and strain into chilled cocktail glass. Garnish with a maraschino cherry or lemon zest.

🍸 THE NORMANDY

1½ oz. Calvados (Père Magloire or Apple Brandy)

1½ oz. Dubonnet Rouge

1 oz. Fresh Apple Cider

¼ oz. Lime Juice

Shake with ice and strain into chilled cocktail glass. Garnish with a slice of red apple.

🍸 OLYMPIC COCKTAIL

¾ oz. Orange Juice

¾ oz. Triple Sec

¾ oz. Brandy

Shake with ice and strain into chilled cocktail glass.

🍸 PARADISE COCKTAIL

1 oz. Apricot-flavored Brandy

¾ oz. Gin

1 oz. Orange Juice

Shake with ice and strain into chilled cocktail glass.

⬜ PEACH SANGAREE

1 oz. Peach-flavored Brandy

Club Soda

1 tsp. Port

Pour brandy into ice-filled highball glass. Fill glass with club soda. Stir and float port on top. Garnish with fresh-grated nutmeg on top.

PISCO SOUR

2 oz. Pisco (Peruvian Brandy)

1 oz. Lime Juice

¼ oz. Superfine Sugar (or Simple Syrup)

½ Egg White

1 dash Angostura Bitters

Shake all ingredients except bitters with ice. Strain into champagne flute. Dash with bitters.

POLONAISE

1½ oz. Brandy

½ oz. Blackberry-flavored Brandy

½ oz. Dry Sherry

1 dash Lemon Juice

Shake with ice and strain into ice-filled old-fashioned glass.

POOP DECK COCKTAIL

1 oz. Brandy

1 oz. Port

½ oz. Blackberry-flavored Brandy

Shake with ice and strain into chilled cocktail glass.

PRESTO COCKTAIL

½ oz. Orange Juice

½ oz. Sweet Vermouth

1½ oz. Brandy

¼ tsp. Anisette

Shake with ice and strain into chilled cocktail glass.

PRINCE OF WALES

¾ oz. Madeira

¾ oz. Brandy

¼ oz. Triple Sec

1 dash Angostura Bitters

1 splash Champagne, chilled

Shake first four ingredients and strain into champagne flute. Top with Champagne.

PRINCESS POUSSE CAFÉ

¾ oz. Apricot-flavored Brandy

1½ tsps. Light Cream

Pour cream carefully on top of brandy in a pousse café glass, so that it does not mix.

RENAISSANCE

2 oz. Brandy

1⅓ oz. Sweet Vermouth

⅓ oz. Limoncello

2 dashes Peach Bitters

Stir with ice and strain into chilled cocktail glass. Garnish with a twist of lemon peel.

ROYAL SMILE COCKTAIL

½ oz. Lemon Juice

1 tsp. Grenadine

½ oz. Gin

1 oz. Apple Brandy

Stir with ice and strain into chilled cocktail glass.

☐ ST. CHARLES PUNCH

1 oz. Brandy
½ oz. Triple Sec
2 oz. Lemon Juice
1 tsp. Sugar
3 oz. Port

Shake all ingredients except port with ice. Strain into ice-filled Collins glass. Top with port. Add a slice of lemon and a maraschino cherry.

☐ SARATOGA COCKTAIL

2 oz. Brandy
2 dashes Bitters
1 tsp. Lemon Juice
1 tsp. Pineapple Juice
½ tsp. Maraschino Liqueur

Shake with ice and strain into chilled cocktail glass.

☐ SAUCY SUE COCKTAIL

½ tsp. Apricot-flavored Brandy
½ tsp. Pernod
2 oz. Apple Brandy

Stir with ice and strain into chilled cocktail glass.

☐ SEVILLA 75

1 oz. Brandy (Spanish)
½ oz. Fresh Lemon Juice
1 tsp. Simple Syrup
2 oz. Cava

Shake first three ingredients and strain into chilled red-wine glass. Top with Cava.

☐ SHRINER COCKTAIL

1½ oz. Brandy
1½ oz. Sloe Gin
2 dashes Bitters
½ tsp. Superfine Sugar (or Simple Syrup)

Stir with ice and strain into chilled cocktail glass. Add a twist of lemon peel.

☐ SIDECAR COCKTAIL

½ oz. Lemon Juice
1 oz. Triple Sec
1 oz. Brandy

Shake with ice and strain into chilled cocktail glass.

☐ SINGAPORE SLING

1½ oz. Gin
½ oz. Cherry-flavored Brandy
¼ oz. Triple Sec
¼ oz. Bénédictine
4 oz. Pineapple Juice
½ oz. Lime Juice
⅓ oz. Grenadine
1 dash Bitters

Shake with ice and strain into ice-filled Collins glass. Garnish with a fresh or maraschino cherry and a slice of pineapple.

As served at the Raffles Hotel, Singapore.

☐ SLOPPY JOE'S COCKTAIL NO. 2

¾ oz. Pineapple Juice
¾ oz. Brandy
¾ oz. Port
¼ tsp. Triple Sec
¼ tsp. Grenadine

Shake with ice and strain into chilled cocktail glass.

SMART ALEC

2 oz. Cognac
1 oz. Triple Sec
1 oz. Chartreuse (Yellow)
1 dash Orange Bitters

Stir and strain into champagne coupe.

SOMBRERO

1½ oz. Coffee-flavored Brandy
1 oz. Light Cream

Pour brandy into ice-filled old-fashioned glass. Float cream on top.

SOOTHER COCKTAIL

½ oz. Brandy
½ oz. Apple Brandy
½ oz. Triple Sec
1 oz. Lemon Juice
1 tsp. Superfine Sugar (or Simple Syrup)

Shake with ice and strain into chilled cocktail glass.

SPECIAL ROUGH COCKTAIL

1½ oz. Apple Brandy
1½ oz. Brandy
½ tsp. Anisette

Stir with ice and strain into chilled cocktail glass.

STAR COCKTAIL

1 oz. Apple Brandy
1 oz. Sweet Vermouth
1 dash Bitters

Stir with ice and strain into chilled cocktail glass. Add a twist of lemon peel.

STINGER

½ oz. Crème de Menthe (White)
1½ oz. Brandy

Shake with ice and strain into chilled cocktail glass.

STIRRUP CUP

1 oz. Cherry-flavored Brandy
1 oz. Brandy
1 oz. Lemon Juice
1 tsp. Sugar

Shake with ice and strain into ice-filled old-fashioned glass.

THE TANTRIS SIDECAR

1 oz. Cognac (VS)
½ oz. Calvados (Apple Brandy)
½ oz. Triple Sec
½ oz. Lemon Juice
½ oz. Superfine Sugar (or Simple Syrup)
¼ oz. Pineapple Juice
¼ oz. Chartreuse (Green)

Shake all ingredients and strain into chilled, sugar-rimmed cocktail glass. Garnish with a lemon twist.

TEMPTER COCKTAIL

1 oz. Port
1 oz. Apricot-flavored Brandy

Stir with ice and strain into chilled cocktail glass.

⅄ THANKSGIVING SPECIAL

¾ oz. Apricot-flavored
Brandy

¾ oz. Gin

¾ oz. Dry Vermouth

¼ tsp. Lemon Juice

Shake with ice and strain
into chilled cocktail glass.
Garnish with a maraschino
cherry.

⅄ TULIP COCKTAIL

1½ tsps. Lemon Juice

1½ tsps. Apricot-flavored
Brandy

¾ oz. Sweet Vermouth

¾ oz. Apple Brandy

Shake with ice and strain
into chilled cocktail glass.

⅄ VALENCIA COCKTAIL

½ oz. Orange Juice

1½ oz. Apricot-flavored
Brandy

2 dashes Orange Bitters

Shake with ice and strain
into chilled cocktail glass.

⅄ VANDERBILT COCKTAIL

¾ oz. Cherry-flavored Brandy

1½ oz. Brandy

1 tsp. Superfine Sugar (or
Simple Syrup)

2 dashes Bitters

Stir with ice and strain into
chilled cocktail glass.

⅄ WHIP COCKTAIL

¾ oz. Dry Vermouth

½ oz. Sweet Vermouth

1½ oz. Brandy

¼ tsp. Anisette

1 tsp. Triple Sec

Stir with ice and strain into
chilled cocktail glass.

⅄ WIDOW'S KISS

2 oz. Calvados (Apple
Brandy)

1 oz. Chartreuse (Yellow)

1 oz. Bénédictine

1 dash Angostura Bitters

Stir with ice and strain into
chilled cocktail glass.

⅄ WINDY-CORNER COCKTAIL

2 oz. Blackberry-flavored
Brandy

Stir brandy with ice and
strain into chilled cocktail
glass. Garnish with fresh-
grated nutmeg on top.

GIN

GIN WAS CREATED OVER 300 YEARS AGO by a Dutch chemist named Dr. Franciscus Sylvius in an attempt to enhance the therapeutic properties of juniper in a medicinal beverage. He called it *genièvre*, French for "juniper," a term that was anglicized by English soldiers fighting in the Netherlands, who also nicknamed it "Dutch courage." The popularity of gin in England became such that the "London dry" style evolved into the benchmark of quality. The clear spirit is made from a mash of cereal grain (primarily corn, rye, barley, and wheat) that is flavored with botanicals (primarily juniper), which gives it its unique taste. Other botanicals employed in top-secret recipes include coriander, lemon and orange peel, cassia root, anise, and fennel seeds, to name only a few.

Gin, like many other spirits, changed in character in the early nineteenth century, when advances made in distilling equipment revolutionized the way it was made. Today, it's changing again. A new international style called "New Western dry" has emerged in the past decade; it's lighter and more balanced, meant to be sipped as well as mixed into cocktails. Historical styles of gin are making a comeback too, such as "Old Tom" (a sweeter version of London dry) and the lower-proof Dutch original genièvre, which is distilled from malted grain mash similar to whiskey and aged in oak casks.

Regardless of the classification, probably the best way to compare gins is to mix them with tonic or vermouth and imagine the myriad possibilities.

▽ ABBEY COCKTAIL

1½ oz. Gin
1 oz. Orange Juice
1 dash Orange Bitters

Shake with ice and strain into chilled cocktail glass. Add a maraschino cherry.

▽ ADAM AND EVE

2 oz. Citrus-flavored Brandy
1 oz. Gin
1 dash Lemon Juice

Shake with ice and strain into chilled cocktail glass.

▯ ALABAMA FIZZ

1 oz. Lemon Juice
1 tsp. Superfine Sugar (or Simple Syrup)
2 oz. Gin
Club Soda

Shake lemon juice, sugar/syrup, and gin with ice and strain into ice-filled highball glass. Fill with club soda. Garnish with two sprigs of fresh mint.

▽ ALASKA COCKTAIL

2 dashes Orange Bitters
1½ oz. Gin
¾ oz. Chartreuse (Yellow)

Stir with ice and strain into chilled cocktail glass.

▯ ALBEMARLE FIZZ

1 oz. Lemon Juice
2 oz. Gin
1 tsp. Superfine Sugar (or Simple Syrup)
1 tsp. Raspberry Syrup
Club Soda

Shake first four ingredients with ice and strain into ice-filled highball glass. Fill with club soda.

▽ ALEXANDER COCKTAIL NO. 1

1 oz. Gin
1 oz. Crème de Cacao (White)
1 oz. Light Cream

Shake with ice and strain into chilled cocktail glass. Garnish with fresh-grated nutmeg on top.

▽ ALEXANDER'S SISTER COCKTAIL

1 oz. Dry Gin
1 oz. Crème de Menthe (Green)
1 oz. Light Cream

Shake with ice and strain into chilled cocktail glass. Garnish with fresh-grated nutmeg on top.

▽ ALLEN COCKTAIL

1½ tsps. Lemon Juice
¾ oz. Maraschino Liqueur
1½ oz. Gin

Shake with ice and strain into chilled cocktail glass.

ANGLER'S COCKTAIL

2 dashes Bitters

3 dashes Orange Bitters

1½ oz. Gin

1 dash Grenadine

Shake with ice and pour into ice-filled old-fashioned glass.

APRICOT ANISETTE COLLINS

1½ oz. Gin

½ oz. Apricot-flavored Brandy

1½ tsps. Anisette

½ oz. Lemon Juice

Club Soda

Shake first four ingredients with ice and strain into ice-filled Collins glass. Fill with club soda and stir lightly. Garnish with a slice of lemon.

ARCHANGEL

1 Cucumber Slice

2¼ oz. Gin

¾ oz. Aperol

Muddle cucumber. Stir remaining ingredients with ice and strain into chilled cocktail glass. Garnish with a lemon twist.

ARTILLERY

1½ oz. Gin

1½ tsps. Sweet Vermouth

2 dashes Bitters

Stir with ice and strain into chilled cocktail glass.

ASTORIA BIANCO

2 oz. Gin

¾ oz. Dry Vermouth

2 dashes Orange Bitters

Stir with ice and strain into chilled cocktail glass. Garnish with an orange twist.

AUDREY FANNING

2½ oz. Gin

1 oz. Sweet Vermouth

½ oz. Cherry Heering

2 dashes Peychaud's Bitters

Sir with ice and strain into chilled cocktail glass.

AVIATION

2 oz. Gin

½ oz. Maraschino Liqueur

¼ oz. Lemon Juice

Shake with ice and strain into chilled cocktail glass. Garnish with a fresh or maraschino cherry.

BAD-HUMORED OLD-FASHIONED

2 oz. Old Genever

¼ oz. Maple Syrup

2 dashes Angostura Bitters

Stir with ice and strain into chilled old-fashioned glass. Garnish with a lemon twist.

⅄ BARBARY COAST

½ oz. Gin
½ oz. Rum
½ oz. White Crème de Cacao
½ oz. Scotch
½ oz. Light Cream

Shake with ice and strain into chilled cocktail glass.

⅄ BARON COCKTAIL

½ oz. Dry Vermouth
1½ oz. Gin
1½ tsps. Triple Sec
½ tsp. Sweet Vermouth

Stir with ice and strain into chilled cocktail glass. Add a twist of lemon peel.

⅄ BASIL'S BITE

3 Basil Leaves
2 oz. Gin
1 barspoon of Cynar
¾ oz. Aperol

Muddle basil leaves. Add ice and shake remaining ingredients. Strain into chilled cocktail glass. Garnish with a small basil leaf.

⅄ BEAUTY-SPOT COCKTAIL

1 tsp. Orange Juice
½ oz. Sweet Vermouth
½ oz. Dry Vermouth
1 oz. Gin
1 dash Grenadine

Shake first four ingredients with ice and strain into chilled cocktail glass, with a dash of grenadine in bottom of glass.

⅄ BEE'S KNEES

2 oz. Gin
½ oz. Lemon Juice
¾ oz. Honey Syrup

Shake and strain into champagne coupe.

⅄ BEE STING

2 oz. Gin
¾ oz. Lemon Juice
¾ oz. Honey Syrup
1 tsp. Pastis

Shake with ice and strain into chilled cocktail glass. Garnish with a whole star anise pod.

⅄ BELMONT COCKTAIL

2 oz. Gin
1 tsp. Raspberry Syrup
¾ oz. Light Cream

Shake with ice and strain into chilled cocktail glass.

⅄ BENNETT COCKTAIL

½ oz. Lime Juice
1½ oz. Gin
½ tsp. Superfine Sugar (or Simple Syrup)
2 dashes Orange Bitters

Shake with ice and strain into chilled cocktail glass.

BERLINER

1½ oz. Gin
½ oz. Dry Vermouth
½ oz. Kümmel
½ oz. Lemon Juice

Shake and serve up in a caraway/sugar-rimmed cocktail glass. Garnish with a lemon twist.

BERMUDA BOUQUET

1 oz. Orange Juice
1 oz. Lemon Juice
1 tsp. Superfine Sugar (or Simple Syrup)
1½ oz. Gin
1 oz. Apricot-flavored Brandy
1 tsp. Grenadine
½ tsp. Triple Sec

Shake with ice and strain into ice-filled highball glass.

BERMUDA HIGHBALL

¾ oz. Gin
¾ oz. Brandy
¾ oz. Dry Vermouth
Ginger Ale or Club Soda

Pour gin, brandy, and vermouth into ice-filled highball glass. Fill with ginger ale or club soda. Add a twist of lemon peel and stir.

BERMUDA ROSE

1¼ oz. Gin
1½ tsps. Apricot-flavored Brandy
1½ tsps. Grenadine

Shake with ice and strain into chilled cocktail glass.

BIJOU COCKTAIL

¾ oz. Gin
¾ oz. Chartreuse (Green)
¾ oz. Sweet Vermouth
1 dash Orange Bitters

Stir with ice and strain into chilled cocktail glass. Add a maraschino cherry on top.

BILLY TAYLOR

Club Soda
½ oz. Lime Juice
2 oz. Gin

Fill Collins glass with club soda and ice. Stir in lime juice and gin.

BLOODHOUND COCKTAIL

½ oz. Dry Vermouth
½ oz. Sweet Vermouth
1 oz. Gin

Shake with ice and strain into chilled cocktail glass. Garnish with two or three crushed strawberries.

BLOOD ORANGE

1½ oz. Gin
⅓ oz. Campari
⅓ oz. Amaro
1 oz. Orange Juice

Shake with ice and strain into chilled cocktail glass.

GIN

▽ BLOOMSBURY

2 oz. Gin
½ oz. Licor 43
½ oz. Lillet Blonde
2 dashes Peychaud's Bitters

Stir with ice and strain into chilled cocktail glass. Garnish with a lemon twist.

▽ BLUEBIRD

1½ oz. Gin
½ oz. Triple Sec
1 dash Bitters

Stir with ice and strain into chilled cocktail glass. Add a twist of lemon peel and a maraschino cherry.

▽ BLUE CANARY

¾ oz. Gin
3 tbsps. Grapefruit Juice
1 tbsp. Blue Curaçao

Stir all ingredients with ice. Strain into chilled cocktail glass filled with crushed ice. Garnish with a mint sprig.

▽ BLUE DEVIL COCKTAIL

1 oz. Gin
1 oz. Lemon Juice
1 tbsp. Maraschino Liqueur
½ tsp. Blue Curaçao

Shake with ice and strain into chilled cocktail glass.

▽ BLUE MOON COCKTAIL

1½ oz. Gin
¾ oz. Blue Curaçao

Stir with ice and strain into chilled cocktail glass. Add a twist of lemon peel.

▽ BOBBO'S BRIDE

1 oz. Gin
1 oz. Vodka
⅓ oz. Peach Liqueur
⅙ oz. Campari

Stir with ice and strain into chilled cocktail glass. Garnish with a slice of fresh peach.

▽ BOOMERANG

1 oz. Dry Vermouth
1½ oz. Gin
1 dash Bitters
1 dash Maraschino Liqueur

Stir with ice cubes and strain into chilled cocktail glass. Add a twist of lemon peel.

▽ BOSTON COCKTAIL

¾ oz. Gin
¾ oz. Apricot-flavored Brandy
½ oz. Lemon Juice
1½ tsps. Grenadine

Shake with ice and strain into chilled cocktail glass.

▽ BRIDAL

2 oz. Gin
1 oz. Sweet Vermouth
¼ oz. Maraschino Liqueur
1 dash Orange Bitters

Stir with ice and strain into chilled cocktail glass. Garnish with a maraschino cherry.

BRONX COCKTAIL

1 oz. Gin
½ oz. Dry Vermouth
½ oz. Sweet Vermouth
1 oz. Orange Juice

Shake with ice and strain into chilled cocktail glass. Garnish with a slice of orange.

BRONX COCKTAIL (DRY)

1 oz. Gin
1 oz. Dry Vermouth
½ oz. Orange Juice

Shake with ice and strain into chilled cocktail glass. Garnish with a slice of orange.

BRONX TERRACE COCKTAIL

1½ oz. Gin
1½ oz. Dry Vermouth
½ oz. Lime Juice

Shake with ice and strain into chilled cocktail glass. Add a maraschino cherry.

BROWN COCKTAIL

¾ oz. Gin
¾ oz. Light Rum
¾ oz. Dry Vermouth

Stir with ice and strain into chilled cocktail glass.

BULLDOG HIGHBALL

2 oz. Orange Juice
2 oz. Gin
Ginger Ale

Pour orange juice and gin into ice-filled highball glass. Fill with ginger ale and stir.

CABARET

1½ oz. Gin
2 dashes Bitters
½ tsp. Dry Vermouth
¼ tsp. Bénédictine

Stir with ice and strain into chilled cocktail glass. Garnish with a maraschino cherry.

CAPRICIOUS

1½ oz. Gin
½ oz. Elderflower Liqueur
½ oz. Dry Vermouth
2 dashes Peychaud's Bitters

Stir with ice and strain into chilled cocktail glass.

THE CARICATURE COCKTAIL

1½ oz. Gin
½ oz. Sweet Vermouth
¾ oz. Triple Sec
½ oz. Campari
½ oz. Grapefruit Juice

Shake with ice and strain into chilled cocktail glass. Garnish with an orange twist.

GIN

CARUSO

1½ oz. Gin

1 oz. Dry Vermouth

½ oz. Crème de Menthe (Green)

Stir with ice and strain into chilled cocktail glass.

CASINO COCKTAIL

2 dashes Orange Bitters

¼ tsp. Maraschino Liqueur

¼ tsp. Lemon Juice

2 oz. Gin

Shake with ice and strain into chilled cocktail glass. Garnish with a maraschino cherry.

CHELSEA SIDECAR

½ oz. Lemon Juice

¾ oz. Triple Sec

¾ oz. Gin

Shake with ice and strain into chilled cocktail glass.

CHIN UP

½ inch Cucumber Wheel

2 oz. Gin

½ oz. Cynar

½ oz. Dry Vermouth

½ pinch Salt

Muddle cucumber in mixing glass, add rest of ingredients, cover with ice, and stir thoroughly. Strain into cocktail glass. Garnish with a paper-thin wheel of cucumber.

CHOCOLATE NEGRONI

1½ oz. Gin

1 oz. Campari

¾ oz. Punt e Mes

½ oz. Crème de Cacao (white)

Stir with ice and strain into ice-filled old-fashioned glass. Garnish with an orange twist.

CLARIDGE COCKTAIL

¾ oz. Gin

¾ oz. Dry Vermouth

1 tbsp. Apricot-flavored Brandy

1 tbsp. Triple Sec

Stir with ice and strain into chilled cocktail glass.

CLOISTER

1½ oz. Gin

½ oz. Chartreuse (Yellow)

½ oz. Grapefruit Juice

¼ oz. Lemon Juice

¼ oz. Simple Syrup

Shake and strain into cocktail glass. Garnish with a grapefruit twist.

CLOVER CLUB

1½ oz. Gin

¼ oz. Grenadine

¾ oz. Lemon Juice

1 Egg White

Shake with ice and strain into chilled red-wine glass.

CLUB COCKTAIL

1½ oz. Gin
¾ oz. Sweet Vermouth

Stir with ice and strain into chilled cocktail glass. Add a maraschino cherry or olive.

COLONIAL COCKTAIL

½ oz. Grapefruit Juice
1 tsp. Maraschino Liqueur
1½ oz. Gin

Shake with ice and strain into chilled cocktail glass. Garnish with an olive.

THE COLONIAL COOLER

1½ oz. Gin
1½ oz. Sweet Vermouth
1 dash Angostura Bitters
¼ oz. Triple Sec
Club Soda

Pour all ingredients into ice-filled Collins glass. Top with club soda, and garnish with a mint sprig and a pineapple wedge.

CONFIDENTIAL COCKTAIL

¾ oz. Gin
¾ oz. Dry Vermouth
½ oz. Strega
½ oz. Cherry Marnier (Flavored Cognac)

Stir with ice and strain into chilled cocktail glass.

COOPERSTOWN COCKTAIL

½ oz. Dry Vermouth
½ oz. Sweet Vermouth
1 oz. Gin

Shake with ice and strain into chilled cocktail glass. Add a sprig of mint.

CORNWALL NEGRONI

2 oz. Gin
½ oz. Punt e Mes
½ oz. Sweet Vermouth
½ oz. Campari

Stir with ice and strain into chilled cocktail glass. Garnish with a flamed orange twist.

CORPSE REVIVER

¾ oz. Gin
¾ oz. Lemon Juice
¾ oz. Triple Sec
¾ oz. Lillet Blonde
1 dash Pastis (or Pernod or other Absinthe substitute)

Shake with ice and strain into chilled cocktail glass.

THE CORRECT COCKTAIL

1½ oz. Gin
½ oz. Ginger Liqueur
½ oz. Triple Sec
½ oz. Lemon Juice
2 dashes Orange Bitters

Shake with ice and strain into chilled champagne flute. Garnish with a lemon twist.

GIN

COUNT CURREY

1½ oz. Gin

1 tsp. Superfine Sugar
(or Simple Syrup)

Champagne, chilled

Shake gin and sugar/syrup with ice and strain into chilled champagne flute. Fill with Champagne.

CREAM FIZZ

1 oz. Lemon Juice

1 tsp. Superfine Sugar
(or Simple Syrup)

2 oz. Gin

1 tsp. Light Cream

Club Soda

Shake first four ingredients with ice and strain into ice-filled highball glass. Fill with club soda and stir.

CRIMSON COCKTAIL

1½ oz. Gin

2 tsps. Lemon Juice

1 tsp. Grenadine

¾ oz. Port

Shake first three ingredients with ice and strain into chilled cocktail glass. Float the port on top.

CRYSTAL SLIPPER COCKTAIL

½ oz. Blue Curaçao

2 dashes Orange Bitters

1½ oz. Gin

Stir with ice and strain into chilled cocktail glass.

CUCUMBER CANTALOUPE SOUR

1½ oz. Gin

¾ oz. Lemon Juice

½ oz. Honey Syrup

2 oz. Cantaloupe Juice

Shake with ice and strain into chilled cocktail glass. Garnish with a cucumber slice.

DAISY MAE

2 oz. Gin

1 oz. Lime Juice

¾ oz. Chartreuse (Green)

¾ oz. Simple Syrup

Shake and strain into a red-wine glass with ice. Garnish with a mint sprig.

DALI

1½ oz. Gin

1 oz. Sherry (Manzanilla)

½ oz. Orange Curaçao

2 dashes Orange Bitters

1 pinch Sea Salt

Stir with ice and strain into chilled cocktail glass. Garnish with roasted red pepper strip.

DAMN-THE-WEATHER COCKTAIL

1 tsp. Triple Sec

1 tbsp. Orange Juice

1 tbsp. Sweet Vermouth

1 oz. Gin

Shake with ice and strain into chilled cocktail glass.

DARB COCKTAIL

1 tsp. Lemon Juice
¾ oz. Dry Vermouth
¾ oz. Gin
¾ oz. Apricot-flavored
   Brandy

Shake with ice and strain
into chilled cocktail glass.

THE DEEP BLUE SEA

2 oz. Gin
¾ oz. Lillet Blanc
¼ oz. Crème de Violette
1 dash Orange Bitters

Stir with ice and strain into
chilled cocktail glass. Garnish with a lemon twist.

DEEP SEA COCKTAIL

1 oz. Dry Vermouth
¼ tsp. Anisette
1 dash Orange Bitters
1 oz. Gin

Stir with ice and strain into
chilled cocktail glass.

DELILAH

1½ oz. Gin
¾ oz. Triple Sec
¾ oz. Lemon Juice

Shake with ice and strain
into chilled cocktail glass.

DELMONICO NO. 1

¾ oz. Gin
½ oz. Dry Vermouth
½ oz. Sweet Vermouth
½ oz. Brandy

Stir with ice and strain
into chilled cocktail glass.
Garnish with a twist of
lemon peel.

DELMONICO NO. 2

1 dash Orange Bitters
1 oz. Dry Vermouth
1½ oz. Gin

Stir with ice and strain
into chilled cocktail glass.
Garnish with a twist of
lemon peel.

DEMPSEY COCKTAIL

1 oz. Gin
1 oz. Apple Brandy
½ tsp. Anisette
½ tsp. Grenadine

Stir with ice and strain into
chilled cocktail glass.

DIAMOND FIZZ

1 oz. Lemon Juice
1 tsp. Superfine Sugar
   (or Simple Syrup)
2 oz. Gin
Champagne, chilled

Shake first three ingredients
with ice and strain into ice-
filled highball glass. Fill with
Champagne and stir.

GIN

DIVA QUARANTA

1½ oz. Gin

½ oz. Simple Syrup

1 oz. Pomegranate Juice

½ oz. Campari

Shake first three ingredients with ice and strain into chilled cocktail glass. Top with Campari, and garnish with an orange twist.

DIXIE COCKTAIL

1 oz. Orange Juice

1 tbsp. Anisette

½ oz. Dry Vermouth

1 oz. Gin

Shake with ice and strain into chilled cocktail glass.

DOC DANEEKA ROYALE

2 oz. Gin

½ oz. Lemon Juice

½ oz. Maple Syrup

Shake and strain into chilled cocktail glass. Top with Champagne. Garnish with a grapefruit twist.

DU BARRY COCKTAIL

1 dash Bitters

¾ oz. Dry Vermouth

½ tsp. Anisette

1½ oz. Gin

Stir with ice and strain into chilled cocktail glass. Garnish with a slice of orange.

DUTCH AND BUTTERSCOTCH

1½ oz. Corenwyn

½ oz. Butterscotch Liqueur

2 dashes of Angostura Bitters

Stir with ice and strain into chilled cocktail glass. Garnish with a flamed orange peel.

EARL GREY MAR-TEA-NI

¾ oz. Lemon Juice

1 oz. Superfine Sugar (or Simple Syrup)

1½ oz. Earl Grey–Infused Gin*

1 Egg White

Shake all ingredients with ice and strain into chilled, sugar-rimmed cocktail glass. Garnish with lemon zest and a lemon twist.

* To infuse gin: Combine 1 tbsp. loose tea with 1 cup gin. Agitate and let stand for 2 hours. Strain and stir.

EASTSIDE

3 slices Cucumber

6–8 Mint Leaves

1 oz. Lime Juice

¾ oz. Superfine Sugar (or Simple Syrup)

2 oz. Gin (Cucumber Flavored)

Muddle cucumber and mint with lime juice and sugar/syrup. Add gin and ice and then shake. Strain into chilled cocktail glass. Garnish with a cucumber slice.

Martini Cocktail

LEFT: Bistro Sidecar
ABOVE: Singapore Sling

ABOVE: The Tantris Sidecar

RIGHT: Easy Like Sunday Morning Cocktail

LEFT: Aviation
ABOVE: Clover Club

Bajito (Bahito)

EASY LIKE SUNDAY MORNING COCKTAIL

1½ oz. Gin

¾ oz. Superfine Sugar (or Simple Syrup)

½ oz. Lemon Juice

1¼ oz. Pineapple Juice

1 dash Bitters

Shake first four ingredients with ice and strain into ice-filled Collins glass. Add dash of bitters and stir.

EDEN

2 oz. Gin

½ oz. Lemon Juice

½ oz. Rose Syrup

¼ oz. Campari

Shake with ice and strain into ice-filled old-fashioned glass. Garnish with a lemon twist.

EMERALD

1½ oz. Gin

½ oz. Chartreuse (Green)

½ oz. Sweet Vermouth

1 dash Orange Bitters

Stir and strain into cocktail glass. Garnish with a lemon twist.

EMERALD ISLE COCKTAIL

2 oz. Gin

1 tsp. Crème de Menthe (Green)

3 dashes Bitters

Stir with ice and strain into chilled cocktail glass.

EMERSON

1½ oz. Gin

1 oz. Sweet Vermouth

½ oz. Lime Juice

1 tsp. Maraschino Liqueur

Shake with ice and strain into chilled cocktail glass.

ENGLISH HIGHBALL

¾ oz. Gin

¾ oz. Brandy

¾ oz. Sweet Vermouth

Ginger Ale or Club Soda

Pour gin, brandy, and vermouth into ice-filled highball glass. Fill with ginger ale or club soda and stir. Garnish with a twist of lemon peel.

ENGLISH ROSE COCKTAIL

1½ oz. Gin

¾ oz. Apricot-flavored Brandy

¾ oz. Dry Vermouth

1 tsp. Grenadine

¼ tsp. Lemon Juice

Prepare rim of glass by rubbing with lemon and dipping in granulated sugar. Shake all ingredients with ice and strain into chilled cocktail glass. Garnish with a maraschino cherry.

GIN

Y FALLEN ANGEL

1 oz. Lime Juice

1½ oz. Gin

1 dash Bitters

½ tsp. Crème de Menthe (White)

Shake with ice and strain into chilled cocktail glass. Garnish with a maraschino cherry.

Y FANCY GIN

2 oz. Gin

1 dash Bitters

¼ tsp. Triple Sec

¼ tsp. Superfine Sugar (or Simple Syrup)

Shake with ice and strain into chilled cocktail glass. Add a twist of lemon peel.

Y FARE THEE WELL

1½ oz. Gin

½ oz. Dry Vermouth

1 dash Sweet Vermouth

1 dash Triple Sec

Shake with ice and strain into chilled cocktail glass.

Y FARMER'S COCKTAIL

1 oz. Gin

½ oz. Dry Vermouth

½ oz. Sweet Vermouth

2 dashes Bitters

Stir with ice and strain into chilled cocktail glass.

Y FAVORITE COCKTAIL

¾ oz. Apricot-flavored Brandy

¾ oz. Dry Vermouth

¾ oz. Gin

¼ tsp. Lemon Juice

Shake with ice and strain into chilled cocktail glass.

Y FIFTY-FIFTY COCKTAIL

1½ oz. Gin

1½ oz. Dry Vermouth

Stir with ice and strain into chilled cocktail glass.

Y FINE-AND-DANDY COCKTAIL

½ oz. Lemon Juice

½ oz. Triple Sec

1½ oz. Gin

1 dash Bitters

Shake with ice and strain into chilled cocktail glass. Garnish with a maraschino cherry.

Y FINO MARTINI

2 oz. Gin

2 tsps. Fino Sherry

Stir gin and sherry with ice in mixing glass. Strain into chilled cocktail glass. Garnish with a twist of lemon peel.

FITZGERALD

1½ oz. Gin
1 oz. Simple Syrup
¾ oz. Lemon Juice
2 dashes Angostura Bitters

Shake with ice and strain into chilled old-fashioned glass. Garnish with a lemon wedge.

FLAMINGO COCKTAIL

½ oz. Lime Juice
½ oz. Apricot-flavored Brandy
1½ oz. Gin
1 tsp. Grenadine

Shake with ice and strain into chilled cocktail glass.

FLORADORA COOLER

1 oz. Lime Juice
½ tsp. Superfine Sugar (or Simple Syrup)
1 tbsp. Grenadine
2 oz. Gin
2 oz. Club Soda or Ginger Ale

Stir first three ingredients in Collins glass. Top with ice and add gin. Fill with club soda or ginger ale and stir again.

FLORIDA

½ oz. Gin
1½ tsps. Kirschwasser
1½ tsps. Triple Sec
1 oz. Orange Juice
1 tsp. Lemon Juice

Shake with ice and strain into chilled cocktail glass.

FLYING DUTCHMAN

2 oz. Gin
1 dash Triple Sec

Shake with ice and strain into ice-filled old-fashioned glass.

FOG HORN

½ oz. Lime Juice
1½ oz. Gin
Ginger Ale

Pour lime juice and gin into ice-filled highball glass. Fill with ginger ale and stir. Garnish with a slice of lime.

FRANKENJACK COCKTAIL

1 oz. Gin
¾ oz. Dry Vermouth
½ oz. Apricot-flavored Brandy
1 tsp. Triple Sec

Stir with ice and strain into chilled cocktail glass. Garnish with a maraschino cherry.

FREE SILVER

½ oz. Lemon Juice
½ tsp. Superfine Sugar (or Simple Syrup)
1½ oz. Gin
½ oz. Dark Rum
1 tbsp. Milk
Club Soda

Shake first five ingredients with ice and strain into ice-filled Collins glass. Fill with club soda and stir.

GIN

FRENCH "75"

2 oz. Lemon Juice

2 tsps. Superfine Sugar
(or Simple Syrup)

2 oz. Gin

Champagne, chilled

Stir first three ingredients in Collins glass. Add ice cubes, fill with Champagne, and stir. Garnish with a slice of lemon or orange and a maraschino cherry. Serve with straws.

G-TANG

1½ oz. Gin

1½ oz. Campari

1 oz. Orange Juice

1 oz. Sweet Vermouth

Combine all ingredients in ice-filled old-fashioned glass. Garnish with a twist of lemon peel.

GARNET

1½ oz. Gin

¾ oz. Triple Sec

1 oz. Pomegranate Juice

1 oz. Grapefruit Juice

Shake with ice and strain into chilled cocktail glass. Garnish with a flamed orange peel.

GERSHWIN

2 oz. Gin

½ oz. Ginger Liqueur

½ oz. Simple Syrup

¾ oz. Lemon Juice

3 drops Rose Water

Shake with ice and strain into chilled cocktail glass. No garnish.

GIBSON

2½ oz. Gin

½ oz. Dry Vermouth

Stir with ice and strain into chilled cocktail glass. Garnish with a cocktail onion.

GIMLET

1 oz. Lime Juice

1 tsp. Superfine Sugar
(or Simple Syrup)

1½ oz. Gin

Shake with ice and strain into chilled cocktail glass.

GIN ALOHA

1½ oz. Gin

1½ oz. Triple Sec

1 tbsp. Unsweetened
Pineapple Juice

1 dash Orange Bitters

Shake with ice and strain into chilled cocktail glass.

GIN AND BITTERS

½ tsp. Bitters

Gin

Pour bitters into cocktail glass and revolve the glass until it is entirely coated with the bitters. Then fill with gin. (No ice is used in this drink.)

GIN BUCK

1 oz. Lemon Juice

1½ oz. Gin

Ginger Ale

Pour lemon juice and gin into ice-filled old-fashioned glass. Fill with ginger ale and stir.

GIN COBBLER

1 tsp. Superfine Sugar (or Simple Syrup)

2 oz. Club Soda

2 oz. Gin

Dissolve sugar/syrup and club soda in red-wine glass, fill with ice, and add gin. Stir and garnish with seasonal fruits. Serve with straws.

GIN COCKTAIL

2 oz. Gin

2 dashes Bitters

Stir with ice and strain into chilled cocktail glass. Garnish with a twist of lemon peel.

GIN COOLER

½ tsp. Superfine Sugar (or Simple Syrup)

2 oz. Club Soda

2 oz. Gin

Club Soda or Ginger Ale

In Collins glass, stir sugar/syrup with club soda. Fill glass with ice and add gin. Fill with club soda or ginger ale and stir again. Insert a spiral of orange or lemon peel (or both) and dangle end over rim of glass.

GIN DAISY

1 oz. Lemon Juice

½ tsp. Superfine Sugar (or Simple Syrup)

1 tsp. Grenadine

2 oz. Gin

Shake with ice and strain into chilled beer mug or metal cup. Add ice cubes and garnish with fruit.

GIN FIX

1 oz. Lemon Juice

1 tsp. Superfine Sugar (or Simple Syrup)

1 tsp. Water

2½ oz. Gin

Mix lemon juice, sugar/syrup, and water in highball glass. Stir and top with ice. Add gin and stir again. Garnish with a slice of lemon. Serve with straws.

GIN FIZZ

1 oz. Lemon Juice

1 tsp. Superfine Sugar
(or Simple Syrup)

2 oz. Gin

Club Soda

Shake first three ingredients
with ice and strain into ice-
filled highball glass. Fill with
club soda and stir.

GIN GIN MULE

6–8 sprigs Mint

¾ oz. Lime Juice

1 oz. Superfine Sugar
(or Simple Syrup)

1½ oz. Gin

1 oz. Ginger Beer

In a mixing glass, mud-
dle mint with lime juice and
sugar/syrup. Add gin and ice
and shake well. Strain into
ice-filled highball glass and
fill with ginger beer.

GIN HIGHBALL

2 oz. Gin

Ginger Ale or Club Soda

Pour gin into ice-filled highball glass and fill with ginger
ale or club soda. Stir. Garnish
with a twist of lemon peel.

GIN AND IT

2 oz. Gin

1 oz. Sweet Vermouth

Stir ingredients in cocktail
glass. (No ice is used in this
drink.)

GIN RICKEY

½ oz. Lime Juice

1½ oz. Gin

Club Soda

Pour lime juice and gin into
ice-filled highball glass and
fill with club soda. Stir. Add a
wedge of lime.

GIN SANGAREE

½ tsp. Superfine Sugar
(or Simple Syrup)

1 tsp. Water

2 oz. Gin

Club Soda

1 tbsp. Port

Dissolve sugar/syrup in
water and gin in highball
glass. Top with ice, and then
fill with club soda and stir.
Float port on top. Garnish
with fresh-grated nutmeg
on top.

GIN AND SIN

1 oz. Gin

1 oz. Lemon Juice

1 tbsp. Orange Juice

1 dash Grenadine

Shake with ice and strain
into chilled cocktail glass.

GIN AND SIP

2½ oz. Gin
½ oz. Amaro
1 splash Absinthe

Stir gin and amaro with ice and strain into chilled old-fashioned glass rinsed with absinthe.

GIN SLING

1 tsp. Superfine Sugar (or Simple Syrup)
1 tsp. Water
1 oz. Lemon Juice
2 oz. Gin

Dissolve sugar/syrup in water and lemon juice in old-fashioned glass. Add gin. Top with ice and stir. Garnish with a twist of orange peel.

GIN SMASH

1 cube Sugar
1 oz. Club Soda
4 sprigs Mint
2 oz. Gin

Muddle sugar with club soda and mint in old-fashioned glass. Add gin, top with ice, and stir. Garnish with a slice of orange and/or a maraschino cherry and a twist of lemon peel.

GIN SOUR

1 oz. Lemon Juice
½ tsp. Superfine Sugar (or Simple Syrup)
2 oz. Gin

Shake with ice and strain into chilled sour glass. Garnish with a half-slice of lemon and a maraschino cherry.

GIN SQUIRT

1½ oz. Gin
1 tbsp. Superfine Sugar (or Simple Syrup)
1 tsp. Grenadine
Club Soda

Stir first three ingredients with ice and strain into ice-filled highball glass. Fill with club soda and stir. Garnish with cubes of pineapple and strawberries.

GIN SWIZZLE

1 oz. Lime Juice
1 tsp. Superfine Sugar (or Simple Syrup)
2 oz. Club Soda
2 dashes Bitters
2 oz. Gin

Combine first three ingredients in Collins glass. Fill with ice and stir. Add bitters and gin. Serve with swizzle stick.

GIN

GIN THING

1½ oz. Gin
½ oz. Lime Juice
Ginger Ale

Pour gin and lime juice into ice-filled highball glass and fill with ginger ale.

GIN TODDY

½ tsp. Superfine Sugar (or Simple Syrup)
2 tsps. Water
2 oz. Gin

In old-fashioned glass, mix sugar/syrup and water. Add gin and one ice cube. Stir and add a twist of lemon peel.

GIN AND TONIC

2 oz. Gin
Tonic Water

Pour gin into ice-filled highball glass and fill with tonic water. Stir.

GOLDEN DAZE

1½ oz. Gin
½ oz. Peach-flavored Brandy
1 oz. Orange Juice

Shake with ice and strain into chilled cocktail glass.

GOLF COCKTAIL

1½ oz. Gin
¾ oz. Dry Vermouth
2 dashes Bitters

Stir with ice and strain into chilled cocktail glass.

GRAND ROYAL FIZZ

2 oz. Orange Juice
1 oz. Lemon Juice
1 tsp. Superfine Sugar (or Simple Syrup)
2 oz. Gin
½ tsp. Maraschino Liqueur
2 tsps. Light Cream
Club Soda

Shake first six ingredients with ice and strain into ice-filled highball glass. Fill with club soda and stir.

GRAPEFRUIT COCKTAIL

1 oz. Grapefruit Juice
1 oz. Gin
1 tsp. Maraschino Liqueur

Shake with ice and strain into chilled cocktail glass. Garnish with a maraschino cherry.

GREENBACK

1½ oz. Gin
1 oz. Crème de Menthe (Green)
1 oz. Lemon Juice

Shake with ice and strain into ice-filled old-fashioned glass.

GREEN DEVIL

1½ oz. Gin
1½ oz. Crème de Menthe (Green)
1 tbsp. Lime Juice

Shake with ice and strain into ice-filled old-fashioned glass. Garnish with mint leaves.

GREEN DRAGON

1 oz. Lemon Juice
½ oz. Kümmel
½ oz. Crème de Menthe (Green)
1½ oz. Gin
4 dashes Orange Bitters

Shake with ice and strain into chilled cocktail glass.

GREYHOUND

1½ oz. Gin
5 oz. Grapefruit Juice

Pour into highball glass over ice cubes. Stir well.

GYPSY COCKTAIL

1½ oz. Sweet Vermouth
1½ oz. Gin

Stir with ice and strain into chilled cocktail glass. Garnish with a maraschino cherry.

HARLEM COCKTAIL

¾ oz. Pineapple Juice
1½ oz. Gin
½ tsp. Maraschino Liqueur

Shake with ice and strain into chilled cocktail glass. Garnish with two pineapple chunks.

HASTY COCKTAIL

¾ oz. Dry Vermouth
1½ oz. Gin
¼ tsp. Anisette
1 tsp. Grenadine

Stir with ice and strain into chilled cocktail glass.

HAWAIIAN COCKTAIL

2 oz. Gin
1 tbsp. Pineapple Juice
½ oz. Triple Sec

Shake with ice and strain into chilled cocktail glass.

HAYS FIZZ

2 oz. Gin
¾ oz. Lemon Juice
¾ oz. Simple Syrup
1 splash Pastis
Club Soda

Shake with ice and strain into Collins glass rinsed with pastis. Top with club soda and garnish with a cherry/orange flag.

HOFFMAN HOUSE COCKTAIL

¾ oz. Dry Vermouth
1½ oz. Gin

Stir with ice and strain into chilled cocktail glass. Garnish with an olive.

HOKKAIDO COCKTAIL

1½ oz. Gin
1 oz. Sake
½ oz. Triple Sec

Shake with ice and strain into chilled cocktail glass.

HOMESTEAD COCKTAIL

1½ oz. Gin
¾ oz. Sweet Vermouth

Stir with ice and strain into chilled cocktail glass. Garnish with a slice of orange.

GIN

☍ HONEYCOMB

2 oz. Gin
¾ oz. Honey Syrup
¾ oz. Lemon Juice
1 splash Pastis (or Pernod or other Absinthe substitute)

Combine gin, honey syrup, and lemon juice over ice and shake thoroughly. Strain into chilled, pastis-rinsed cocktail glass. Garnish with star anise.

☍ HONOLULU COCKTAIL NO. 1

1 dash Bitters
¼ tsp. Orange Juice
¼ tsp. Pineapple Juice
¼ tsp. Lemon Juice
½ tsp. Superfine Sugar (or Simple Syrup)
1½ oz. Gin

Shake with ice and strain into chilled cocktail glass.

☍ HONOLULU COCKTAIL NO. 2

¾ oz. Gin
¾ oz. Maraschino Liqueur
¾ oz. Bénédictine

Stir with ice and strain into chilled cocktail glass.

☍ HOSKINS

2 oz. Gin
¾ oz. Torani Amer
¾ oz. Maraschino Liqueur
¼ oz. Triple Sec
1 dash Orange Bitters

Stir with ice and strain into chilled cocktail glass. Flame an orange peel over the drink and garnish with the peel.

☍ H. P. W. COCKTAIL

1½ tsps. Dry Vermouth
1½ tsps. Sweet Vermouth
1½ oz. Gin

Stir with ice and strain into chilled cocktail glass. Garnish with a twist of orange peel.

☍ HUDSON BAY

1 oz. Gin
½ oz. Cherry-flavored Brandy
1½ tsps. 151-proof Rum
1 tbsp. Orange Juice
1½ tsps. Lime Juice

Shake with ice and strain into chilled cocktail glass.

☍ HULA-HULA COCKTAIL

¾ oz. Orange Juice
1½ oz. Gin
¼ tsp. Superfine Sugar (or Simple Syrup)

Shake with ice and strain into chilled cocktail glass.

HUMMINGBIRD DOWN

2 oz. Gin
¾ oz. Lemon Juice
¾ oz. Honey Syrup
¼ oz. Green Chartreuse

Shake with ice and strain
into chilled cocktail glass.
Garnish with a mint leaf.

IDEAL COCKTAIL

1 oz. Dry Vermouth
1 oz. Gin
¼ tsp. Maraschino Liqueur
¼ tsp. Grapefruit or Lemon
  Juice

Shake with ice and strain
into chilled cocktail glass.
Garnish with a maraschino
cherry.

IMPERIAL COCKTAIL

1½ oz. Dry Vermouth
1½ oz. Gin
½ tsp. Maraschino Liqueur
1 dash Bitters

Stir with ice and strain into
chilled cocktail glass. Garnish with a maraschino
cherry.

INCOME TAX COCKTAIL

1½ tsps. Dry Vermouth
1½ tsps. Sweet Vermouth
1 oz. Gin
1 dash Bitters
1 oz. Orange Juice

Shake with ice and strain
into chilled cocktail glass.

JABBERWOCKY FIZZ

1½ oz. Gin
1 oz. Drambuie
½ oz. Lemon Juice
½ oz. Lime Juice
Club Soda

Shake with ice and strain
into ice-filled Collins glass.
Top with club soda. No
garnish.

JAMAICA GLOW

1 oz. Gin
1 tbsp. Claret
1 tbsp. Orange Juice
1 tsp. Jamaican Rum

Shake with ice and strain
into chilled cocktail glass.

JASMINE

1½ oz. Gin
1 oz. Triple Sec
¾ oz. Campari
½ oz. Lemon Juice

Shake with ice and strain
into chilled cocktail glass.

JEWEL COCKTAIL

¾ oz. Chartreuse (Green)
¾ oz. Sweet Vermouth
¾ oz. Gin
1 dash Orange Bitters

Stir with ice and strain into
chilled cocktail glass. Garnish with a maraschino
cherry.

GIN

Y JEYPLAK COCKTAIL

1½ oz. Gin
¾ oz. Sweet Vermouth
¼ tsp. Anisette

Shake with ice and strain into chilled cocktail glass. Garnish with a maraschino cherry.

Y JOCKEY CLUB COCKTAIL

1 dash Bitters
¼ tsp. Crème de Cacao (White)
½ oz. Lemon Juice
1½ oz. Gin

Shake with ice and strain into chilled cocktail glass.

Y THE JOLLITY BUILDING

1½ oz. Gin
½ oz. Amaro
¼ oz. Maraschino Liqueur
1 dash Orange Bitters

Stir with ice and strain into chilled cocktail glass. Garnish with an orange twist.

Y JOULOUVILLE

1 oz. Gin
½ oz. Apple Brandy
1½ tsps. Sweet Vermouth
½ oz. Lemon Juice
2 dashes Grenadine

Shake with ice and strain into chilled cocktail glass.

Y JOURNALIST COCKTAIL

1½ tsps. Dry Vermouth
1½ tsps. Sweet Vermouth
1½ oz. Gin
½ tsp. Lemon Juice
½ tsp. Triple Sec
1 dash Bitters

Shake with ice and strain into chilled cocktail glass.

Y JUDGE JR. COCKTAIL

¾ oz. Gin
¾ oz. Light Rum
½ oz. Lemon Juice
½ tsp. Superfine Sugar (or Simple Syrup)
¼ tsp. Grenadine

Shake with ice and strain into chilled cocktail glass.

Y JUDGETTE COCKTAIL

¾ oz. Peach-flavored Brandy
¾ oz. Gin
¾ oz. Dry Vermouth
¼ oz. Lime Juice

Shake with ice and strain into chilled cocktail glass. Garnish with a maraschino cherry.

Y JUNIPER BREEZE NO. 1

1½ oz. Gin
1 oz. Grapefruit Juice
½ oz. Cranberry Juice
½ oz. Elderflower Liqueur
1 dash Lime Juice

Build and roll over ice in cocktail glass with an orange twist.

☐ JUNIPER BREEZE NO. 2

2 oz. Gin
2 oz. Cranberry Juice
1 oz. Grapefruit Juice

Build in ice-filled highball glass. Garnish with half a grapefruit wheel.

☐ JUPITER

2 oz. Gin
1 oz. Dry Vermouth
1 tsp. Orange Juice
1 tsp. Parfait Amour

Shake with ice and strain into chilled cocktail glass.

☐ KISS IN THE DARK

¾ oz. Gin
¾ oz. Cherry-flavored Brandy
¾ oz. Dry Vermouth

Stir with ice and strain into chilled cocktail glass.

☐ KNICKERBOCKER COCKTAIL

¼ tsp. Sweet Vermouth
¾ oz. Dry Vermouth
1½ oz. Gin

Stir with ice and strain into chilled cocktail glass. Garnish with a twist of lemon peel.

☐ KNOCKOUT COCKTAIL

½ oz. Anisette
¾ oz. Gin
¾ oz. Dry Vermouth
1 tsp. Crème de Menthe (White)

Stir with ice and strain into chilled cocktail glass. Garnish with a maraschino cherry.

☐ KUP'S INDISPENSABLE COCKTAIL

½ oz. Light Vermouth
½ oz. Dry Vermouth
1½ oz. Gin
1 dash Bitters

Stir with ice and strain into chilled cocktail glass.

☐ LA BICYCLETTE

2 oz. Gin
¾ oz. Sweet Vermouth
½ oz. Elderflower Liqueur
2 dashes Peach Bitters

Stir with ice and strain into chilled cocktail glass. No garnish.

☐ LA LOUCHE

1½ oz. Gin
½ oz. Lillet Rouge
¼ oz. Yellow Chartreuse
¼ oz. Lime Juice

Shake with ice and strain into chilled cocktail glass. Garnish with a lime twist.

☐ LA TAZZA D'EVA

6 Fresh Mint Leaves
1 oz. Amaro
1 oz. Gin
1 oz. Apple Juice
1 oz. Tonic

Muddle mint leaves in highball glass. Add ice and the rest of ingredients. Stir and garnish with a slice of apple and a sprig of fresh rosemary.

GIN

LADY FINGER

1 oz. Gin
½ oz. Kirschwasser
1 oz. Cherry-flavored Brandy

Shake with ice and strain
into chilled cocktail glass.

LAST WORD

½ oz. Gin
½ oz. Maraschino Liqueur
½ oz. Chartreuse
½ oz. Lime Juice

Shake with ice and strain
into chilled cocktail glass.

LEAPFROG HIGHBALL

1 oz. Lemon Juice
2 oz. Gin
Ginger Ale

Pour lemon juice and gin
into ice-filled highball glass
and fill with ginger ale. Stir.

LEAPYEAR

2 oz. Gin
½ oz. Sweet Vermouth
½ oz. Grand Marnier
1 dash Lemon Juice

Shake with ice and strain
into chilled cocktail glass.

LEAVE-IT-TO-ME COCKTAIL NO. 1

½ oz. Apricot-flavored
  Brandy
½ oz. Dry Vermouth
1 oz. Gin
¼ tsp. Lemon Juice
¼ tsp. Grenadine

Shake with ice and strain
into chilled cocktail glass.

LEAVE-IT-TO-ME COCKTAIL NO. 2

1 tsp. Raspberry Syrup
1 tsp. Lemon Juice
¼ tsp. Maraschino Liqueur
1½ oz. Gin

Stir with ice and strain into
chilled cocktail glass.

THE LEMONY SNICKET COCKTAIL

2½ oz. Gin
½ oz. Limoncello
½ oz. Yellow Chartreuse
½ oz. Lemon Juice

Shake with ice and strain
into chilled cocktail glass.
Garnish with a cherry.

LEO DI JANEIRO

2 oz. Gin
2 oz. Pineapple Juice
4 dashes of Angostura
  Bitters

Shake with ice and strain
into ice-filled Collins glass.
Garnish with a pineapple
wedge.

Y THE LIBATION GODDESS

2 oz. Gin

¾ oz. Crème de Cacao (White)

½ oz. Cranberry Juice

Stir and strain into chilled cocktail glass. Garnish with a lime wedge.

Y LIGHT AND DAY

2 oz. Gin

½ oz. Yellow Chartreuse

¼ oz. Maraschino Liqueur

¼ oz. Orange Juice

3 dashes Peychaud's Bitters

Stir with ice and strain into chilled cocktail glass.

🍺 LONDON BUCK

2 oz. Gin

1 oz. Lemon Juice

Ginger Ale

Pour gin and lemon juice into ice-filled highball glass. Fill with ginger ale and stir.

Y LONDON COCKTAIL

2 oz. Gin

2 dashes Orange Bitters

½ tsp. Superfine Sugar (or Simple Syrup)

½ tsp. Maraschino Liqueur

Stir with ice and strain into chilled cocktail glass. Add a twist of lemon peel.

Y THE LONDONER

2 oz. Gin

½ oz. Grand Marnier

½ oz. Sweet Vermouth

1 dash Orange Bitters

Shake and strain into cocktail glass. Garnish with a flamed orange twist.

Y LONE TREE COCKTAIL

¾ oz. Sweet Vermouth

1½ oz. Gin

Stir with ice and strain into chilled cocktail glass.

🍺 LONE TREE COOLER

½ tsp. Superfine Sugar (or Simple Syrup)

2 oz. Club Soda

2 oz. Gin

1 tbsp. Dry Vermouth

Club Soda or Ginger Ale

Stir sugar/syrup and club soda in Collins glass. Fill glass with ice, and add gin and vermouth. Fill with club soda or ginger ale and stir again. Garnish with a spiral of orange or lemon peel (or both) and dangle end over rim of glass.

Y MAIDEN'S BLUSH COCKTAIL

¼ tsp. Lemon Juice

1 tsp. Triple Sec

1 tsp. Grenadine

1½ oz. Gin

Shake with ice and strain into chilled cocktail glass.

GIN

Y MAIDEN'S PLEA

1½ oz. Gin
½ oz. Triple Sec
1 oz. Lemon Juice

Shake with ice and strain into chilled cocktail glass.

☐ MAJOR BAILEY

1½ tsps. Lime Juice
1½ tsps. Lemon Juice
½ tsp. Superfine Sugar (or Simple Syrup)
12 Mint Leaves
2 oz. Gin

Muddle first four ingredients, pour into ice-filled Collins glass, and add gin. Stir until glass is frosted. Garnish with sprig of mint, and serve with straws.

☐ MAMIE'S SISTER

1 oz. Lime Juice
2 oz. Gin
Ginger Ale

Pour the lime juice and a lime twist into Collins glass, and add gin. Fill glass with ginger ale and ice. Stir.

Y MARTINEZ COCKTAIL

1 dash Orange Bitters
1 oz. Dry Vermouth
¼ tsp. Triple Sec
1 oz. Gin´

Stir with ice and strain into chilled cocktail glass. Garnish with a maraschino cherry.

Y MARTINI (TRADITIONAL 2-TO-1)

1½ oz. Gin
¾ oz. Dry Vermouth

Stir with ice and strain into chilled cocktail glass. Garnish with a twist of lemon peel or olive.

Y MARTINI (DRY) (5-TO-1)

1⅔ oz. Gin
⅓ oz. Dry Vermouth

Follow directions for Martini (Traditional 2-to-1) preparation.

Y MARTINI (EXTRA DRY) (8-TO-1)

2 oz. Gin
¼ oz. Dry Vermouth

Follow directions for Martini (Traditional 2-to-1) preparation.

Y MARTINI (MEDIUM)

1½ oz. Gin
½ oz. Dry Vermouth
½ oz. Sweet Vermouth

Follow directions for Martini (Traditional 2-to-1) preparation.

Y MARTINI (SWEET)

1 oz. Gin
1 oz. Sweet Vermouth

Follow directions for Martini (Traditional 2-to-1) preparation.

⍦ MAURICE COCKTAIL

1 oz. Orange Juice
½ oz. Sweet Vermouth
½ oz. Dry Vermouth
1 oz. Gin
1 dash Bitters

Shake with ice and strain into chilled cocktail glass.

⍦ MAXIM

1½ oz. Gin
1 oz. Dry Vermouth
1 dash Crème de Cacao (White)

Shake with ice and strain into chilled cocktail glass. Garnish with a maraschino cherry.

⎕ MAXWELL'S RETURN

15 Rosemary Leaves
2 oz. Gin
1 oz. Pineapple Juice
½ oz. Simple Syrup
½ oz. Lime Juice
¼ oz. Green Chartreuse

Muddle rosemary in mixing glass. Add rest of the ingredients. Shake with ice and double-strain into ice-filled old-fashioned glass. Garnish with a rosemary sprig.

⍦ MELON COCKTAIL

2 oz. Gin
¼ tsp. Lemon Juice
¼ tsp. Maraschino Liqueur

Shake with ice and strain into chilled cocktail glass. Garnish with a maraschino cherry.

⎕ MELON STAND

2 oz. Gin
½ oz. Aperol
½ oz. Simple Syrup
¾ oz. Lemon Juice
4 chunks Watermelon

Muddle watermelon in mixing glass. Add rest of the ingredients. Shake with ice and strain into Collins glass filled with crushed ice. Garnish with a watermelon ball.

GIN

⍦ MERCY, MERCY

2 oz. Gin
½ oz. Aperol
½ oz. Lillet Blanc
1 dash Angostura Bitters

Stir with ice and strain into chilled cocktail glass. Garnish with an orange twist.

⍦ MERRY WIDOW COCKTAIL NO. 1

1¼ oz. Gin
1¼ oz. Dry Vermouth
½ tsp. Bénédictine
½ tsp. Anisette
1 dash Orange Bitters

Stir with ice and strain into chilled cocktail glass. Garnish with a twist of lemon peel.

∇ MR. MANHATTAN COCKTAIL

1 cube Sugar
4 sprigs Mint
¼ tsp. Lemon Juice
1 tsp. Orange Juice
1½ oz. Gin

Muddle ingredients. Shake with ice and strain into chilled cocktail glass.

∇ MONARCH

4 Mint Leaves
1 Grapefruit Twist
2 oz. Gin
1 oz. Lemon Juice
¾ oz. Elderflower Syrup
2 tsps. Castor Sugar

Tear mint leaves in a mixing glass, add grapefruit twist. Shake rest of ingredients with ice and double-strain into cocktail glass.

∇ THE MONEYPENNY

½ oz. Lillet Blanc
1 oz. Gin
½ oz. Lemon Juice
1 oz. Grapefruit Juice
1 dash Grapefruit Bitters

Shake with ice and strain into cocktail glass with a demerara sugar rim. Garnish with a grapefruit twist.

∇ MONKEY GLAND

2 oz. Gin
1 oz. Orange Juice
¼ oz. Grenadine
1 dash Pernod (or Absinthe substitute)

Shake with ice and strain into chilled cocktail glass. Garnish with an orange twist.

▢ MONTE CARLO IMPERIAL HIGHBALL

2 oz. Gin
½ oz. Crème de Menthe (White)
½ oz. Lemon Juice
Champagne, chilled

Shake first three ingredients with ice and strain into ice-filled highball glass. Fill glass with Champagne and stir.

∇ MONTMARTRE COCKTAIL

1¼ oz. Dry Gin
½ oz. Sweet Vermouth
½ oz. Triple Sec

Stir with ice and strain into chilled cocktail glass. Garnish with a maraschino cherry.

▢ MONTREAL CLUB BOUNCER

1½ oz. Gin
½ oz. Anisette

Pour into ice-filled old-fashioned glass and stir.

⅄ MOONDREAM

1½ oz. Gin

1 oz. Manzanilla Sherry

¼ oz. Crème de Peche

Stir with ice and strain into chilled cocktail glass.

▢ MORRO

1 oz. Gin

½ oz. Dark Rum

1 tbsp. Pineapple Juice

1 tbsp. Lime Juice

½ tsp. Superfine Sugar (or Simple Syrup)

Shake with ice and strain into sugar-rimmed, ice-filled old-fashioned glass.

⅄ NEGRONI

¾ oz. Gin

¾ oz. Campari

¾ oz. Sweet or Dry Vermouth

1 splash Club Soda (optional)

Stir first three ingredients with ice and strain into chilled cocktail glass, or into ice-filled old-fashioned glass. Add club soda, if desired. Garnish with a twist of lemon peel.

⅄ NEW AMSTERDAM

2 oz. Old Genever

1 oz. Kirschwasser

1 barspoon Simple Syrup

2 dashes Peychaud's bitters

Stir with ice and strain into chilled cocktail glass. Garnish with a lemon twist.

⅄ NIGHTMARE

1½ oz. Gin

½ oz. Madeira

½ oz. Cherry-flavored Brandy

1 tsp. Orange Juice

Shake with ice and strain into chilled cocktail glass.

⅄ NINETEENTH HOLE

1½ oz. Gin

1 oz. Dry Vermouth

1 tsp. Sweet Vermouth

1 dash Bitters

Stir with ice and strain into chilled cocktail glass. Garnish with an olive.

⅄ NON CI CREDO

2 oz. Gin

¾ oz. Aperol

¼ oz. Simple Syrup

¾ oz. Lemon Juice

3 dashes Peach Bitters

1 Egg White

Shake without ice. Shake with ice and strain into chilled cocktail glass.

⅄ NOVARA

1½ oz. Gin

½ oz. Campari

½ oz. Passion Fruit Nectar

½ oz. Lemon Juice

Shake with ice and strain into chilled cocktail glass.

GIN

⊻ OBITUARY COCKTAIL

2 oz. Gin
¼ oz. Dry Vermouth
¼ oz. Pastis (or Pernod or other Absinthe substitute)

Stir with ice and strain into chilled cocktail glass.

⊔ THE OLD GOAT

1½ oz. Old Genever
¾ oz. Crème de Cassis
3 oz. Ginger Ale

Combine all ingredients in ice-filled Collins glass. Squeeze a lime wedge into the drink and drop it in.

⊻ OPAL COCKTAIL

1 oz. Gin
½ oz. Triple Sec
1 tbsp. Orange Juice
¼ tbsp. Superfine Sugar (or Simple Syrup)

Shake with ice and strain into chilled cocktail glass.

⊻ OPERA

2 oz. Gin
½ oz. Dubonnet
¼ oz. Maraschino Liqueur
1 dash Orange Bitters

Stir with ice and strain into chilled cocktail glass. Garnish with a lemon twist.

⊻ ORANGE BLOSSOM

1 oz. Gin
1 oz. Orange Juice
¼ tsp. Superfine Sugar (or Simple Syrup)

Shake with ice and strain into chilled cocktail glass.

⊔ ORANGE BUCK

1½ oz. Gin
1 oz. Orange Juice
1 tbsp. Lime Juice
Ginger Ale

Shake first three ingredients with ice and strain into ice-filled highball glass. Fill with ginger ale and stir.

Pour in View

Make drinks in front of the guest whenever possible. This was a tradition that started in the 19th century when a patron wanted to be sure he was getting the genuine product, but the whole cocktail experience is incomplete if the visual and the interaction with the bartender are missing.

—DALE DEGROFF (a.k.a. King Cocktail), author of The Craft of the Cocktail

ORANGE OASIS

1½ oz. Gin
½ oz. Cherry-flavored Brandy
4 oz. Orange Juice
Ginger Ale

Shake first three ingredients with ice and strain into ice-filled highball glass. Fill with ginger ale and stir.

ORIENT EXPRESS

2 oz. Gin
1 oz. Sake
½ oz. Lemongrass Syrup*

Chill and stir and serve in chilled cocktail glass. Garnish with a thin green apple slice.

* Lemongrass Syrup: Peel five stalks of lemongrass and cut into small segments. Add to ½ liter of water and bring to boil. Transfer to sterile container and refrigerate.

THE OUTSIDER

2 oz. Gin
1 oz. Lemon Juice
¾ oz. Superfine Sugar
(or Simple Syrup)
1 oz. Fresh Apple Cider
1 splash Ginger Ale

Shake first four ingredients with ice and strain into ice-filled Collins glass. Top with splash of ginger ale. Garnish with a slice of red apple.

PAISLEY MARTINI

2 oz. Gin
½ oz. Dry Vermouth
1 tsp. Scotch

Stir in ice-filled old-fashioned glass. Garnish with a twist of lemon peel.

PALL MALL

1½ oz. Gin
½ oz. Sweet Vermouth
½ oz. Dry Vermouth
½ oz. Crème de Menthe
(White)

Stir in ice-filled old-fashioned glass.

PALM BEACH COCKTAIL

1½ oz. Gin
1½ tsps. Sweet Vermouth
1½ tsps. Grapefruit Juice

Shake with ice and strain into chilled cocktail glass.

PAPAYA SLING

1½ oz. Gin
1 dash Bitters
1 oz. Lime Juice
1 tbsp. Papaya Syrup
Club Soda

Shake first four ingredients with ice and strain into ice-filled Collins glass. Fill with club soda and stir. Garnish with skewered pineapple chunks.

GIN

Y PARISIAN

1 oz. Gin
1 oz. Dry Vermouth
¼ oz. Crème de Cassis

Shake with ice and strain into chilled cocktail glass.

Y PARK AVENUE

1½ oz. Gin
¼ oz. Sweet Vermouth
1 tbsp. Pineapple Juice

Stir with ice and strain into chilled cocktail glass.

Y PEARL WHITE

6 Mint Leaves
2 oz. Gin
½ oz. Lillet Blanc
½ oz. Lemon Juice
¼ oz. Simple Syrup

Muddle the mint in mixing glass. Add the other ingredients. Shake with ice and double-strain into chilled cocktail glass. No garnish.

Y PEGU

2 oz. Gin
1 oz. Orange Curaçao
1 tsp. Lime Juice
1 dash Angostura Bitters
1 dash Orange Bitters

Stir with ice and strain into chilled cocktail glass.

Y PEGU CLUB

2 oz. Gin
½ oz. Lemon Juice
½ oz. Triple Sec
4 dashes Angostura Bitters

Shake with ice and strain into chilled cocktail glass.

Y PERFECT COCKTAIL

1½ tsps. Dry Vermouth
1½ tsps. Sweet Vermouth
1½ oz. Gin
1 dash Bitters

Stir with ice and strain into chilled cocktail glass.

Y PERFECT 10

1 oz. Gin
½ oz. Triple Sec
½ oz. Campari
¼ oz. Lemon Juice
¼ oz. Superfine Sugar
   (or Simple Syrup)

Shake with ice and strain into chilled cocktail glass. Run a lemon twist along lip of glass, and then drop lemon twist in cocktail.

Y PETER PAN COCKTAIL

2 dashes Bitters
¾ oz. Orange Juice
¾ oz. Dry Vermouth
¾ oz. Gin

Shake with ice and strain into chilled cocktail glass.

PICCADILLY COCKTAIL

¾ oz. Dry Vermouth

1½ oz. Gin

¼ tsp. Anisette

¼ tsp. Grenadine

Stir with ice and strain into chilled cocktail glass.

PINK GIN

1½ oz. Gin

3–4 dashes Angostura Bitters

Stir with ice and strain into chilled cocktail glass.

PINK LADY

1½ oz. Gin

½ oz. Applejack

¾ oz. Lemon Juice

¼ oz. Grenadine

1 Egg White

Shake with ice and strain into chilled red-wine glass.

PLAZA COCKTAIL

¾ oz. Sweet Vermouth

¾ oz. Dry Vermouth

¾ oz. Gin

Shake with ice and strain into chilled cocktail glass. Garnish with a wedge of pineapple.

POET'S DREAM

¾ oz. Gin

¾ oz. Dry Vermouth

¾ oz. Bénédictine

Stir with ice and strain into chilled cocktail glass. Garnish with a twist of lemon peel.

POLLYANNA

3 slices Orange

3 slices Pineapple

2 oz. Gin

½ oz. Sweet Vermouth

½ tsp. Grenadine

Muddle ingredients. Shake with ice and strain into chilled cocktail glass.

POLO COCKTAIL

1 tbsp. Lemon Juice

1 tbsp. Orange Juice

1 oz. Gin

Shake with ice and strain into chilled cocktail glass.

POMPANO

1 oz. Gin

½ oz. Dry Vermouth

1 oz. Grapefruit Juice

Shake with ice and strain into chilled cocktail glass.

POPPY COCKTAIL

¾ oz. Crème de Cacao (White)

1½ oz. Gin

Shake with ice and strain into chilled cocktail glass.

PRINCE'S SMILE

½ oz. Apricot-flavored Brandy

½ oz. Apple Brandy

1 oz. Gin

¼ tsp. Lemon Juice

Shake with ice and strain into chilled cocktail glass.

GIN

PRINCETON COCKTAIL

1 oz. Gin
1 oz. Dry Vermouth
½ oz. Lime Juice

Stir with ice and strain into chilled cocktail glass.

PROHIBITION

1½ oz. Gin
1½ oz. Lillet Blanc
¼ oz. Orange Juice
¼ oz. Apricot Brandy

Shake and strain into cocktail glass. Garnish with a lemon twist.

QUEEN ELIZABETH

1½ oz. Gin
½ oz. Dry Vermouth
1½ tsps. Bénédictine

Stir with ice and strain into chilled cocktail glass.

RAMOS GIN FIZZ

1½ oz. Gin
½ oz. Lemon Juice
½ oz. Lime Juice
2 tbsp. Cream
1 Egg White
1 tbsp. Superfine Sugar (or Simple Syrup)
3–4 dashes Orange Flower Water
¼ oz. Club Soda

Shake first seven ingredients with ice for at least one minute (or blend on low in a blender) until foamy. Strain into chilled red-wine glass, top with club soda, and stir.

RED BARON

1½ oz. Gin
½ oz. Sweet Vermouth
½ oz. Amaro
¼ oz. Maraschino Liqueur

Stir with ice and strain into chilled cocktail glass. Garnish with a lemon twist.

RED CLOUD

1½ oz. Gin
½ oz. Apricot-flavored Brandy
1 tbsp. Lemon Juice
1 tsp. Grenadine

Shake with ice and strain into chilled cocktail glass.

RED SNAPPER

2 oz. Gin
4 oz. Tomato Juice
½ oz. Lemon Juice
1 pinch Salt
1 pinch Pepper
2–3 dashes Worcestershire Sauce
2–3 drops Tabasco Sauce
Celery stalk

Stir with ice in a chilled highball or delmonico glass. Garnish with a celery stalk and a lemon wedge.

REMSEN COOLER

½ tsp. Superfine Sugar
(or Simple Syrup)

2 oz. Club Soda

2 oz. Gin

Club Soda or Ginger Ale

Combine sugar/syrup and club soda in Collins glass. Stir. Add ice and gin. Fill with club soda or ginger ale and stir again. Garnish with a spiral of orange or lemon peel (or both) and dangle end over rim of glass.

RENAISSANCE COCKTAIL

1½ oz. Gin

½ oz. Dry Sherry

1 tbsp. Light Cream

Shake with ice and strain into chilled cocktail glass. Garnish with fresh-grated nutmeg on top.

RESOLUTE COCKTAIL

½ oz. Lemon Juice

½ oz. Apricot-flavored Brandy

1 oz. Gin

Shake with ice and strain into chilled cocktail glass.

ROBERT E. LEE COOLER

½ oz. Lime Juice

½ tsp. Superfine Sugar
(or Simple Syrup)

2 oz. Club Soda

¼ tsp. Anisette

2 oz. Gin

Ginger Ale

Stir first three ingredients in Collins glass. Add ice, anisette, and gin. Fill with ginger ale and stir again. Add a spiral of orange or lemon peel (or both) and dangle end over rim of glass.

ROLLS-ROYCE

½ oz. Dry Vermouth

½ oz. Sweet Vermouth

1½ oz. Gin

¼ tsp. Bénédictine

Stir with ice and strain into chilled cocktail glass.

ROSE COCKTAIL (ENGLISH)

½ oz. Apricot-flavored Brandy

½ oz. Dry Vermouth

1 oz. Gin

½ tsp. Lemon Juice

1 tsp. Grenadine

Shake with ice and strain into chilled, sugar-rimmed cocktail glass.

GIN

ROSE COCKTAIL (FRENCH)

½ oz. Cherry-flavored Brandy
½ oz. Dry Vermouth
1½ oz. Gin

Stir with ice and strain into chilled cocktail glass.

ROSELYN COCKTAIL

¾ oz. Dry Vermouth
1½ oz. Gin
½ tsp. Grenadine

Stir with ice and strain into chilled cocktail glass. Garnish with a twist of lemon peel.

RUM RUNNER

1½ oz. Gin
1 oz. Lime Juice
1 oz. Pineapple Juice
1 tsp. Superfine Sugar (or Simple Syrup)
1 dash Bitters

Shake with ice and strain into ice-filled, salt-rimmed old-fashioned glass.

RUSTY MONK

2 oz. Gin
1 oz. Dubonnet
½ oz. Yellow Chartreuse
2 dashes Orange Bitters

Stir and strain into chilled cocktail glass. Garnish with an orange twist.

SALTY DOG

1½ oz. Gin
5 oz. Grapefruit Juice
¼ tsp. Salt

Pour into ice-filled highball glass. Stir well. (Vodka may be substituted for the gin.)

SAND-MARTIN COCKTAIL

1 tsp. Chartreuse (Green)
1½ oz. Sweet Vermouth
1½ oz. Gin

Stir with ice and strain into chilled cocktail glass.

SAN SEBASTIAN

1 oz. Gin
1½ tsps. Light Rum
1 tbsp. Grapefruit Juice
1½ tsps. Triple Sec
1 tbsp. Lemon Juice

Shake with ice and strain into chilled cocktail glass.

SATAN'S WHISKERS

¾ oz. Gin
¾ oz. Dry Vermouth
¾ oz. Sweet Vermouth
½ oz. Orange Juice
½ oz. Grand Marnier
1 dash Orange Bitters

Shake with ice and strain into chilled cocktail glass.

SENSATION COCKTAIL

½ oz. Lemon Juice
1½ oz. Gin
1 tsp. Maraschino Liqueur

Shake with ice and strain
into chilled cocktail glass.
Garnish with two sprigs of
fresh mint.

SEVENTH HEAVEN COCKTAIL

2 tsps. Grapefruit Juice
1 tbsp. Maraschino Liqueur
1½ oz. Gin

Shake with ice and strain
into chilled cocktail glass.
Garnish with a sprig of
fresh mint.

SHADY GROVE

1½ oz. Gin
1 oz. Lemon Juice
1 tsp. Superfine Sugar
    (or Simple Syrup)
Ginger Beer

Shake gin, lemon juice, and
sugar/syrup with ice and
strain into ice-filled highball
glass. Fill with ginger beer.

SHISO NO NATSU

4 Shiso Leaves
1½ oz. Sake
1 oz. Gin
½ oz. Dry Vermouth

Muddle the shiso leaves.
Add the other ingredients.
Stir with ice and double-
strain into chilled cocktail
glass. Garnish with a
shiso leaf.

SILVER BULLET

1 oz. Gin
1 oz. Kümmel
1 tbsp. Lemon Juice

Shake with ice and strain
into chilled cocktail glass.

SILVER COCKTAIL

1 oz. Dry Vermouth
1 oz. Gin
2 dashes Orange Bitters
¼ tsp. Superfine Sugar
    (or Simple Syrup)
½ tsp. Maraschino Liqueur

Stir with ice and strain
into chilled cocktail glass.
Garnish with a twist of
lemon peel.

SILVER KING FIZZ

2 oz. Gin
1 oz. Fresh Lemon Juice
1 tsp. Simple Syrup
1 Egg White
4 dashes Orange Bitters
Club Soda

Shake first five ingredients
vigorously. Strain into ice-
filled highball glass. Top
with club soda. Garnish with
orange slice flat on rim
of glass.

GIN

Y SILVER STAR DAISY

1 oz. Gin
½ oz. Apple Brandy
1 oz. Fresh Lemon Juice
½ oz. Orange Curaçao
½ oz. Simple Syrup
1 Egg White
1 dash Orange Bitters

Shake all but bitters without ice. Then shake with ice and strain into chilled cocktail glass. Add bitters on top.

Y SILVER STREAK

1½ oz. Gin
1 oz. Kümmel

Shake with ice and strain into chilled cocktail glass.

Y SMILE COCKTAIL

1 oz. Grenadine
1 oz. Gin
½ tsp. Lemon Juice

Shake with ice and strain into chilled cocktail glass.

Y SMILER COCKTAIL

½ oz. Sweet Vermouth
½ oz. Dry Vermouth
1 oz. Gin
1 dash Bitters
¼ tsp. Orange Juice

Shake with ice and strain into chilled cocktail glass.

Y SNOWBALL

1½ oz. Gin
½ oz. Anisette
1 tbsp. Light Cream

Shake with ice and strain into chilled cocktail glass.

Y SNYDER

1½ oz. Gin
½ oz. Dry Vermouth
½ oz. Triple Sec

Shake with ice and strain into chilled cocktail glass. Garnish with a twist of lemon peel.

Y SOCIETY COCKTAIL

1½ oz. Gin
¾ oz. Dry Vermouth
¼ tsp. Grenadine

Stir with ice and strain into chilled cocktail glass.

Y SO CUE

1 oz. Gin
1 oz. Soju
1 oz. White Vermouth
½ oz. Lime Juice
¾ oz. Simple Syrup

Stir with ice and strain into chilled cocktail glass. Garnish with a cucumber slice.

SOLOMON SLING

1½ oz. Gin
¾ oz. Lemon Juice
½ oz. Simple Syrup
½ oz. Kirschwasser
¼ oz. Cherry Heering
1 dash Angostura Bitters

Shake with ice and strain into Collins glass filled with ice. Garnish with 2 straws, each with a cherry skewered at the bottom.

SOUTHERN BRIDE

1½ oz. Gin
1 oz. Grapefruit Juice
1 dash Maraschino Liqueur

Shake with ice and strain into chilled cocktail glass.

SOUTHERN GIN COCKTAIL

2 oz. Gin
2 dashes Orange Bitters
½ tsp. Triple Sec

Stir with ice and strain into chilled cocktail glass. Garnish with a twist of lemon peel.

SOUTH-SIDE COCKTAIL

1 oz. Lemon Juice
1 tsp. Superfine Sugar (or Simple Syrup)
1½ oz. Gin

Shake with ice and strain into chilled cocktail glass. Garnish with two sprigs of fresh mint.

SOUTH-SIDE FIZZ

1 oz. Lemon Juice
1 tsp. Superfine Sugar (or Simple Syrup)
2 oz. Gin
Club Soda

Shake lemon juice, sugar/syrup, and gin with ice and strain into ice-filled highball glass. Fill with club soda and stir. Garnish with fresh mint leaves.

GIN

SPENCER COCKTAIL

¾ oz. Apricot-flavored Brandy
1½ oz. Gin
1 dash Bitters
¼ tsp. Orange Juice

Shake with ice and strain into chilled cocktail glass. Garnish with a maraschino cherry and a twist of orange peel.

SPHINX COCKTAIL

1½ oz. Gin
1½ tsps. Sweet Vermouth
1½ tsps. Dry Vermouth

Stir with ice and strain into chilled cocktail glass. Garnish with a slice of lemon.

SPRING FEELING COCKTAIL

1 tbsp. Lemon Juice
½ oz. Chartreuse (Green)
1 oz. Gin

Shake with ice and strain into chilled cocktail glass.

Y STANLEY COCKTAIL

½ oz. Lemon Juice

1 tsp. Grenadine

¾ oz. Gin

¼ oz. Light Rum

Shake with ice and strain into chilled cocktail glass.

STAR DAISY

1 oz. Lemon Juice

½ tsp. Superfine Sugar (or Simple Syrup)

1 tsp. Grenadine

1 oz. Gin

1 oz. Apple Brandy

Shake with ice and strain into chilled beer mug or metal cup. Add an ice cube and garnish with seasonal fruit.

Y STRAIGHT LAW COCKTAIL

¾ oz. Gin

1½ oz. Dry Sherry

Stir with ice and strain into chilled cocktail glass.

STRAITS SLING

2 oz. Gin

½ oz. Cherry Brandy (Dry)

½ oz. Bénédictine

1 oz. Lemon Juice

2 dashes Orange Bitters

2 dashes Angostura Bitters

Club Soda

Shake all ingredients except club soda with ice. Strain into ice-filled tumbler or Collins glass. Fill with club soda and stir.

Y SUMMER CABINET

1½ oz. Gin

½ oz. Apricot Liqueur

1 oz. Olorosso Sherry

1 oz. Lemon Juice

1 dash Lemon Bitters

Shake with ice and strain into chilled cocktail glass.

Y SUNSHINE COCKTAIL

¾ oz. Sweet Vermouth

1½ oz. Gin

1 dash Bitters

Stir with ice and strain into chilled cocktail glass. Garnish with a twist of orange peel.

Y SWEET BASIL MARTINI

3 Basil Leaves

1 Lemon Wedge

1½ oz. Gin

¾ oz. Lillet Blanc

½ oz. Simple Syrup

Muddle the basil and lemon wedge in mixing glass. Add the other ingredients. Shake with ice and strain into chilled cocktail glass. Garnish with a lemon wheel.

T & T

2 oz. Tanqueray Gin

Tonic Water

Pour gin into ice-filled highball glass and fill with tonic water. Stir. Garnish with a lime wedge.

GIN

TAILSPIN

¾ oz. Gin

¾ oz. Sweet Vermouth

¾ oz. Chartreuse (Green)

1 dash Campari

Stir with ice and strain into chilled cocktail glass. Garnish with a lemon twist and a maraschino cherry.

TANGO COCKTAIL

1 tbsp. Orange Juice

½ oz. Dry Vermouth

½ oz. Sweet Vermouth

1 oz. Gin

½ tsp. Triple Sec

Shake with ice and strain into chilled cocktail glass.

THE TART GIN COOLER

2 oz. Gin

2 oz. Pink Grapefruit Juice

2 oz. Tonic Water

Peychaud's Bitters to taste

Build, in order given, in ice-filled Collins glass.

THIRD-DEGREE COCKTAIL

1½ oz. Gin

¾ oz. Dry Vermouth

1 tsp. Anisette

Stir with ice and strain into chilled cocktail glass.

THREE CARD MONTY

1 oz. Gin

1 oz. Campari

1 oz. Tawny Port

Stir with ice and strain into chilled cocktail glass. No garnish.

THREE STRIPES COCKTAIL

1 oz. Gin

½ oz. Dry Vermouth

1 tbsp. Orange Juice

Shake with ice and strain into chilled cocktail glass.

THUNDERCLAP

¾ oz. Gin

¾ oz. Blended Whiskey

¾ oz. Brandy

Shake with ice and strain into chilled cocktail glass.

TILLICUM

2¼ oz. Gin

¾ oz. Dry Vermouth

2 dashes Peychaud's Bitters

Stir with ice and strain into chilled cocktail glass. Garnish with a slice of smoked salmon skewered flat on a pick.

TOM COLLINS

1 oz. Lemon Juice
1 tsp. Superfine Sugar
(or Simple Syrup)
2 oz. Gin
Club Soda

Shake lemon juice, sugar/syrup, and gin with ice and strain into Collins glass. Add several ice cubes, fill with club soda, and stir. Garnish with slices of lemon and orange, and a maraschino cherry. Serve with a straw.

TROPICAL SPECIAL

1½ oz. Gin
1 oz. Orange Juice
1 oz. Lime Juice
2 oz. Grapefruit Juice
½ oz. Triple Sec

Shake with ice and strain into ice-filled highball glass. Garnish with fruit slices and a maraschino cherry.

TURF COCKTAIL

¼ tsp. Anisette
2 dashes Bitters
1 oz. Dry Vermouth
1 oz. Gin

Stir with ice and strain into chilled cocktail glass. Add a twist of orange peel.

TUXEDO COCKTAIL

1½ oz. Gin
1½ oz. Dry Vermouth
¼ tsp. Maraschino Liqueur
¼ tsp. Anisette
2 dashes Orange Bitters

Stir with ice and strain into chilled cocktail glass. Garnish with a maraschino cherry.

TWENTIETH-CENTURY COCKTAIL

1½ oz. Gin
¾ oz. Lillet Blonde
¾ oz. Lemon Juice
½ oz. Crème de Cacao (White)

Shake with ice and strain into chilled cocktail glass.

TYPHOON

1 oz. Gin
½ oz. Anisette
1 oz. Lime Juice
Champagne, chilled

Shake first three ingredients with ice and strain into ice-filled Collins glass. Top with Champagne.

UNION COCKTAIL

¾ oz. Sloe Gin
1½ oz. Gin
½ tsp. Grenadine

Shake with ice and strain into chilled cocktail glass.

Y UNION JACK

2 oz. Gin

½ oz. Pimm's

½ oz. Crème de Violette

2 dashes Orange Bitters

Stir with ice and strain into chilled cocktail glass. Garnish with an orange twist.

Y THE VALENTINO

2 oz. Gin

½ oz. Campari

½ oz. Sweet Vermouth

Stir over ice and strain into chilled cocktail glass. Garnish with a twist of orange peel.

Y VESPER

3 oz. Gin

1 oz. Vodka

½ oz. Lillet Blonde

Stir with ice and strain into chilled cocktail glass. Garnish with a twist of orange peel.

As mentioned in James Bond, *Casino Royale*

Y VICTOR

1½ oz. Gin

½ oz. Brandy

½ oz. Sweet Vermouth

Shake with ice and strain into chilled cocktail glass.

Y VIEUX MOT

1½ oz. Gin

¾ oz. Lemon Juice

½ oz. Elderflower Liqueur

½ oz. Simple Syrup

Shake with ice and strain into chilled cocktail glass.

Y VOW OF SILENCE

1½ oz. Gin

¾ oz. Grapefruit Juice

½ oz. Lime Juice

½ oz. Yellow Chartreuse

¼ oz. Amaro

¼ oz. Simple Syrup

Shake with ice and strain into chilled cocktail glass.

Y WAIKIKI BEACHCOMBER

¾ oz. Gin

¾ oz. Triple Sec

1 tbsp. Fresh Pineapple Juice

Shake with ice and strain into chilled cocktail glass.

Y WALLICK COCKTAIL

1½ oz. Dry Vermouth

1½ oz. Gin

1 tsp. Triple Sec

Stir with ice and strain into chilled cocktail glass.

GIN

WALLIS BLUE COCKTAIL

1 oz. Triple Sec
1 oz. Gin
1 oz. Lime Juice

Moisten rim of old-fashioned glass with lime juice and dip into superfine sugar (or simple syrup). Shake ingredients with ice and strain into ice-filled glass.

WATER LILY

¾ oz. Gin
¾ oz. Triple Sec
¾ oz. Crème de Violette
¾ oz. Lemon Juice

Shake with ice and strain into chilled cocktail glass. Garnish with an orange twist.

WEBSTER COCKTAIL

½ oz. Lime Juice
1½ tsps. Apricot-flavored Brandy
½ oz. Dry Vermouth
1 oz. Gin

Shake with ice and strain into chilled cocktail glass.

WEMBLY COCKTAIL

¾ oz. Dry Vermouth
1½ oz. Gin
¼ tsp. Apricot-flavored Brandy
½ tsp. Apple Brandy

Stir with ice and strain into chilled cocktail glass.

WESTERN ROSE

½ oz. Apricot-flavored Brandy
1 oz. Gin
½ oz. Dry Vermouth
¼ tsp. Lemon Juice

Shake with ice and strain into chilled cocktail glass.

WHAT THE HELL

1 oz. Gin
1 oz. Dry Vermouth
1 oz. Apricot-flavored Brandy
1 dash Lemon Juice

Stir into ice-filled old-fashioned glass.

WHITE LADY

2 oz. Gin
1 oz. Triple Sec
½ oz. Lemon Juice

Shake with ice and strain into chilled cocktail glass.

WHITE SPIDER

1 oz. Gin
1 oz. Lemon Juice
½ oz. Triple Sec
1 tsp. Superfine Sugar (or Simple Syrup)

Shake with ice and strain into chilled cocktail glass.

WHITE WAY COCKTAIL

¾ oz. Crème de Menthe (White)

1½ oz. Gin

Shake with ice and strain into chilled cocktail glass.

WHY NOT?

1 oz. Gin

1 oz. Apricot-flavored Brandy

½ oz. Dry Vermouth

1 dash Lemon Juice

Shake with ice and strain into chilled cocktail glass.

WILL ROGERS

1½ oz. Gin

1 tbsp. Orange Juice

½ oz. Dry Vermouth

1 dash Triple Sec

Shake with ice and strain into chilled cocktail glass.

THE WINK

2 oz. Gin

¼ oz. Simple Syrup

¼ oz. Triple Sec

2 dashes Peychaud's Bitters

1 splash Absinthe

Stir all but absinthe with ice and strain into chilled, absinthe-rinsed old-fashioned glass. Garnish with a wink.

THE WINKLE

3 Sage Leaves

2 oz. Gin

½ oz. Limoncello

1 oz. Lime Juice

½ oz. Simple Syrup

4 Whole Raspberries

Muddle sage in mixing glass. Add rest of ingredients. Shake with ice and double-strain into chilled cocktail glass. Garnish with a lemon twist.

WOLF'S BITE

1½ oz. Gin

1 oz. Grapefruit Juice

½ oz. Green Chartreuse

Shake with ice and strain into chilled cocktail glass.

WOODSTOCK

1½ oz. Gin

1 oz. Lemon Juice

1½ tsps. Maple Syrup

1 dash Orange Bitters

Shake with ice and strain into chilled cocktail glass.

XANTHIA COCKTAIL

¾ oz. Cherry-flavored Brandy

¾ oz. Chartreuse (Yellow)

¾ oz. Gin

Stir with ice and strain into chilled cocktail glass.

GIN

YALE COCKTAIL

1½ oz. Gin
½ oz. Dry Vermouth
1 dash Bitters
1 tsp. Blue Curaçao

Stir with ice and strain into chilled cocktail glass.

YELLOW RATTLER

1 oz. Gin
1 tbsp. Orange Juice
½ oz. Dry Vermouth
½ oz. Sweet Vermouth

Shake with ice and strain into chilled cocktail glass. Garnish with a cocktail onion.

YOKAHAMA ROMANCE

2½ oz. Sake
1 oz. Gin
¼ oz. Maraschino Liqueur

Stir with ice and strain into chilled cocktail glass. Garnish with a rose petal.

YOLANDA

½ oz. Brandy
½ oz. Gin
½ oz. Anisette
1 oz. Sweet Vermouth
1 dash Grenadine

Shake with ice and strain into chilled cocktail glass. Garnish with a twist of orange peel.

Educate the Customer

Too often a customer walks into a bar and orders the same cocktail they always do. This is generally out of habit, or lack of a better idea. A well-informed bartender will have a selection of great cocktails to recommend to their patrons. By turning the customer on to a new cocktail, whether it is an original creation or a classic, you are both educating your guest and making sure to create repeat business. Get them addicted to your special cocktails, and let them have that vodka tonic at any other bar; I guarantee you will see their faces again.

—JULIE REINER,
owner, Flatiron Lounge, New York City

RUM

RUM WAS FIRST PRODUCED IN BRAZIL, Barbados, and Jamaica after Columbus introduced sugarcane to the West Indies in the late fifteenth century; within two centuries it was the favorite spirit of New England. Today this spirit, made from molasses, sugarcane juice, or syrup made by reducing the free-run juice of sugarcane, is among the most popular in the United States.

Rums can be divided into three stylistic types: Light rums, sometimes called white or silver, are traditionally produced in southern Caribbean islands (like Puerto Rico, Trinidad, and Barbados) and aged up to a year in barrels. Medium rums, sometimes called gold or amber, are smoother as a result of either congeners (organic compounds produced during fermentation), the addition of caramel, or occasionally through aging in wood barrels. Dark rums, which take their color from being aged anywhere from 3 to 12 years (and in some cases from the addition of caramel), are produced in the tropics: Jamaica, Haiti, or Martinique. And speaking of the French island of Martinique, if you see the words "rhum agricole" on a bottle or menu it refers to how pure-cane rum is known there—and pure-cane rums are suddenly all the rage. Brazilians call their pure-cane spirit "cachaça," which is synonymous with Caipirinha cocktails.

Subcategories of rum include spiced or flavored rums, which are infused with spices or aromatics while being distilled. There are also 151-proof rums, also called high-proof rums, which are often added to complete a mixed drink or in desserts or dessert cocktails that call for flaming—literally igniting the spirit. (Obviously, one should be very careful when playing with fire and high-proof rum!)

A DAY AT THE BEACH

1 oz. Coconut-flavored Rum
½ oz. Amaretto
4 oz. Orange Juice
½ oz. Grenadine

Shake rum, amaretto, and orange juice with ice and pour into ice-filled highball glass. Top with grenadine and garnish with a pineapple wedge and a strawberry.

AGRICOLE RUM PUNCH

2 oz. Aged Rhum Agricole
1 oz. Lime Juice
1 oz. Simple Syrup
2 dashes Angostura Bitters
¼ oz. Allspice Liqueur

Shake with ice and strain into ice-filled Collins glass. Garnish with ground nutmeg.

AIR MAIL

1 oz. White Rum
½ oz. Lime Juice
½ oz. Honey Syrup
1 splash Champagne, chilled

Shake first three ingredients, then strain into champagne flute. Top with Champagne.

ANCIENT MARINER

1 oz. Aged Rum
1 oz. Dark Rum
¾ oz. Lime Juice
½ oz. Grapefruit Juice
½ oz. Simple Syrup
¼ oz. Allspice Liqueur

Shake with ice and strain into old-fashioned glass filled with crushed ice. Garnish with lime wedge and mint sprig.

APPLE PIE NO. 1

¾ oz. Light Rum
¾ oz. Sweet Vermouth
1 tsp. Apple Brandy
½ tsp. Grenadine
1 tsp. Lemon Juice

Shake with ice and strain into chilled cocktail glass.

BAHAMA MAMA

½ oz. Dark Rum
½ oz. Coconut Liqueur
¼ oz. 151-proof Rum
¼ oz. Coffee Liqueur
½ oz. Lemon Juice
4 oz. Pineapple Juice

Combine all ingredients and pour into ice-filled highball glass. Garnish with a strawberry or a maraschino cherry.

BAJITO (BAHITO)

4 Fresh Mint Leaves

4 Fresh Basil Leaves

5 slices Fresh Lime

1 tbsp. Superfine Sugar
(or Simple Syrup)

3 oz. Dark Rum

In shaker glass muddle mint and basil with lime slices and sugar/syrup. Top with ice and then rum. Shake well and strain into ice-filled old-fashioned glass. Garnish with a basil leaf.

BANANA COW

1 oz. Light Rum

1 oz. Crème de Banana

1½ oz. Cream

1 dash Grenadine

Shake ingredients with crushed ice and strain into chilled cocktail glass. Garnish with a banana slice and fresh-grated nutmeg on top.

THE BEACHBUM

1 oz. Light Rum

1 oz. Dark Rum

½ oz. Apricot Brandy

½ oz. Almond Syrup

¾ oz. Lime Juice

1 oz. Pineapple Juice

Shake with ice and strain into ice-filled Collins glass. Garnish with cherry/orange flag.

BEACHCOMBER

1½ oz. Light Rum

½ oz. Triple Sec

½ oz. Grenadine

½ oz. Superfine Sugar
(or Simple Syrup)

½ oz. Lemon Juice

Shake with ice and strain into chilled, sugar-rimmed cocktail glass. Garnish with a lime wheel.

THE BEAUTY BENEATH

2 oz. Aged Rum

½ oz. Sweet Vermouth

½ oz. Campari

½ oz. Triple Sec

1 dash Angostura Bitters

Shake with ice and strain into chilled cocktail glass. Garnish with orange twist.

BEE'S KISS

1½ oz. White Rum

1 oz. Heavy Cream

¾ oz. Honey Syrup

Shake and strain into a champagne flute.

BENJAMIN BARKER DAIQUIRI

2 oz. Dark Rum

½ oz. Lime Juice

½ oz. Simple Syrup

½ oz. Campari

2 dashes Absinthe

Shake with ice and strain into chilled cocktail glass. Garnish with lime wedge.

RUM

BERMUDA RUM SWIZZLE

2 oz. Dark Rum
1 oz. Lime Juice
1 oz. Pineapple Juice
1 oz. Orange Juice
¼ oz. Falernum

Shake with ice and strain into ice-filled highball glass. Garnish with a slice of orange and a maraschino cherry.

BERMUDA TRIANGLE

1 oz. Peach Schnapps
½ oz. Spiced Rum
3 oz. Orange Juice

Pour ingredients into ice-filled old-fashioned glass.

BITCHES' BREW

1 oz. Aged Rum
1 oz. White Rhum Agricole
1 oz. Lime Juice
½ oz. Simple Syrup
½ oz. Allspice Liqueur
1 Egg

Shake without ice. Then shake with ice and strain into highball glass. Garnish with grated nutmeg.

BITTERLY DARK

1 oz. Blood Orange Juice
1½ oz. Aged Rum
1 oz. Amaro
¼ oz. Crème de Cassis

Shake and strain into chilled cocktail glass. Garnish with a slice of blood orange.

BLACK DEVIL

2 oz. Light Rum
½ oz. Dry Vermouth

Stir with ice and strain into chilled cocktail glass. Add a black olive.

BLACK MARIA

2 oz. Coffee-flavored Brandy
2 oz. Light Rum
4 oz. Strong Black Coffee
2 tsps. Superfine Sugar (or Simple Syrup)

Stir in brandy snifter and add ice.

BLACK WIDOW

3 oz. Dark Rum
1 oz. White Crème de Menthe

Shake with ice and strain into old-fashioned glass filled with ice.

BLOOD AND SAMBA

¾ oz. Cachaça
¾ oz. Orange Juice
¾ oz. Sweet Vermouth
¾ oz. Cherry Heering
2 dashes Peychaud's Bitters

Shake with ice and strain into chilled cocktail glass. Garnish with flamed orange twist.

BLUE HAWAIIAN

1 oz. Light Rum
1 oz. Blue Curaçao
2 oz. Pineapple Juice
1 oz. Cream of Coconut

Combine all ingredients with 1 cup crushed ice in blender on high speed. Pour into chilled highball glass. Garnish with a slice of pineapple and a maraschino cherry.

BOLERO

1½ oz. Light Rum
¼ oz. Apple Brandy
¼ tsp. Sweet Vermouth

Stir with ice and strain into chilled cocktail glass.

THE BONAIRE

1½ oz. Spiced Rum
¾ oz. Orange Curaçao
¾ oz. Cranberry Juice
½ oz. Lime Juice
2 dashes Angostura Bitters

Shake with ice and strain into chilled cocktail glass. Garnish with orange twist.

BORINQUEN

1½ oz. Light Rum
1 tbsp. Passion Fruit Syrup
1 oz. Lime Juice
1 oz. Orange Juice
1 tsp. 151-proof Rum

Combine all ingredients with half a cup of ice in blender on low speed. Pour into chilled old-fashioned glass.

BOSSA NOVA SPECIAL COCKTAIL

1 oz. Rum
1 oz. Galliano
¼ oz. Apricot Liqueur
2 oz. Pineapple Juice
¼ oz. Lemon Juice
1 Egg White

Shake and strain into an ice-filled highball glass. Garnish with a maraschino cherry.

BOSTON COOLER

1 oz. Lemon Juice
1 tsp. Superfine Sugar (or Simple Syrup)
2 oz. Club Soda
2 oz. Light Rum
Club Soda or Ginger Ale

Into Collins glass pour lemon juice, sugar/syrup, and club soda. Stir. Fill glass with ice and add rum. Fill with club soda or ginger ale and stir again. Add spiral of orange or lemon peel and dangle end over rim of glass.

BOSTON SIDECAR

¾ oz. Brandy
¾ oz. Light Rum
¾ oz. Triple Sec
½ oz. Lime Juice

Shake with ice and strain into chilled cocktail glass.

RUM

BUCCANEER

1½ oz. Spiced Rum
½ oz. White Crème de Cacao
½ oz. Falernum
¾ oz. Lime Juice
¾ oz. Pineapple Juice
1 dash Angostura Bitters

Shake with ice and strain into chilled cocktail glass. Garnish with grated nutmeg.

BUCK JONES

1½ oz. Light Rum
1 oz. Sweet Sherry
½ oz. Lime Juice
Ginger Ale

Pour first three ingredients into ice-filled highball glass and stir. Fill with ginger ale.

BULL'S BLOOD

¾ oz. Aged Rum
¾ oz. Orange Curaçao
¾ oz. Spanish Brandy
1½ oz. Orange Juice

Shake with ice and strain into chilled cocktail glass. Garnish with flamed orange twist.

BURGUNDY BISHOP

½ oz. Lemon Juice
1 tsp. Superfine Sugar (or Simple Syrup)
1 oz. Light Rum
Red Wine

Shake lemon juice, sugar/syrup, and rum with ice and strain into ice-filled highball glass. Fill with red wine and stir. Garnish with fruits.

CABLE CAR

2 oz. Spiced Rum
1 oz. Triple Sec
⅓ oz. Lemon Juice

Shake with ice and strain into chilled, cinnamon-sugar-rimmed cocktail glass. Garnish with a twist of lemon peel and a dust of cinnamon.

CAIPIRINHA

1 Whole Lime
1 tsp. Sugar
2 oz. Cachaça (Brazilian White Rum)

Wash the lime and cut it into quarters. Muddle sugar and lime in highball glass. Add cachaça and stir. Fill with ice and stir again.

CANADO SALUDO

1½ oz. Light Rum
1 oz. Orange Juice
1 oz. Pineapple Juice
½ oz. Lemon Juice
½ oz. Grenadine
5 dashes Bitters

Combine all ingredients in ice-filled highball glass. Garnish with pineapple slices, an orange slice, and a maraschino cherry.

CAPTAIN'S BLOOD

1½ oz. Dark Rum

¼ oz. Lime Juice

¼ oz. Superfine Sugar
(or Simple Syrup)

2 dashes Angostura Bitters

Shake with ice and strain
into chilled cocktail glass.
Garnish with a spiral of
lemon peel.

CARIBBEAN
CHAMPAGNE

½ oz. Light Rum

½ oz. Crème de Banana

Champagne, chilled

Pour rum and banana
liqueur into champagne
flute. Fill with Champagne
and stir gently. Add a slice of
banana.

CARIBBEAN ROMANCE

1½ oz. Light Rum

1 oz. Amaretto

1½ oz. Orange Juice

1½ oz. Pineapple Juice

1 splash Grenadine

Shake rum, amaretto, and
juices with ice and strain into
ice-filled highball glass. Float
grenadine on top and gar-
nish with an orange, lemon,
or lime slice.

CASA BLANCA

2 oz. Light Rum

1½ tsps. Lime Juice

1½ tsps. Triple Sec

1½ tsps. Maraschino Liqueur

Shake with ice and strain
into chilled cocktail glass.

CASTAWAY

1½ oz. Aged Rum

3 oz. Pineapple Juice

¾ oz. Coffee Liqueur

Shake with ice and strain
into hurricane glass filled
with crushed ice. Garnish
with cherry speared to pineapple wedge.

CHANTILLY COCKTAIL

1½ oz. Rum

¾ oz. Apricot-flavored
Brandy

2 dashes Peach Bitters

1 oz. Lemon Juice

1 oz. Superfine Sugar
(or Simple Syrup)

Shake with ice and strain
into chilled, cinnamon-sugar-
rimmed cocktail glass. Garnish with an orange peel
spiral wrapped around a
cinnamon stick.

CHERIE

1 oz. Lime Juice

½ oz. Triple Sec

1 oz. Light Rum

½ oz. Cherry-flavored Brandy

Shake with ice and strain
into chilled cocktail glass.
Add a maraschino cherry.

RUM

CHERRY RUM

1¼ oz. Light Rum

1½ tsps. Cherry-flavored Brandy

1 tbsp. Light Cream

Shake with ice and strain into chilled cocktail glass.

CHET BAKER

1 cube Sugar

2 dashes Angostura Bitters

2 oz. Aged Rum

¼ oz. Punt e Mes

¼ oz. Honey Syrup

Muddle sugar cube with bitters in mixing glass. Add ice, then other ingredients and stir briefly. Strain over fresh ice in old-fashioned glass. Garnish with a lemon twist.

CHINESE COCKTAIL

1 tbsp. Grenadine

1½ oz. Jamaican Rum

1 dash Bitters

1 tsp. Maraschino Liqueur

1 tsp. Triple Sec

Shake with ice and strain into chilled cocktail glass.

CHOCOLATE RUM

1 oz. Light Rum

½ oz. Crème de Cacao (Brown)

½ oz. Crème de Menthe (White)

1 tbsp. Light Cream

1 tsp. 151-proof Rum

Shake with ice and strain into ice-filled old-fashioned glass.

COCOMACOQUE

1 oz. Lemon Juice

2 oz. Pineapple Juice

2 oz. Orange Juice

1½ oz. Light Rum

2 oz. Red Wine

Shake all ingredients except wine. Pour into ice-filled Collins glass and top with wine. Add a pineapple stick.

COFFEY PARK SWIZZLE

1 oz. Aged Rum

1 oz. Amontillado Sherry

¾ oz. Ginger Liqueur

¾ oz. Lime Juice

¼ oz. Falernum

4 dashes Angostura Bitters

Build in Collins glass filled with crushed ice. Swizzle, and top with crushed ice. Garnish with a mint sprig.

CONTINENTAL

1¾ oz. Light Rum

1 tbsp. Lime Juice

1½ tsps. Crème de Menthe (Green)

½ tsp. Superfine Sugar (or Simple Syrup)

Shake with ice and strain into chilled cocktail glass. Add a twist of lemon peel.

COOL CARLOS

1½ oz. Dark Rum

2 oz. Cranberry Juice

2 oz. Pineapple Juice

1 splash Superfine Sugar (or Simple Syrup)

1 splash Lemon Juice

1 oz. Orange Curaçao

Shake first five ingredients with ice. Strain into ice-filled Collins glass and float curaçao on top. Garnish with pineapple and orange slices and a maraschino cherry.

CORKSCREW

1½ oz. Light Rum

½ oz. Dry Vermouth

½ oz. Peach-flavored Brandy

Shake with ice and strain into chilled cocktail glass. Garnish with a lime slice.

CREAM PUFF

2 oz. Light Rum

1 oz. Light Cream

½ tsp. Superfine Sugar (or Simple Syrup)

Club Soda

Shake first three ingredients with ice and strain into chilled highball glass over two ice cubes. Fill with club soda and stir.

CREOLE

1½ oz. Light Rum

1 dash Tabasco Sauce

1 tsp. Lemon Juice

1½ oz. Beef Bouillon

Salt and Pepper as needed

Shake with ice and strain into ice-filled old-fashioned glass.

CREOLE CLUB COCKTAIL

2 oz. Aged Rhum Agricole

1 oz. Creole Shrubb

¾ oz. Lime Juice

1 dash Angostura Bitters

1 dash Orange Bitters

Shake with ice and strain into chilled cocktail glass. Garnish with grated nutmeg and a whole star anise pod.

CUBA LIBRE

½ oz. Lime Juice

2 oz. Light Rum

Cola

Put lime juice and twist of lime into highball glass and add rum. Top with ice and fill with cola.

CUBAN COCKTAIL NO. 1

½ oz. Lime Juice

½ tsp. Superfine Sugar (or Simple Syrup)

2 oz. Light Rum

Shake with ice and strain into chilled cocktail glass.

RUM

☐ CUBAN SPECIAL

1 tbsp. Pineapple Juice
½ oz. Lime Juice
1 oz. Light Rum
½ tsp. Triple Sec

Shake with ice and strain into chilled cocktail glass. Garnish with a slice of pineapple and a maraschino cherry.

☐ DAIQUIRI

1 oz. Lime Juice
1 tsp. Superfine Sugar (or Simple Syrup)
1½ oz. Light Rum

Shake with ice and strain into chilled cocktail glass.

☐ DAISY DE SANTIAGO

2 oz. Dark Rum
¾ oz. Superfine Sugar (or Simple Syrup)
¾ oz. Lime Juice
1 oz. Chartreuse (Yellow)

Shake first three ingredients and strain into ice-filled red-wine glass. Pour chartreuse over an inverted bar spoon to float. Garnish with a sprig of mint.

☐ DARK 'N' STORMY

2 oz. Dark Rum
4 oz. Ginger Beer

Mix in an old-fashioned glass over ice.

Dark 'n' Stormy is a registered trademark of Gosling Brothers Limited, Hamilton, Bermuda.

Get in Their Heads

If a bartender has time, it's always good to try to get "inside the head" of his or her customer, to try to discern their individual tastes. For instance, if somebody orders a Negroni, the bartender might ask, "Traditional gin Negroni?" since many people in the 21st century seem to prefer vodka (some people might not condone this, but facts are facts). This can lead to asking which brand of gin the customer prefers, and in turn, when the guest returns to the bar, the bartender might suggest another cocktail made with the same gin. Thus the bartender better understands the customer, and the customer enjoys the bar more.

—GARY REGAN,
co-publisher, ArdentSpirits.com

DERBY DAIQUIRI

1½ oz. Light Rum
1 oz. Orange Juice
1 tbsp. Lime Juice
1 tsp. Sugar

Combine all ingredients with ½ cup of shaved ice in blender on low speed. Pour into champagne flute.

DIABOLO

2 oz. Rum
½ oz. Triple Sec
½ oz. Dry Vermouth
2 dashes Angostura Bitters

Stir with ice and strain into chilled cocktail glass. Garnish with a twist of orange peel.

DINGO

½ oz. Light Rum
½ oz. Amaretto
½ oz. Whiskey (Tennessee Sour Mash)
1 oz. Superfine Sugar (or Simple Syrup)
1 oz. Lemon Juice
2 oz. Orange Juice
1 splash Grenadine

Shake with ice and pour into ice-filled highball glass. Garnish with an orange slice.

DOCTOR FUNK #2

1½ oz. Dark Rum
½ oz. Falernum
½ oz. Grenadine
¾ oz. Lime Juice
1 dash Absinthe
1 dash Angostura Bitters
Club Soda

Shake first six ingredients with ice and strain into hurricane glass. Top with club soda and garnish with a lime wedge.

DOMINICANA

1½ oz. Coffee Liqueur
1½ oz. Dark Rum (Reserve)
1 oz. Heavy Cream

Stir and strain first two ingredients into champagne flute. Pour heavy cream slowly over an inverted spoon to float.

EL PRESIDENTE COCKTAIL NO. 1

1 oz. Lime Juice
1 tsp. Pineapple Juice
1 tsp. Grenadine
1½ oz. Light Rum

Shake with ice and strain into chilled cocktail glass.

EL PRESIDENTE COCKTAIL NO. 2

¾ oz. Dry Vermouth
1½ oz. Light Rum
1 dash Bitters

Stir with ice and strain into chilled cocktail glass.

RUM

FAIR-AND-WARMER COCKTAIL

¾ oz. Sweet Vermouth

1½ oz. Light Rum

½ tsp. Triple Sec

Stir with ice and strain into chilled cocktail glass.

FAT LIKE BUDDHA

2 oz. Aged Rum

¾ oz. Dubonnet Rouge

¼ oz. Bénédictine

¼ oz. Triple Sec

Stir with ice and strain into chilled cocktail glass. Garnish with a flamed orange twist.

FIREMAN'S SOUR

½ tsp. Superfine Sugar (or Simple Syrup)

½ tbsp. Grenadine

2 oz. Lime Juice

2 oz. Light Rum

Club Soda (optional)

Shake sugar/syrup, grenadine, lime juice, and rum with ice and strain into chilled sour glass. Fill with club soda, if desired. Garnish with a half-slice of lemon and a maraschino cherry.

FLORIDITA

1½ oz. Rum

½ oz. Lime Juice

½ oz. Sweet Vermouth

⅛ oz. Crème de Cacao (White)

⅛ oz. Grenadine

Shake with ice and strain into chilled cocktail glass. Garnish with a lime twist.

FLORIDITA NO. 3

2 oz. White Rum

¾ oz. Lime Juice

½ oz. Grapefruit Juice

½ oz. Maraschino Liqueur

½ oz. Superfine Sugar (or Simple Syrup)

Shake and strain into champagne flute. Garnish with a lime wheel.

FOG CUTTER

1½ oz. Light Rum

½ oz. Brandy

½ oz. Gin

1 oz. Orange Juice

1½ oz. Lemon Juice

1½ tsps. Orgeat Syrup (Almond Syrup)

1 tsp. Sweet Sherry

Shake all ingredients except sherry and strain into ice-filled Collins glass. Top with sherry.

FORT LAUDERDALE

1½ oz. Light Rum
½ oz. Sweet Vermouth
1 oz. Orange Juice
¼ oz. Lime Juice

Shake with ice and strain into ice-filled old-fashioned glass. Add a slice of orange.

GAUGUIN

2 oz. Light Rum
1 tbsp. Passion Fruit Syrup
1 tbsp. Lemon Juice
1 tbsp. Lime Juice

Combine all ingredients with a cup of crushed ice in blender on low speed. Serve in chilled old-fashioned glass. Garnish with a maraschino cherry.

GINGER GRAPEFRUIT RICKEY

2 oz. Light Rum
2 oz. Grapefruit Juice
1 oz. Ginger Liqueur
½ oz. Lime Juice
Club Soda

Shake everything but the club soda with ice. Strain into highball glass and top with club soda.

GOLDEN FRIENDSHIP

EQUAL PARTS

Amaretto
Sweet Vermouth
Light Rum
Ginger Ale

Mix first three ingredients in Collins glass with ice, then fill with ginger ale. Garnish with an orange spiral and a maraschino cherry.

GORILLA MILK

1 oz. Light Rum
½ oz. Coffee Liqueur
½ oz. Irish Cream Liqueur
½ oz. Crème de Banana
1 oz. Light Cream

Shake with ice and pour into ice-filled hurricane or parfait glass. Garnish with a banana slice.

GRANDE GUIGNOL

1½ oz. Aged Rum
¾ oz. Lime Juice
¾ oz. Yellow Chartreuse
¾ oz. Cherry Heering

Shake with ice and strain into chilled cocktail glass. Garnish with a lime wheel.

RUM

HAI KARATE

1 oz. Lime Juice
1 oz. Pineapple Juice
1 oz. Orange Juice
1 barspoon Maple Syrup
1 dash Angostura Bitters
2 oz. Aged Rum

Shake with ice and strain into ice-filled Collins glass. Garnish with a cherry/orange flag.

HARVEST NECTAR

1½ oz. Rum
1 oz. Pineapple Juice
1 oz. Cranberry Juice
1 oz. Orange Juice
1 oz. Lemon-lime Soda

Shake with ice and strain into ice-filled beer mug.

HAVANA COCKTAIL

1½ oz. Pineapple Juice
½ tsp. Lemon Juice
¾ oz. Light Rum

Shake with ice and strain into chilled cocktail glass.

HOP TOAD

½ oz. Lime Juice
¾ oz. Apricot-flavored Brandy
¾ oz. Light Rum

Stir with ice and strain into chilled cocktail glass.

HURRICANE

1 oz. Dark Rum
1 oz. Light Rum
1 tbsp. Passion Fruit Syrup
2 tsps. Lime Juice

Shake with ice and strain into chilled cocktail glass.

HURRICANE LEAH

¼ oz. Light Rum
¼ oz. Gin
¼ oz. Vodka
¼ oz. Tequila
¼ oz. Blue Curaçao
1 dash Cherry Brandy
1½ oz. Superfine Sugar (or Simple Syrup)
1½ oz. Lemon Juice
3 oz. Orange Juice

Pour into ice-filled hurricane or parfait glass and stir. Garnish with an orange wheel.

HUSH AND WONDER

2 oz. Light Rum
¾ oz. Lime Juice
¾ oz. Simple Syrup
3 dashes Grapefruit Bitters
1 splash Crème de Violette

Shake first four ingredients with ice and strain into chilled, crème de violette–rinsed cocktail glass.

IRRESISTIBLE

1½ oz. White Rum
½ oz. Sweet Vermouth
¼ oz. Bénédictine
¼ oz. Lemon Juice

Shake and strain into cocktail glass. Garnish with a lemon twist.

JACK SPARROW FLIP

2 oz. Aged Rum
¾ oz. Simple Syrup
¾ oz. Madeira
2 dashes Angostura Bitters
1 Whole Egg

Shake without ice. Then shake with ice and strain into highball glass. Garnish with grated nutmeg.

JACQUELINE

1 oz. Triple Sec
2 oz. Dark Rum
1 oz. Lime Juice
1 pinch Superfine Sugar (or Simple Syrup)

Shake with ice and ͜ ain into chilled cocktail glass.

JADE

1½ oz. Light Rum
½ tsp. Crème de Menthe (Green)
½ tsp. Triple Sec
1 tbsp. Lime Juice
1 tsp. Superfine Sugar (or Simple Syrup)

Shake with ice and strain into chilled cocktail glass. Add a lime slice.

JAMAICAN CRAWLER

1 oz. Light Rum
1 oz. Melon Liqueur
3 oz. Pineapple Juice
1 splash Grenadine

Combine first three ingredients with ice and stir well. Pour into Collins glass, and float grenadine on top.

JAMAICAN GINGER

1½ oz. Light Rum
1 oz. Aged Rum
½ oz. Falernum
½ oz. Lime Juice
4 dashes Angostura Bitters
Ginger Ale

Combine first five ingredients in ice-filled Collins glass. Top with ginger ale and garnish with a lime wheel.

KNICKERBOCKER SPECIAL COCKTAIL

1 tsp. Raspberry Syrup
1 tsp. Lemon Juice
1 tsp. Orange Juice
2 oz. Light Rum
½ tsp. Triple Sec

Shake with ice and strain into chilled cocktail glass. Garnish with a small slice of pineapple.

RUM

KO ADANG

2 oz. Aged Rum

1 oz. Coconut Rum

½ oz. Ginger Liqueur

½ oz. Mango Nectar

½ oz. Coconut Cream

½ oz. Lime Juice

Shake with ice and strain into ice-filled Collins glass. Garnish with a lime wheel.

KOLA NUT

1 oz. Light Rum

½ oz. Dry Vermouth

¼ oz. Bénédictine

Stir with ice and strain into ice-filled old-fashioned glass. Garnish with a lemon twist.

LEMON-COCONUT COLADA

1½ oz. Citrus-flavored Rum

1½ oz. Coconut-flavored Rum

2 oz. Coco Lopez

1 oz. Heavy Cream

4 oz. Pineapple Juice

½ oz.–1 oz. Lemon Juice

Shake all ingredients with ice and strain into ice-filled hurricane glass. Garnish with lemon zest or fresh toasted coconut.

LEVELHEADED COCKTAIL

1½ oz. Aged Rhum Agricole

1 oz. Chilled Brewed Coffee

½ oz. Allspice Liqueur

¼ oz. Simple Syrup

2 dashes Angostura Bitters

Shake with ice and strain into snifter.

LITTLE DEVIL COCKTAIL

½ oz. Lemon Juice

1½ tsps. Triple Sec

¾ oz. Light Rum

¾ oz. Gin

Shake with ice and strain into chilled cocktail glass.

LITTLE PRINCESS COCKTAIL

1½ oz. Sweet Vermouth

1½ oz. Light Rum

Shake with ice and strain into chilled cocktail glass.

LOOK OUT BELOW

1½ oz. 151-proof Rum

¼ oz. Lime Juice

1 tsp. Grenadine

Shake with ice and strain into ice-filled old-fashioned glass.

LOUNGE LIZARD

1 oz. Dark Rum
½ oz. Amaretto
Cola

Pour rum and amaretto into ice-filled Collins glass. Fill with cola. Garnish with a slice of lime.

LUMINATION

2 slices Ginger
1 oz. Superfine Sugar (or Simple Syrup)
2 oz. Dark Rum
1 oz. Cognac (V.S.)
1 oz. Lemon Juice
1 dash Angostura Bitters

Muddle ginger in sugar/syrup, top with ice, add rest of ingredients and shake. Strain into champagne flute. Garnish with a lemon twist.

MAI-TAI

1 oz. Light Rum
1 oz. Gold Rum
½ oz. Orange Curaçao
½ oz. Orgeat Syrup (Almond Syrup)
½ oz. Lime Juice
1 oz. Dark Rum

Shake all but the dark rum with ice. Strain into chilled old-fashioned glass. Top with the dark rum. Garnish with a maraschino cherry.

Created by Victor "Trader Vic" Bergeron.

MAI-TAI (ORIGINAL TRADER VIC FORMULA)

2 oz. Jamaican Rum
½ oz. French Garnier Orgeat
½ oz. Orange Curaçao
¼ oz. Rock Candy Syrup
1 oz. Lime Juice

Shake ingredients in mixing glass and strain into ice-filled old-fashioned glass. Garnish with half of the lime shell inside the glass and float a sprig of fresh mint at the edge of the glass.

MALMAISON

1 oz. Lemon Juice
1 oz. Light Rum
½ oz. Cream Sherry

Shake with ice and strain into chilled, anisette-rimmed cocktail glass.

MANDEVILLE

1½ oz. Light Rum
1 oz. Dark Rum
1 tsp. Anisette
1 tbsp. Lemon Juice
1 tbsp. Cola
¼ tsp. Grenadine

Shake with ice and strain into ice-filled old-fashioned glass.

RUM

MARIPOSA

1 oz. Light Rum
½ oz. Brandy
1 tbsp. Lemon Juice
1 tbsp. Orange Juice
1 dash Grenadine

Shake with ice and strain into chilled cocktail glass.

MARTINIQUE ROSE

2 oz. Aged Rhum Agricole
½ oz. Amaretto
¾ oz. Lime Juice
½ oz. Orgeat
¾ oz. Grapefruit Juice

Shake with ice and strain into chilled cocktail glass.

MARY PICKFORD COCKTAIL

1 oz. Light Rum
1 oz. Pineapple Juice
¼ tsp. Grenadine
¼ tsp. Maraschino Liqueur

Shake with ice and strain into chilled cocktail glass.

MIAMI

1½ oz. Light Rum
½ oz. Crème de Menthe (White)
1 dash Lemon Juice

Shake with ice and strain into chilled cocktail glass.

MIDNIGHT EXPRESS

1½ oz. Dark Rum
½ oz. Triple Sec
¾ oz. Lime Juice
1 splash Superfine Sugar (or Simple Syrup)
1 splash Lemon Juice

Shake with ice and pour into ice-filled old-fashioned glass.

MISSISSIPPI PLANTER'S PUNCH

1 tbsp. Superfine Sugar (or Simple Syrup)
1 oz. Lemon Juice
½ oz. Light Rum
½ oz. Bourbon
1 oz. Brandy
Club Soda

Shake all but club soda with ice and strain into ice-filled Collins glass. Fill with club soda and stir.

MOJITO

2 tsps. Sugar
4 sprigs Fresh Mint
1 Lime, halved
2 oz. Light Rum
Club Soda

Muddle sugar and mint in beer mug. Squeeze both halves of lime into the glass, leaving one hull in the mixture. Add rum, stir, and fill with ice. Top with club soda. Garnish with a mint sprig.

MONKEY WRENCH

1½ oz. Light Rum
Grapefruit Juice

Pour rum into ice-filled Collins glass. Fill with grapefruit juice and stir.

MOON QUAKE SHAKE

1½ oz. Dark Rum
1 oz. Coffee-flavored Brandy
1 tbsp. Lemon Juice

Shake with ice and strain into chilled cocktail glass.

NEVADA COCKTAIL

1½ oz. Light Rum
1 oz. Grapefruit Juice
1 oz. Lime Juice
1 dash Bitters
3 tsps. Superfine Sugar
  (or Simple Syrup)

Shake with ice and strain into chilled cocktail glass.

NEW ORLEANS BUCK

1½ oz. Light Rum
1 oz. Orange Juice
½ oz. Lemon Juice
Ginger Ale

Shake all ingredients except ginger ale with ice and strain into ice-filled Collins glass. Fill with ginger ale and stir.

NIGHT CAP

2 oz. Light Rum
1 tsp. Superfine Sugar
  (or Simple Syrup)
Warm Milk

Pour rum and sugar/syrup in Irish coffee glass, fill with warm milk, and stir. Garnish with fresh-grated nutmeg on top.

OH, GOSH!

1½ oz. Light Rum
1½ oz. Triple Sec
1 oz. Lime Juice

Shake with ice and strain into chilled cocktail glass. Garnish with a lemon twist.

THE OLD CUBAN

¾ oz. Lime Juice
1 oz. Superfine Sugar
  (or Simple Syrup)
6 Mint Leaves
1½ oz. Rum (Aged)
2 dashes Angostura Bitters
2 oz. Champagne

In a mixing glass, muddle lime juice, sugar/syrup, and mint. Add rum and bitters, top with ice, and shake well. Strain into chilled cocktail glass and top with Champagne. Garnish with a sugar-dried vanilla bean and mint flecks.

RUM

PADDINGTON

1½ oz. Light Rum
½ oz. Lillet Blanc
½ oz. Grapefruit Juice
½ oz. Lemon Juice
1 barspoon Orange Marmalade
1 splash Absinthe

Shake with ice and strain into chilled, absinthe-rinsed cocktail glass. Garnish with a grapefruit twist.

PALMETTO COCKTAIL

1½ oz. Light Rum
1½ oz. Dry Vermouth
2 dashes Bitters

Stir with ice and strain into chilled cocktail glass.

PARIS WHEN IT SIZZLES

2 oz. Aged Rum
½ oz. Lime Juice
¾ oz. Elderflower Liqueur
1 dash Angostura Bitters

Shake with ice and strain into chilled cocktail glass. Garnish with a lime wedge.

PASSION DAIQUIRI

1½ oz. Light Rum
1 oz. Lime
1 tsp. Superfine Sugar (or Simple Syrup)
1 tbsp. Passion Fruit Juice

Shake with ice and strain into chilled cocktail glass.

PEARL BUTTON

2 oz. Cachaça
½ oz. Lime Juice
¾ oz. Lillet Blanc
Lemon Soda

Shake with ice and strain into ice-filled Collins glass. Top with soda and garnish with half a grapefruit wheel.

PIÑA COLADA

3 oz. Light Rum
3 tbsps. Coconut Milk
3 tbsps. Crushed Pineapple

Combine all ingredients with 2 cups of crushed ice in blender on high speed. Strain into chilled Collins glass and serve with a straw.

PINEAPPLE COCKTAIL

¾ oz. Pineapple Juice
1½ oz. Light Rum
½ tsp. Lemon Juice

Shake with ice and strain into chilled cocktail glass.

PINEAPPLE FIZZ

1 oz. Pineapple Juice
½ tsp. Superfine Sugar (or Simple Syrup)
2 oz. Light Rum
Club Soda

Shake juice, sugar/syrup, and rum with ice and strain into chilled highball glass over two ice cubes. Fill with club soda and stir.

Y PINK CREOLE

1½ oz. Light Rum
1 tbsp. Lime Juice
1 tsp. Grenadine
1 tsp. Light Cream

Shake with ice and strain into chilled cocktail glass. Add a black cherry soaked in rum.

PINK PARADISE

1½ oz. Coconut-flavored Rum
1 oz. Amaretto
3 oz. Cranberry Juice
1½ oz. Pineapple Juice

Combine all ingredients in ice-filled hurricane or parfait glass. Garnish with a pineapple wedge and a maraschino cherry.

Y PLANTER'S COCKTAIL

½ oz. Lemon Juice
½ tsp. Superfine Sugar (or Simple Syrup)
1½ oz. Jamaican Rum

Shake with ice and strain into chilled cocktail glass.

PLANTER'S PUNCH NO. 1

2 oz. Lime Juice
2 tsps. Superfine Sugar (or Simple Syrup)
2 oz. Club Soda
2 dashes Bitters
2½ oz. Light Rum
1 dash Grenadine

Mix first three ingredients in ice-filled Collins glass, and stir until glass is frosted. Add bitters and rum. Stir and top with grenadine. Garnish with slices of lemon, orange, and pineapple, and a maraschino cherry. Serve with a straw.

RUM

Tend to People

As bartenders, we are there to tend to peoples' needs. Mixing up a great drink, although very important, is only a part of that equation. Being considered a great bartender should be as important as being a talented mixologist. They call it the hospitality industry for a reason: You need to be able to tune into people, and then follow through with them. Folks who choose to sit at your bar rather than at a floor table are doing so for a reason—often they are looking for interaction.

—Audrey Saunders (a.k.a. Libation Goddess), owner, Pegu Club, New York City

PLANTER'S PUNCH NO. 2

1 oz. Lime Juice
¼ oz. Lemon Juice
2 oz. Orange Juice
1 tsp. Pineapple Juice
2 oz. Light Rum
1 oz. Jamaican Rum
2 dashes Triple Sec
1 dash Grenadine

Pour first five ingredients into ice-filled Collins glass. Stir until glass is frosted. Add Jamaican Rum, stir, and top with Triple Sec and grenadine. Garnish with slices of orange, lemon, and pineapple, a maraschino cherry, and a sprig of mint dipped in sugar. Serve with a straw.

POKER COCKTAIL

1½ oz. Sweet Vermouth
1½ oz. Light Rum

Stir with ice and strain into chilled cocktail glass.

PUERTO RICAN RUM DAISY

1½ oz. Aged Rum
¼ oz. Orange Curaçao
¾ oz. Lemon Juice
½ oz. Orange Juice
½ oz. Simple Syrup
1 dash Angostura Bitters

Shake with ice and strain into chilled cocktail glass. Garnish with grated nutmeg and a slice of orange.

QUAKER'S COCKTAIL

¾ oz. Light Rum
¾ oz. Brandy
½ oz. Lemon Juice
2 tsps. Raspberry Syrup

Shake with ice and strain into chilled cocktail glass.

QUARTER DECK COCKTAIL

½ oz. Cream Sherry
1½ oz. Light Rum
½ oz. Lime Juice

Stir with ice and strain into chilled cocktail glass.

RAIN MAN

1¼ oz. 151-proof Rum
¾ oz. Melon Liqueur
4 oz. Orange Juice

Shake and pour into ice-filled hurricane or parfait glass.

RED STRING BIKINI

1 oz. Apple Rum
2 oz. Cranberry Juice

Pour into ice-filled highball glass and stir.

RESTLESS NATIVE

2 oz. Coconut Rum
1½ oz. Lime Juice
¾ oz. Crème de Cacao (White)

Shake with ice and strain into chilled cocktail glass. Garnish with a spiral-cut length of lime peel.

RINGO STARR

3 Red Grapes
½ Lemon
6 Mint Leaves
1 cube Sugar
¾ oz. Superfine Sugar
  (or Simple Syrup)
2 oz. Rum (African)

Muddle fruit, mint leaves, and sugar in shaker. Add rum and cracked ice and shake briefly. Strain into old-fashioned glass.

RIO FIX

1½ oz. Cachaça
½ oz. Maraschino Liqueur
¾ oz. Lime Juice
½ oz. Pineapple Juice
1 splash Pastis

Shake with ice and strain into pastis-rinsed champagne flute.

ROBSON COCKTAIL

2 tsps. Lemon Juice
1 tbsp. Orange Juice
1½ tsps. Grenadine
1 oz. Jamaican Rum

Shake with ice and strain into chilled cocktail glass.

RUM COBBLER

1 tsp. Superfine Sugar
  (or Simple Syrup)
2 oz. Club Soda
2 oz. Light Rum

In red-wine glass, dissolve sugar/syrup in club soda. Fill glass with shaved ice and add rum. Stir and garnish with fruits in season. Serve with a straw.

RUM COLLINS

1 oz. Lime Juice
1 tsp. Superfine Sugar
  (or Simple Syrup)
2 oz. Light Rum
Club Soda

Shake juice, sugar/syrup, and rum with ice and strain into chilled Collins glass. Add several ice cubes, fill with club soda, and stir. Garnish with a slice of lemon and a maraschino cherry. Serve with a straw.

RUM COOLER

½ tsp. Superfine Sugar
  (or Simple Syrup)
2 oz. Club Soda
2 oz. Light Rum
Club Soda or Ginger Ale

In Collins glass, dissolve sugar/syrup in club soda. Stir. Fill glass with ice and add rum. Fill with club soda or ginger ale and stir again. Insert a spiral of orange or lemon peel (or both) and dangle end over rim of glass.

RUM

RUM DAISY

½ oz. Lemon Juice

½ tsp. Superfine Sugar (or Simple Syrup)

1 tsp. Grenadine

2 oz. Light Rum

Shake with ice and strain into chilled beer mug or metal cup. Add one large ice cube and garnish with fruit.

RUM FIX

1 oz. Lemon Juice (or Lime Juice)

1 tsp. Superfine Sugar (or Simple Syrup)

1 tsp. Water (if not using Simple Syrup)

2½ oz. Light Rum

Stir juice, sugar, and water together in highball glass and fill glass with ice. Add rum. Stir and add a slice of lemon. Serve with a straw.

RUM HIGHBALL

2 oz. Light or Dark Rum

Ginger Ale or Club Soda

Pour rum into highball glass over ice cubes and fill with ginger ale or club soda. Add a twist of lemon peel and stir.

RUM MARTINI

4–5 parts Light Rum

1 dash Dry Vermouth

Serve over ice in cocktail glass with a twist of lemon.

RUM OLD-FASHIONED

½ tsp. Superfine Sugar (or Simple Syrup)

1 dash Bitters

1 tsp. Water

1½ oz. Light Rum

1 tsp. 151-proof Rum

Stir sugar/syrup, bitters, and water in old-fashioned glass. When sugar is dissolved, add ice cubes and light rum. Add a twist of lime peel and float the 151-proof rum on top.

RUM RELAXER

1½ oz. Light Rum

1 oz. Pineapple Juice

½ oz. Grenadine

Lemon-lime Soda

Shake first three ingredients with ice and pour into hurricane or parfait glass. Fill glass with lemon-lime soda. Garnish with an orange slice and a maraschino cherry.

RUM RICKEY

½ oz. Lime Juice

1½ oz. Light Rum

Club Soda

Pour lime juice and rum into ice-filled highball glass and fill with club soda. Stir. Add a wedge of lime.

RUM SCREWDRIVER

1½ oz. Light Rum

5 oz. Orange Juice

Combine ingredients in ice-filled highball glass.

RUM SOUR

1 oz. Lemon Juice
½ tsp. Superfine Sugar (or Simple Syrup)
2 oz. Light Rum

Shake with ice and strain into chilled sour glass. Garnish with a half-slice of lemon and a maraschino cherry.

RUM SWIZZLE

1 oz. Lime Juice
1 tsp. Superfine Sugar (or Simple Syrup)
2 oz. Club Soda
2 dashes Bitters
2 oz. Light or Dark Rum

Put lime juice, sugar/syrup, and club soda into Collins glass. Fill glass with ice and stir. Add bitters and rum. Fill with club soda and serve with a swizzle stick.

RUM TODDY

½ tsp. Superfine Sugar (or Simple Syrup)
2 tsps. Water
2 oz. Light or Dark Rum

In old-fashioned glass, dissolve sugar/syrup in water. Stir and add rum and a large cube of ice. Stir again and add a twist of lemon peel.

S & V

1½ oz. Light Rum
½ oz. Creole Shrubb
½ oz. Ruby Port
½ oz. Lime Juice

Shake with ice and strain into chilled cocktail glass. Garnish with a lime wheel.

SAINT LUCY BRACER

½ oz. Butterscotch Schnapps
½ oz. Sweet Vermouth
2 oz. Aged Rum
2 dashes Angostura Bitters

Stir with ice and strain into chilled cocktail glass. Garnish with a flower.

SANTIAGO COCKTAIL

½ tsp. Superfine Sugar (or Simple Syrup)
¼ tsp. Grenadine
1 oz. Lime Juice
1½ oz. Light Rum

Shake with ice and strain into chilled cocktail glass.

SARGASSO

2 oz. Aged Rhum Agricole
¾ oz. Dry Sherry
½ oz. Aperol
2 dashes Angostura Bitters

Stir with ice and strain into chilled cocktail glass. Garnish with an orange twist.

RUM

☐ SAXON COCKTAIL

½ oz. Lime Juice
½ tsp. Grenadine
1¾ oz. Light Rum

Shake with ice and strain
into chilled cocktail glass.
Serve with a twist of orange
peel.

☐ SEWER WATER

1 splash Grenadine
1 oz. 151-proof Rum
½ oz. Gin
¾ oz. Melon Liqueur
Pineapple Juice
Lime Juice

In hurricane or parfait glass,
splash grenadine. Add ice,
then rum, gin, and melon
liqueur. Fill with pineapple
juice and float lime juice
on top.

☐ SHANGHAI COCKTAIL

½ oz. Lemon Juice
1 tsp. Anisette
1 oz. Jamaican Light Rum
½ tsp. Grenadine

Shake with ice and strain
into chilled cocktail glass.

☐ SIR WALTER COCKTAIL

¾ oz. Light Rum
¾ oz. Brandy
1 tsp. Grenadine
1 tsp. Triple Sec
1 tsp. Lemon Juice

Shake with ice and strain
into chilled cocktail glass.

☐ SLOPPY JOE'S COCKTAIL NO. 1

1 oz. Lime Juice
¼ tsp. Triple Sec
¼ tsp. Grenadine
¾ oz. Light Rum
¾ oz. Dry Vermouth

Shake with ice and strain
into chilled cocktail glass.

Be Pithy (but Hold the Pith)

When a recipe calls for a twist of lemon or lime,
you want the skin, not the pith. This can be hard
to do with a knife, but easy with a sharp carrot
grater/potato peeler, especially the small, plastic-
handled Swiss peeler made by Kuhn Rikon.

—WILLIAM GRIMES,
author of *Straight Up or On the Rocks:
The Story of the American Cocktail*

SPANISH TOWN COCKTAIL

2 oz. Light Rum
1 tsp. Triple Sec

Stir with ice and strain into chilled cocktail glass.

STONE COCKTAIL

½ oz. Light Rum
½ oz. Sweet Vermouth
1 oz. Dry Sherry

Stir with ice and strain into chilled cocktail glass.

STONE WALL

¼ oz. Fresh Skinned Ginger
¾ oz. Demerara Syrup (Cane Syrup)
1½ oz. Fresh Apple Cider
1½ oz. Rum
1½ oz. Jamaican Ginger Beer

Muddle ginger and syrup in mixing glass. Add cider and rum and shake with ice. Strain into ice-filled old-fashioned glass and top with ginger beer. Garnish with a lime squeeze and a green apple slice.

STORMY COLADA

2 oz. Rum
2 oz. Pineapple Juice
Ginger Beer

Fill 10-oz. highball glass with ice. Add rum and pineapple juice and top with ginger beer. Garnish with pineapple wedge, mint leaves, and candied ginger on skewer.

STRAWBERRY DAIQUIRI

1 oz. Light Rum
½ oz. Strawberry Schnapps
1 oz. Lime Juice
1 tsp. Superfine Sugar (or Simple Syrup)
1 oz. Fresh or Frozen Strawberries

Shake with ice and strain into chilled cocktail glass.

SUNSET AT GOWANUS

2 oz. Aged Rum
¾ oz. Lime Juice
½ oz. Maple Syrup
¼ oz. Apple Brandy
¼ oz. Yellow Chartreuse

Shake with ice and strain into chilled cocktail glass.

SUSIE TAYLOR

½ oz. Lime Juice
2 oz. Light Rum
Ginger Ale

Pour lime juice and rum into ice-filled Collins glass and fill with ginger ale. Stir.

TAHITI CLUB

2 oz. Light Rum
1 tbsp. Lemon Juice
1 tbsp. Lime Juice
1 tbsp. Pineapple Juice
½ tsp. Maraschino Liqueur

Shake with ice and strain into ice-filled old-fashioned glass. Add a slice of lemon.

RUM

THIRD-RAIL COCKTAIL

¾ oz. Light Rum
¾ oz. Apple Brandy
¾ oz. Brandy
¼ tsp. Anisette

Shake with ice and strain into chilled cocktail glass.

THE THOMAS TRIBUTE

3 Eggs (whites and yolks separated)
2 oz. Rum
1 tsp. Cinnamon
½ tsp. Cloves
½ tsp. Allspice
½ tsp. Cream of Tartar
1 lb. Sugar
2 oz. Brandy

Beat egg whites to stiff peaks and yolks until they are as thin as water. Mix yolks and whites together, and then add the rum, spices, and cream of tartar. Thicken with sugar until consistency of a light batter. Serve in an Irish coffee glass, combining 1 tablespoonful of the above mixture and 2 ounces of brandy, and then fill the glass with boiling water. Garnish with fresh-grated nutmeg on top.

THREE MILLER COCKTAIL

1½ oz. Light Rum
¾ oz. Brandy
1 tsp. Grenadine
¼ tsp. Lemon Juice

Shake with ice and strain into chilled cocktail glass.

TOMATO DAIQUIRI

3 Fresh Cherry Tomatoes
2 oz. Aged Rum
1 oz. Lime Juice
1 oz. Simple Syrup
1 dash Angostura Bitters

Muddle tomatoes in mixing glass. Add remaining ingredients. Shake with ice and strain into chilled cocktail glass.

TORRIDORA COCKTAIL

1½ oz. Light Rum
½ oz. Coffee-flavored Brandy
1½ tsps. Light Cream
1 tsp. 151-proof Rum

Shake all but 151-proof rum with ice and strain into chilled cocktail glass. Float 151-proof rum on top.

TROPICA COCKTAIL

1¼ oz. Light Rum
5 oz. Pineapple Juice
2 oz. Grapefruit Juice
1 dash Grenadine

Mix ingredients in ice-filled Collins glass. Garnish with a pineapple wedge.

Harvest Nectar

LEFT: Lemon-Coconut Colada
ABOVE: Stone Wall

ABOVE: Diablo
RIGHT: Shady Lady

LEFT: Caesar
ABOVE: Cubeltini

The Big Crush

THE VACATION COCKTAIL

1 tsp. Ginger, chopped
¾ oz. Lime Juice
1 tsp. Superfine Sugar (or Simple Syrup)
1 oz. Mango Puree
½ oz. Cranberry Juice
½ oz. Orange Juice
½ oz. Light Rum
½ oz. Dark Rum
½ oz. Spiced Rum

Muddle ginger, lime juice, and sugar/syrup in mixing glass. Add all but spiced rum, cover with ice, and shake. Strain into chilled cocktail glass and float spiced rum on top. Garnish with a mango slice.

VAN VLEET

3 oz. Light Rum
1 oz. Maple Syrup
1 oz. Lemon Juice

Shake with ice and strain into ice-filled old-fashioned glass.

VIRGINIA DARE

2 slices Pear
2 oz. Aged Rum
½ oz. Bénédictine
2 dashes Angostura Bitters

Muddle 1 pear slice in mixing glass. Add other ingredients. Shake with ice and double-strain into chilled cocktail glass. Garnish with remaining pear slice.

WHITE LILY COCKTAIL

¾ oz. Triple Sec
¾ oz. Light Rum
¾ oz. Gin
¼ tsp. Anisette

Shake with ice and strain into chilled cocktail glass.

WHITE LION COCKTAIL

1 oz. Lemon Juice
1 tsp. Superfine Sugar (or Simple Syrup)
2 dashes Bitters
½ tsp. Grenadine
1½ oz. Light Rum

Shake with ice and strain into chilled cocktail glass.

WIKI WAKI WOO

½ oz. Vodka
½ oz. Rum
½ oz. 151-proof Rum
½ oz. Tequila
½ oz. Triple Sec
1 oz. Amaretto
1 oz. Orange Juice
1 oz. Pineapple Juice
1 oz. Cranberry Juice

Combine all ingredients with ice and pour into hurricane or parfait glass. Garnish with an orange slice and a maraschino cherry.

X.Y.Z. COCKTAIL

1 tbsp. Lemon Juice
½ oz. Triple Sec
1 oz. Light Rum

Shake with ice and strain into chilled cocktail glass.

RUM

ZOMBIE

- 1 tsp. Brown Sugar
- 1 oz. Lemon Juice
- 1 oz. Lime Juice
- 1 oz. Pineapple Juice
- 1 oz. Passion Fruit Syrup
- 1 dash Angostura Bitters
- 1 oz. Gold Rum
- 1 oz. 151-proof Rum
- 1 oz. White Rum

Dissolve brown sugar in juices. Shake all ingredients with ice and pour into chilled Collins glass. Garnish with a mint sprig.

TEQUILA

TEQUILA IS MADE FROM THE BLUE AGAVE PLANT, an aloe vera–like plant that takes between eight and ten years to mature. Then, it can only be harvested once by stripping away its leaves and cooking what's left: a core that weighs on average forty to seventy pounds (and it takes fifteen pounds of core to produce only one quart of tequila). The cooked cores are fermented with yeast (which converts the sugar to alcohol), then distilled twice—the second time yielding what will become tequila.

Like Scotch and bourbon, tequila takes its name from its place of origin, in this case the town of Tequila in Mexico's state of Jalisco. By Mexican law, it can only be produced in this region under strict guidelines—though that doesn't stop less scrupulous producers from making it outside those boundaries with whatever they want. There are two kinds of tequila: 100 percent blue agave and *mixto*, the former made purely from agave, the latter distilled with a mixture of 60 percent blue agave plus "other sugars." Just look for "100 percent agave" and you're safe.

Finally, there are four official classifications for tequila, though some have confusing subtitles. At the bottom is blanco (also called "silver" or "white"), which is clear, transparent, and bottled immediately after distillation. Next comes oro ("gold" or "joven"), which is blanco blended with caramel and other additives to *appear* aged; then reposado, which is blanco aged in white oak barrels for up to one year. At the top there's añejo, which is blanco aged in white oak barrels for at least one year, though often much longer.

ALAMO SPLASH

1½ oz. Tequila
1 oz. Orange Juice
½ oz. Pineapple Juice
1 splash Lemon-lime Soda

Mix with ice and strain into
chilled Collins glass.

AMANTE PICANTE

2 slices Cucumber
2 sprigs Cilantro
2 oz. Blanco Tequila
1 oz. Lime Juice
1 oz. Simple Syrup
2 dashes Green Tabasco
  Sauce

Muddle cucumber and cilantro in mixing glass. Add rest
of the ingredients. Shake
with ice and double-strain
into chilled cocktail glass.
Garnish with a cucumber
wheel.

AÑEJO BRAVO

2 oz. Añejo Tequila
¼ oz. Agave Nectar
2 dashes Angostura Bitters
1 dash Orange Bitters

Stir with ice and strain into
chilled old-fashioned glass.
Garnish with a grapefruit
twist.

BIG RED HOOTER

1 oz. Tequila
¾ oz. Amaretto
Pineapple Juice
1 oz. Grenadine

Pour tequila and amaretto
into ice-filled Collins glass.
Fill with pineapple juice and
top with grenadine. Garnish
with a maraschino cherry
and serve with a straw.

BLOODY MARIA

1 oz. Tequila
2 oz. Tomato Juice
1 dash Lemon Juice
1 dash Tabasco Sauce
1 dash Celery Salt

Shake all ingredients with
ice. Strain into ice-filled old-
fashioned glass. Add a slice
of lemon.

BLUE MARGARITA

1½ oz. Tequila
½ oz. Blue Curaçao
1 oz. Lime Juice

Shake ingredients with ice
and strain into chilled, salt-
rimmed cocktail glass.

BRAVE BULL

1½ oz. Tequila
1 oz. Coffee Liqueur

Pour into ice-filled old-
fashioned glass and stir. Add
a twist of lemon.

BUM'S RUSH

1½ oz. Blanco Tequila
¾ oz. Triple Sec
¾ oz. Honey Liqueur
1 oz. Lime Juice
1 oz. Apple Cider

Shake with ice and strain into ice-filled Collins glass. Garnish with a lime wedge.

CACTUS BERRY

1¼ oz. Tequila
1¼ oz. Red Wine
1 oz. Triple Sec
3¼ oz. Superfine Sugar (or Simple Syrup)
3¼ oz. Lemon Juice
1 splash Lemon-lime Soda
1 dash Lime Juice

Shake with ice and pour into large, chilled, salt-rimmed cocktail or margarita glass.

CATALINA MARGARITA

1½ oz. Tequila
1 oz. Peach Schnapps
1 oz. Blue Curaçao
2 oz. Superfine Sugar (or Simple Syrup)
2 oz. Lemon Juice

Shake with ice and strain into chilled cocktail or margarita glass.

CHAPALA

1½ oz. Reposado Tequila
1½ oz. Fresh Orange Juice
¾ oz. Fresh Lemon Juice
1 dash Grenadine
1 dash Orange Flower Water

Shake and strain into hurricane glass. Fill glass with crushed ice. Garnish with orange blossoms.

CHINCHONA

1½ oz. Añejo Tequila
¾ oz. Lillet Rouge
½ oz. Orange Curacao
2 dashes Orange Bitters

Stir with ice and strain into chilled cocktail glass. Garnish with an orange twist.

CHUPA CABRA

2 oz. Blanco Tequila
½ oz. Lime Juice
¾ oz. Grapefruit Juice
½ oz. Campari
½ oz. Simple Syrup
1 dash Angostura Bitters

Shake with ice and strain into chilled cocktail glass. Garnish with a lime wheel.

TEQUILA

⏃ COMPANY B

1 Strawberry
1½ oz. Blanco Tequila
½ oz. Campari
½ oz. Triple Sec
½ oz. Lemon Juice
¼ oz. Agave Nectar

Muddle strawberry in mixing glass. Add rest of the ingredients. Shake with ice and double-strain into chilled cocktail glass. Garnish with a slice of strawberry.

COUNT CAMILLOS PALOMA

¾ oz. Blanco Tequila
¾ oz. Sweet Vermouth
¾ oz. Campari
2 oz. Grapefruit Soda

Build in ice-filled Collins glass and stir. Garnish with a sprig of rosemary.

DIABLO

1½ oz. Tequila
¾ oz. Crème de Cassis
½ oz. Lime Juice
Ginger Ale

Shake first three ingredients with ice. Strain into chilled Collins glass. Top with ginger ale. Garnish with a lime wheel.

EL NIÑO

6 Lime Chunks
1 Strawberry
¾ oz. Superfine Sugar (or Simple Syrup)
1 cube Sugar
2 oz. Tequila
5 drops Rose Water

Muddle lime, strawberry, and sugar/syrup. Add rest over cracked ice. Shake briefly and strain into ice-filled old-fashioned glass.

⏃ FLOWER POWER

2 oz. Blanco Tequila
1 oz. Grapefruit Juice
½ oz. Agave Nectar
3 dashes Orange Flower Water
1 Egg White
2 dashes Peychaud's Bitters

Shake without ice. Then shake with ice and strain into chilled cocktail glass.

⏃ FROSTBITE

1 oz. Tequila
¾ oz. Crème de Cacao (White)
¾ oz. Cream

Shake with ice and strain into chilled cocktail glass. Garnish with fresh-grated nutmeg on top.

☐ GUADALAJARA

2 oz. Tequila
1 oz. Dry Vermouth
½ oz. Bénédictine

Stir with ice and strain into chilled cocktail glass. Garnish with a lemon twist.

☐ HAIRY SUNRISE

¾ oz. Tequila
¾ oz. Vodka
½ oz. Triple Sec
3 oz. Orange Juice
2–3 dashes Grenadine

Shake all ingredients with ice except grenadine. Strain into chilled Collins glass. Float grenadine on top and garnish with a lime slice.

☐ HIGH PLAINS DRIFTER NO. 1

2 oz. Blanco Tequila
¾ oz. Fresh Lime Juice
¾ oz. Honey Syrup
1 dash Angostura Bitters
1 splash Campari

Shake first four ingredients with ice and strain into chilled, Campari-rinsed cocktail glass.

☐ HOT PANTS

1½ oz. Tequila
½ oz. Peppermint Schnapps
1 tbsp. Grapefruit Juice
1 tsp. Superfine Sugar (or Simple Syrup)

Shake with ice and pour into salt-rimmed old-fashioned glass.

☐ THE INTERESTING COCKTAIL

2 oz. Blanco Tequila
½ oz. Aperol
½ oz. Crème de Cacao (Dark)
¾ oz. Lemon Juice

Shake with ice and strain into chilled cocktail glass. Garnish with a grapefruit twist.

☐ LA BOMBA

1¼ oz. Gold Tequila
¾ oz. Triple Sec
1½ oz. Pineapple Juice
1½ oz. Orange Juice
2 dashes Grenadine

Combine all ingredients except grenadine with ice and shake just three times. Pour into sugar-rimmed cocktail glass. Add grenadine and garnish with a lime wheel.

☐ LA PERLA

1½ oz. Reposado Tequila
1½ oz. Manzanilla Sherry
¾ oz. Pear Liqueur

Stir with ice and strain into chilled cocktail glass. Garnish with a lemon twist.

TEQUILA

☐ LA ULTIMA PALABRA

¾ oz. Blanco Tequila
¾ oz. Grapefruit Juice
¾ oz. Lime Juice
¾ oz. Yellow Chartreuse
¾ oz. Maraschino Liqueur

Shake with ice and strain into chilled cocktail glass. Garnish with a grapefruit twist.

☐ LILLYPAD

1½ oz. Blanco Tequila
½ oz. Lillet Blanc
½ oz. Lillet Rouge
1½ oz. Apple Juice
¼ oz. Agave Nectar
¾ oz. Lime Juice

Shake with ice and strain into chilled cocktail glass. Garnish with a blood orange wheel.

☐ MARGARITA

1½ oz. Tequila
½ oz. Triple Sec
1 oz. Lemon Juice or Lime Juice

Shake ingredients with ice and strain into chilled, salt-rimmed cocktail glass.

☐ MEXICANA

1½ oz. Tequila
1 oz. Lemon Juice
1 tbsp. Pineapple Juice
1 tsp. Grenadine

Shake with ice and strain into chilled cocktail glass.

☐ MEXICAN FIRING SQUAD

2 oz. Tequila
1 oz. Superfine Sugar (or Simple Syrup)
¾ oz. Lime Juice
1 tsp. Pomegranate Molasses
2 dashes Angostura Bitters

Shake and strain into ice-filled highball glass. Garnish with a lime wheel.

☐ MEXICAN MADRAS

3 oz. Cranberry Juice
½ oz. Orange Juice
1 oz. Gold Tequila
1 dash Lime Juice

Shake with ice and strain into old-fashioned glass. Garnish with an orange slice.

☐ MEXICOLA

2 oz. Tequila
½ oz. Lime Juice
Cola

Pour tequila and lime juice into ice-filled Collins glass. Fill with cola and stir.

NO. 8

2 oz. Reposado Tequila
¾ oz. Palo Cortado Sherry
½ oz. Honey Liqueur
2 dashes Orange Bitters

Stir with ice and strain into chilled cocktail glass. Garnish with a lemon twist.

THE OAXACA OLD-FASHIONED

1½ oz. Reposado Tequila
½ oz. Mezcal
¼ oz. Agave Nectar
2 dashes Angostora Bitters

Stir with ice and strain into chilled old-fashioned glass. Garnish with a flamed orange twist.

OLDEST TEMPTATION

2 oz. Añejo Tequila
1 oz. Apple Juice
½ oz. Lemon Juice
½ oz. Triple Sec
¼ oz. Simple Syrup
1 dash Angostura Bitters

Shake with ice and strain into chilled cocktail glass. Garnish with a flamed lemon zest.

PACIFIC SUNSHINE

1½ oz. Tequila
1½ oz. Blue Curaçao
¾ oz. Superfine Sugar (or Simple Syrup)
¾ oz. Lemon Juice
1 dash Bitters

Mix with ice and pour, with ice, into chilled, salt-rimmed parfait or hurricane glass. Garnish with a lemon wheel.

PANCHO VILLA

1 oz. Añejo Tequila
¾ oz. Aperol
¾ oz. Sweet Vermouth
1 dash Peach Bitters

Stir with ice and strain into chilled cocktail glass. Garnish with a grapefruit twist.

PIÑA AGAVE

2 slices Cucumber
1½ oz. Blanco Tequila
1 oz. Pineapple Juice
¾ oz. Lemon Juice
½ oz. Agave Nectar
Lemon-lime Soda

Muddle cucumber in mixing glass. Add the next four ingredients. Shake with ice and strain into chilled cocktail glass. Top with soda and garnish with a slice of cucumber.

TEQUILA

THE PONCHO

2 oz. Reposado Tequila
½ oz. Dry Vermouth
½ oz. Maraschino Liqueur
2 dashes Peychaud's Bitters

Stir with ice and strain
into chilled cocktail glass.
Garnish with a cherry.

PURPLE GECKO

1½ oz. Tequila
½ oz. Blue Curaçao
½ oz. Red Curaçao
1 oz. Cranberry Juice
½ oz. Superfine Sugar
   (or Simple Syrup)
½ oz. Lemon Juice
½ oz. Lime Juice

Shake with ice and pour into
chilled, salt-rimmed cocktail
or margarita glass. Garnish
with a lime wedge.

PURPLE PANCHO

1 oz. Tequila
½ oz. Blue Curaçao
½ oz. Sloe Gin
2 oz. Lime Juice
1 oz. Superfine Sugar
   (or Simple Syrup)
1 oz. Lemon Juice

Shake with ice and pour into
chilled, salt-rimmed cocktail
or margarita glass. Garnish
with a lime wheel.

THE REFUGE

1½ oz. Blanco Tequila
½ oz. Aperol
¼ oz. Agave Nectar
¼ oz. Fresh Lime Juice
¼ oz. Fresh Grapefruit Juice

Shake with ice and strain
into chilled cocktail glass.

ROSITA

1½ oz. Tequila
½ oz. Sweet Vermouth
½ oz. Dry Vermouth
½ oz. Campari
1 dash Bitters

Stir with ice and strain into
ice-filled old-fashioned
glass. Garnish with lemon
twist.

SANTANA SLING

1½ oz. Reposado Tequila
½ oz. Cherry Heering
¼ oz. Batavia Arak
   (or Rum)
½ oz. Lime Juice
3 oz. Ginger Beer

Build in ice-filled Collins
glass and stir.

SATIN SHEETS

1½ oz. Blanco Tequila
½ oz. Falernum
½ oz. Simple Syrup
¾ oz. Lime Juice

Shake with ice and strain
into chilled cocktail glass.
Garnish with a lime wheel.

SEA OF CORTEZ

1½ oz. Blanco Tequila
1 oz. Lime Juice
¾ oz. Crème de Cassis
¼ oz. Orange Curaçao

Shake with ice and strain
into chilled cocktail glass.

SHADY LADY

1 oz. Tequila
1 oz. Melon Liqueur
4 oz. Grapefruit Juice

Combine all ingredients in
ice-filled highball glass and
stir. Garnish with honeydew
melon, lime, or a maraschino
cherry.

SILK STOCKINGS

1½ oz. Tequila
1 oz. Crème de Cacao
1½ oz. Cream
1 dash Grenadine

Shake ingredients with ice
and strain into chilled cocktail glass. Sprinkle cinnamon
on top.

SLOE TEQUILA

1 oz. Tequila
½ oz. Sloe Gin
1 tbsp. Lime Juice

Combine all ingredients
with ½ cup of crushed ice in
blender on low speed. Pour
into old-fashioned glass.
Add ice cubes and a twist of
cucumber peel.

SMOKED MARGARITA

1 oz. Reposado Tequila
1 oz. Triple Sec
½ oz. Lemon Juice
½ oz. Lime Juice
1 splash Whisky (Scotch,
 heavily peated)

Shake and strain over ice in
old-fashioned glass. Garnish
with a lime wedge.

SOUTH OF THE BORDER

1 oz. Tequila
¾ oz. Coffee-flavored Brandy
½ oz. Lime Juice

Shake with ice and strain
into chilled sour glass. Add a
lime slice.

STRAWBERRY MARGARITA

1 oz. Tequila
½ oz. Triple Sec
½ oz. Strawberry Schnapps
1 oz. Lemon Juice or Lime
 Juice
1 oz. Fresh or Frozen
 Strawberries

Shake with ice and strain
into chilled cocktail glass
(salt-rimmed, if desired).

SUNDAY CONFESSION

1 oz. Blanco Tequila
1 oz. Limoncello
½ oz. Lemon Juice
Ginger Beer

Build first three ingredients
in ice-filled Collins glass.
Stir and top with ginger
beer. Garnish with a lemon
wedge.

TEQUILA

TEQUILA CANYON

1½ oz. Tequila
⅛ oz. Triple Sec
4 oz. Cranberry Juice
¼ oz. Pineapple Juice
¼ oz. Orange Juice

Pour first three ingredients into ice-filled Collins glass and stir gently. Top with pineapple and orange juices. Garnish with a lime wheel. Serve with a straw.

TEQUILA COLLINS

½ oz. Lemon Juice
1 tsp. Superfine Sugar
  (or Simple Syrup)
2 oz. Tequila
Club Soda

Shake first three ingredients with ice and strain into chilled Collins glass. Add several ice cubes, fill with club soda, and stir. Garnish with slices of lemon and orange, and a maraschino cherry. Serve with a straw.

TEQUILA MANHATTAN

2 oz. Tequila
1 oz. Sweet Vermouth
1 dash Lime Juice

Shake with ice and strain into ice-filled old-fashioned glass. Add a maraschino cherry and an orange slice.

TEQUILA MATADOR

1½ oz. Tequila
3 oz. Pineapple Juice
½ oz. Lime Juice

Shake with crushed ice and strain into chilled champagne flute.

TEQUILA MOCKINGBIRD

1½ oz. Tequila
¾ oz. Crème de Menthe
  (Green)
1 oz. Lime Juice

Shake with ice and strain into chilled cocktail glass. Garnish with a lime slice.

Keep Track

Make a check immediately after serving a drink or a round of drinks. The bar can get away from you quickly if you're not organized and methodical about all your tasks—especially billing. No matter how busy the bar gets, keep your tasks ordered and handle one job at a time. Keep the rest of the bar happy with your grace, confidence, and sparkling dialogue.

—DALE DEGROFF (a.k.a. King Cocktail),
author of *The Craft of the Cocktail*

☐ TEQUILA OLD-FASHIONED

½ tsp. Superfine Sugar (or Simple Syrup)

1 dash Bitters

1 tsp. Water

1½ oz. Tequila

1 splash Club Soda

Mix sugar/syrup, bitters, and water in old-fashioned glass. Add tequila, ice, and club soda. Garnish with a pineapple stick.

☐ TEQUILA PINK

1½ oz. Tequila

1 oz. Dry Vermouth

1 dash Grenadine

Shake with ice and strain into chilled cocktail glass.

☐ TEQUILA SMASH

4 Blueberries

4 Cherries

2 oz. Blanco Tequila

½ oz. Lime Juice

½ oz. Maraschino Liqueur

Muddle blueberries and cherries in mixing glass. Add the rest of ingredients. Shake with ice and strain into ice-filled old-fashioned glass. Garnish with a lime wheel skewered with a cherry and a blueberry.

☐ TEQUILA SOUR

1 oz. Lemon Juice

1 tsp. Superfine Sugar (or Simple Syrup)

2 oz. Tequila

Shake with ice and strain into chilled sour glass. Garnish with a half-slice of lemon and a maraschino cherry.

☐ TEQUILA STRAIGHT

1 pinch Salt

1½ oz. Tequila

¼ oz. Lemon (wedge)

Put salt between thumb and index finger on back of left hand. Hold shot glass of tequila in same hand and lemon wedge in right hand. Taste salt, drink the tequila, and then suck the lemon.

☐ TEQUILA SUNRISE

2 oz. Tequila

4 oz. Orange Juice

¾ oz. Grenadine

Stir tequila and orange juice with ice and strain into ice-filled highball glass. Pour in grenadine slowly and allow to settle. Before drinking, stir to complete your sunrise.

☐ TEQUINI

1½ oz. Tequila

½ oz. Dry Vermouth

1 dash Bitters (optional)

Stir with ice and strain into chilled cocktail glass. Serve with a twist of lemon peel and an olive.

TEQUILA

☐ TEQUONIC

2 oz. Tequila
1 oz. Lemon Juice (or ½ oz. Lime Juice)
Tonic Water

Pour tequila into ice-filled old-fashioned glass. Add fruit juice, fill with tonic water, and stir.

☐ TÍA JUANATHAN

1½ oz. Blanco Tequila
½ oz. Lime Juice
½ oz. Aperol
½ oz. Yellow Chartreuse
Club Soda

Shake first four ingredients with ice and strain into ice-filled highball glass. Top with club soda and garnish with half an orange wheel.

☐ TIJUANA TAXI

2 oz. Gold Tequila
1 oz. Blue Curaçao
1 oz. Tropical Fruit Schnapps
Lemon-lime Soda

Pour tequila, curaçao, and schnapps into ice-filled large highball glass. Fill with lemon-lime soda and garnish with an orange slice and a maraschino cherry.

☐ T.N.T. NO. 2

1 oz. Tequila
Tonic Water

Mix with ice in old-fashioned glass.

Keep It Simple

A simple drink that's perfectly executed is far, far more satisfying than a complex, creative one that isn't. If a patron's drink is too warm, too sweet, too weak, or too strong (yes, such a thing is theoretically possible), he or she won't be impressed by its clever name and its innovative use of infusions. On the other hand, strain a subzero-cold mixture of gin and vermouth into a chilled glass and twist a swatch of fresh lemon peel over the top and that patron won't care in the slightest that you're out of shiso-infused vodka and fresh lemongrass juice.

—DAVE WONDRICH,
drinks correspondent, *Esquire* magazine

☍ TOREADOR

1½ oz. Tequila
½ oz. Crème de Cacao
1 tbsp. Light Cream

Shake with ice and strain into chilled cocktail glass. Top with a little whipped cream and sprinkle lightly with cocoa.

☍ TRAFFIC LIGHT COOLER

¾ oz. Melon Liqueur
1 oz. Gold Tequila
1 splash Superfine Sugar (or Simple Syrup)
1 splash Lemon Juice
2 oz. Orange Juice
½ oz. Sloe Gin

Into ice-filled pilsner glass first pour the melon liqueur and then the tequila to create the green layer. Add the sugar/syrup and lemon juice. Slowly pour the orange juice against side of glass to create the yellow layer. Add a few more ice cubes, if needed. Carefully float the sloe gin on top for the red layer. Garnish with a maraschino cherry and lemon and lime wheels. Stir just before drinking.

☍ THE 21ST CENTURY

1½ oz. Blanco Tequila
¾ oz. Lime Juice
¾ oz. White Crème de Cacao
1 splash Pastis

Shake first three ingredients with ice and strain into chilled, pastis-rinsed cocktail glass.

☍ VAGABUNDO

2 oz. Reposado Tequila
1½ oz. Pineapple Juice
1½ oz. Celery Juice
½ oz. Lime Juice

Build in ice-filled hurricane glass and stir. Garnish with a lime wheel.

☍ VENIAL SIN

1½ oz. Blanco Tequila
½ oz. Yellow Chartreuse
¼ oz. Elderflower Liqueur
¼ oz. Maraschino Liqueur
½ oz. Mezcal

Stir with ice and strain into chilled cocktail glass.

☍ VIVA VILLA

1 oz. Lime Juice
1 tsp. Superfine Sugar (or Simple Syrup)
1½ oz. Tequila

Shake with ice and strain into salt-rimmed, ice-filled old-fashioned glass.

☐ WILD THING

1½ oz. Tequila
1 oz. Cranberry Juice
1 oz. Club Soda
½ oz. Lime Juice

Pour into ice-filled old-fashioned glass. Garnish with a lime wheel.

☖ YELLOW ROSE OF TEXAS

2 oz. Blanco Tequila
¾ oz. Lemon Juice
½ oz. Simple Syrup
¼ oz. Yellow Chartreuse

Shake with ice and strain into chilled cocktail glass. Garnish with 3 drops of rose water.

VODKA

ACCORDING TO U.S. LAW, vodkas produced in the country must be pure spirits with no additives except water; nonaged; and basically colorless, tasteless, and odorless. This description may sound lackluster, but it explains why vodka is one of today's most popular spirits: Because of its purity, vodka graciously assumes the characteristics of whatever it's mixed with.

Vodka is generally made from grain (corn, rye, or wheat) or potatoes, with grain accounting for nearly all the vodka available on the international market. It is a rectified spirit, meaning it's distilled at least three times, and then filtered—the most important step—typically through charcoal, although some distillers claim to employ diamond dust and even quartz crystals.

Stylistic differences between one vodka and another are subtle, even at the very high end, given that discernible flavor isn't a factor. Vodka is often described by its texture on the tongue or mouth-feel, ranging from clean and crisp to viscous and silky. Subtle sensations in the finish—after it's swallowed—can range from slightly sweet to medicinal. The finish could also reveal if a vodka is hot, rough, and raw (usually the mark of an inexpensive bulk vodka, or perhaps one with higher-than-normal 80-proof) or, conversely, if it is smooth, round, and rich (one made by a master distiller).

That said, the very best vodkas, the so-called super-premium brands (priced higher than $30 per bottle) are perfect when unadorned, say in a Martini, or for a chilled straight shot to accompany caviar. In the end, vodka mixed in just about any of the following recipes will only enhance whatever it touches.

ALFIE COCKTAIL

1½ oz. Lemon-flavored Vodka

1 tbsp. Pineapple Juice

1 dash Triple Sec

Shake with ice and strain into chilled cocktail glass.

AQUEDUCT

1½ oz. Vodka

1½ tsps. Curaçao (White)

1½ tsps. Apricot-flavored Brandy

1 tbsp. Lime Juice

Shake with ice and strain into chilled cocktail glass. Add a twist of orange peel.

BANANA PUNCH

2 oz. Vodka

1½ tsps. Apricot-flavored Brandy

½ oz. Lime Juice

Club Soda

Pour vodka, brandy, and lime juice into Collins glass filled with crushed ice. Add club soda and top with slices of banana and sprigs of mint.

BASIL 8

3 Basil Leaves

5 White Grapes

1½ oz. Vodka

¾ oz. Lime Juice

1 oz. Simple Syrup

1 dash Angostura Bitters

Ginger Ale

Muddle basil and grapes in Collins glass. Build next four ingredients over ice. Top with ginger ale. Garnish with a sprig of basil and one white grape.

BEER BUSTER

1½ oz. 100-proof Vodka

Chilled Beer or Ale

2 dashes Tabasco Sauce

Pour vodka into highball glass and fill with beer or ale. Add Tabasco Sauce and stir lightly.

BIANCA

1½ oz. Citrus-flavored Vodka

1 splash Superfine Sugar (or Simple Syrup)

1 splash Lemon Juice

¼ oz. Lime Juice

2 oz. Pomegranate Juice

Shake with ice and strain into chilled, sugar-rimmed cocktail glass. Garnish with twist of lemon and fresh pomegranate seeds.

THE BIG CRUSH

2½ oz. Raspberry-flavored Vodka

1 oz. Triple Sec

½ oz. Raspberry-flavored Liqueur

1 splash Lime Juice

Champagne

Shake first four ingredients with ice. Strain into chilled cocktail glass and top with Champagne. Garnish with fresh blackberries and raspberries.

BIKINI

2 oz. Vodka

1 oz. Light Rum

½ oz. Milk

1 tsp. Sugar

1 oz. Lemon Juice

Shake with ice and strain into chilled cocktail glass. Garnish with a twist of lemon peel.

BLACK CHERRY CHOCOLATE

1½ oz. Effen Black Cherry Vodka

1½ oz. White Chocolate Liqueur

1 splash Cherry-flavored Soda or Cherry Juice

Shake with ice and strain into chilled cocktail glass.

BLACK MAGIC

1½ oz. Vodka

¾ oz. Coffee Liqueur

1 dash Lemon Juice

Stir and serve in ice-filled old-fashioned glass. Add a twist of lemon peel.

BLACK RUSSIAN

1½ oz. Vodka

¾ oz. Coffee Liqueur

Pour over ice cubes into old-fashioned glass.

THE BLOOD ORANGE

2 oz. Orange-flavored Vodka

1 oz. Campari

Stir with ice and strain into chilled cocktail glass. Garnish with a half wheel of blood orange.

BLOODY BULL

1 oz. Vodka

2 oz. Tomato Juice

2 oz. Beef Bouillon

Pour into ice-filled highball glass. Stir, and add a squeeze of lemon and a slice of lime.

VODKA

☐ BLOODY MARY

1½ oz. Vodka

3 oz. Tomato Juice

1 dash Lemon Juice

½ tsp. Worcestershire Sauce

2–3 drops Tabasco Sauce

Salt and Pepper as needed

Shake with ice and strain into ice-filled old-fashioned glass. Garnish with a lime wedge or a celery stalk.

☐ BLUE LAGOON

1 oz. Vodka

1 oz. Blue Curaçao

Lemonade

Pour first two ingredients into ice-filled highball glass. Fill with lemonade. Garnish with a maraschino cherry.

☐ BLUE LEMONADE

1½ oz. Effen Vodka

4 oz. Lemonade

¾ oz. Blue Curaçao

Pour into ice-filled highball glass and stir.

☐ BLUE MONDAY COCKTAIL

1½ oz. Vodka

¾ oz. Triple Sec

1 dash Blue Food Coloring

Stir with ice and strain into chilled cocktail glass.

☐ BOLSHOI PUNCH

1 oz. Vodka

2½ oz. Lemon Juice

1 tsp. Superfine Sugar (or Simple Syrup)

¼ oz. Rum

¼ oz. Crème de Cassis

Shake and pour into ice-filled old-fashioned glass.

☐ BORDEAUX COCKTAIL

1½ oz. Citrus-flavored Vodka

½ oz. Lillet Blonde

Stir with ice and strain into chilled cocktail glass. Garnish with a twist of lemon peel.

☐ BOSTON GOLD

1 oz. Vodka

½ oz. Crème de Banana

Orange Juice

Pour vodka and banana liqueur into ice-filled highball glass. Fill with orange juice and stir.

☐ BULLFROG

1½ oz. Vodka

5 oz. Lemonade

Pour into ice-filled Collins glass and garnish with a slice of lime.

☐ BULL SHOT

1½ oz. Vodka

3 oz. Beef Bouillon, chilled

1 dash Worcestershire Sauce

1 dash Salt

1 dash Pepper

Shake with ice and strain into chilled old-fashioned glass.

☐ CAESAR

1 oz. Vodka

4 oz. Tomato-Clam Juice

1 pinch Salt

1 pinch Pepper

1 dash Worcestershire Sauce

2–3 dashes Horseradish

Coat rim of a highball or Delmonico glass with celery salt, and then fill with ice. Shake ingredients with ice and strain mixture into glass. Garnish with a celery stalk and a lemon wedge or cherry tomato.

☐ CAPE CODDER

1½ oz. Vodka

5 oz. Cranberry Juice

Pour into ice-filled highball glass. Stir well. Garnish with a wedge of lime.

☐ CAPPUCCINO COCKTAIL

¾ oz. Coffee-flavored Brandy

¾ oz. Vodka

¾ oz. Light Cream

Shake with ice and strain into chilled cocktail glass.

☐ CARIBBEAN CRUISE

1 oz. Vodka

¼ oz. Light Rum

¼ oz. Coconut-flavored Rum

1 splash Grenadine

4 oz. Pineapple Juice

Shake first four ingredients with ice and pour into ice-filled Collins glass. Fill with pineapple juice. Garnish with a pineapple wedge and a maraschino cherry.

☐ CASCO BAY LEMONADE

1½ oz. Citrus-flavored Vodka

2 oz. Superfine Sugar (or Simple Syrup)

2 oz. Lemon Juice

1 splash Cranberry Juice

1 splash Lemon-lime Soda

Shake first four ingredients with ice. Pour into ice-filled Collins glass. Add lemon-lime soda. Float a lemon slice on top.

☐ CHAMPAGNE FLAMINGO

¾ oz. Vodka

¾ oz. Campari

5 oz. Champagne, chilled

Shake vodka and Campari with ice. Strain into chilled champagne flute and top with Champagne. Garnish with a zest of orange.

VODKA

CHERRY BOMB

- 1 oz. Effen Black Cherry Vodka
- 1 tumbler ¾ full of Energy Drink

Mix in old-fashioned glass with ice and garnish with a maraschino cherry.

CITRONELLA COOLER

- 1 oz. Citrus-flavored Vodka
- 1 dash Lime Juice
- 2 oz. Lemonade
- 1 oz. Cranberry Juice

Pour into ice-filled Collins glass. Top with a squeeze of fresh lime.

COSMOPOLITAN COCKTAIL

- 1¼ oz. Vodka
- ¼ oz. Lime Juice
- ¼ oz. Triple Sec
- ¼ oz. Cranberry Juice

Shake well with ice and strain into chilled cocktail glass. Garnish with a lime wedge.

CROCODILE COOLER

- 1½ oz. Citrus-flavored Vodka
- 1 oz. Melon Liqueur
- ¾ oz. Triple Sec
- 1 oz. Superfine Sugar (or Simple Syrup)
- 1 oz. Lemon Juice
- Lemon-lime Soda

Place first five ingredients into ice-filled parfait or hurricane glass. Fill with soda and stir well. Garnish with a pineapple wedge and a maraschino cherry or lime wheel. Serve with a straw.

CUBELTINI

- 3 Cucumber Slices
- 5–7 Mint Leaves
- 1½ oz. Superfine Sugar (or Simple Syrup)
- 2 oz. Vodka
- 1 oz. Lime Juice

Muddle the cucumber, mint, and sugar/syrup. Add vodka and lime juice. Shake and strain into chilled cocktail glass. Garnish with fresh mint.

DESERT SUNRISE

- 1¼ oz. Vodka
- 1½ oz. Orange Juice
- 1½ oz. Pineapple Juice
- 1 dash Grenadine

Pour first three ingredients over crushed ice in Collins glass. Top with grenadine.

☙ DREAMY DORINI SMOKING MARTINI

2 oz. Vodka
½ oz. Whisky (Scotch)
4 drops Anise Liqueur

Shake and strain into a chilled cocktail glass. Garnish with a lemon twist.

☐ ELECTRIC JAM

1¼ oz. Vodka
½ oz. Blue Curaçao
1 oz. Superfine Sugar (or Simple Syrup)
1 oz. Lemon Juice
Lemon-lime Soda

Pour first four ingredients into ice-filled Collins glass. Fill with soda and stir.

☙ FLATIRON MARTINI

1½ oz. Orange-flavored Vodka
1½ oz. Lillet Blanc
1 splash Triple Sec

Stir vodka and Lillet with ice and strain into Triple Sec–rinsed cocktail glass. Garnish with an orange slice.

☙ FRENCH MARTINI

1½ oz. Vodka
1 oz. Black Raspberry Liqueur

Stir with ice and strain into chilled cocktail glass.

☐ FRISKY WITCH

1 oz. Vodka
1 oz. Sambuca

Pour into ice-filled old-fashioned glass and stir. Garnish with a black licorice stick.

☐ GABLES COLLINS

1½ oz. Vodka
1 oz. Crème de Noyaux
1 tbsp. Lemon Juice
1 tbsp. Pineapple Juice
Club Soda

Shake first four ingredients with ice and strain into ice-filled Collins glass. Fill with club soda. Garnish with a slice of lemon and a pineapple chunk.

☐ GENTLE BEN

1 oz. Vodka
1 oz. Gin
1 oz. Tequila
Orange Juice

Shake first three ingredients with ice and pour into ice-filled Collins glass. Fill with orange juice and stir. Garnish with an orange slice and a maraschino cherry.

VODKA

GEORGIA MULE

1 Peach Slice, skinless
1½ oz. Vodka
½ oz. Lemon Juice
1½ oz. Ginger Beer
2 dashes Peach Bitters

Muddle peach in a Collins glass. Build other ingredients over ice and stir. Garnish with a slice of peach.

GEORGIA PEACH

1½ oz. Vodka
½ oz. Peach Schnapps
1 dash Grenadine
Lemonade

Pour first three ingredients into ice-filled Collins glass. Fill with lemonade.

GLASS TOWER

1 oz. Vodka
1 oz. Peach Schnapps
1 oz. Rum
1 oz. Triple Sec
½ oz. Sambuca
Lemon-lime Soda

Pour first five ingredients into ice-filled Collins glass. Fill with lemon-lime soda and garnish with an orange slice and a maraschino cherry.

GODCHILD

1 oz. Amaretto
1 oz. Vodka
1 oz. Heavy Cream

Shake well with ice and strain into chilled champagne flute.

Make People Happy

Bartenders should never lose sight of the primary mission of their job: To make people happy. This can be done by serving a great cocktail, but it can also be achieved by telling a good joke, commiserating with some unhappy soul, or introducing like-minded people to each other, and in a million other different ways. Some of my favorite bartenders have worked in shot-and-a-beer joints, and wouldn't know how to fix a decent Margarita to save their lives. If a bartender makes the customers happy, he or she is doing a good job.

—GARY REGAN,
co-publisher, AredentSpirits.com

GODMOTHER

1½ oz. Vodka

¾ oz. Amaretto

Combine in ice-filled old-fashioned glass.

GRAPEFRUIT GIMLET ROYALE

2 oz. Vodka

2 oz. Grapefruit Juice

1 splash Fresh Lime Juice

1 splash Superfine Sugar (or Simple Syrup)

Champagne, chilled

Shake first four ingredients with ice and strain into chilled cocktail glass. Top off with Champagne.

GRAPE NEHI (PURPLE HOOTER)

1 oz. Vodka

1 oz. Raspberry-flavored Liqueur

1 oz. Lemon Juice

Shake with ice and strain into chilled cocktail glass.

HANDBALL COOLER

1½ oz. Vodka

Club Soda

1 splash Orange Juice

Pour vodka into ice-filled highball glass. Fill almost to top with club soda. Top with orange juice. Garnish with a lime wedge.

HARRINGTON

1½ oz. Vodka

¼ oz. Triple Sec

⅛ oz. Chartreuse

Stir with ice and strain into chilled cocktail glass. Twist an orange zest over the drink and then float zest in drink.

HARVEY WALLBANGER

1 oz. Vodka

4 oz. Orange Juice

½ oz. Galliano

Pour vodka and orange juice into ice-filled Collins glass. Stir. Float Galliano on top.

HEADLESS HORSEMAN

2 oz. Vodka

3 dashes Bitters

Ginger Ale

Pour vodka and bitters into ice-filled Collins glass. Fill with ginger ale and stir. Garnish with a slice of orange.

HUMPTY DUMPTY

2 oz. Vodka

1 oz. Orange Juice

½ oz. Galliano

1 Whole Egg

3 dashes Peychaud's Bitters

Shake without ice. Then shake with ice and strain into chilled cocktail glass.

VODKA

HUNTSMAN COCKTAIL

1½ oz. Vodka
½ oz. Jamaican Rum
½ oz. Lime Juice
½ tsp. Superfine Sugar
(or Simple Syrup)

Shake with ice and strain
into chilled cocktail glass.

IBIZA

1 oz. Orange-flavored Vodka
½ oz. Campari
1 dash Peach Schnapps
1 dash Apple Schnapps
1 dash Pomegranates au
Merlot Syrup
1 oz. Grapefruit Juice

Shake with ice and strain
into chilled cocktail glass.
Garnish with a grapefruit
twist.

ITALIAN SCREWDRIVER

1½ oz. Citrus-flavored Vodka
3 oz. Orange Juice
2 oz. Grapefruit Juice
1 splash Ginger Ale

Mix and pour into ice-filled,
sugar-rimmed hurricane or
parfait glass. Garnish with a
lime wheel.

JACKIE-O

½ oz. Citrus-flavored Vodka
½ oz. Orange-flavored
Vodka
½ oz. Crème de Cassis
1 oz. Apricot Nectar
3 tsps. Lemon Juice
2 tsps. Cranberry Juice
Champagne, chilled

Shake first six ingredi-
ents with ice and strain into
chilled, pink-sugar-rimmed
10-oz. cocktail glass. Top
with Champagne and gar-
nish with an orange slice and
a lime wheel.

THE JAMAICAN TEN SPEED

1 oz. Vodka
¾ oz. Melon Liqueur
¼ oz. Crème de Banana
¼ oz. Coconut-flavored Rum
½ oz. Half-and-Half

Shake with ice and strain
into chilled cocktail glass.

JERICHO'S BREEZE

1 oz. Vodka
¾ oz. Blue Curaçao
1¼ oz. Superfine Sugar
(or Simple Syrup)
1¼ oz. Lemon Juice
1 splash Lemon-lime Soda
1 splash Orange Juice

Shake with ice until frothy.
Strain into chilled red-wine
glass. Garnish with a pineapple spear and a maraschino
cherry.

JUNGLE JUICE

1 oz. Vodka

1 oz. Rum

½ oz. Triple Sec

1 splash Superfine Sugar (or Simple Syrup)

1 splash Lemon Juice

1 oz. Cranberry Juice

1 oz. Orange Juice

1 oz. Pineapple Juice

Pour into ice-filled Collins glass. Garnish with an orange slice and a maraschino cherry.

KANGAROO COCKTAIL

1½ oz. Vodka

¾ oz. Dry Vermouth

Shake with ice and strain into chilled cocktail glass. Garnish with a twist of lemon peel.

KATANA

3 Thin Cucumber Slices

1½ oz. Vodka

½ oz. Sake

¾ oz. Lime Juice

¾ oz. Simple Syrup

Muddle cucumber in mixing glass. Add rest of ingredients. Shake and double strain into chilled cocktail glass. Garnish with a slice of cucumber.

KRETCHMA COCKTAIL

1 oz. Vodka

1 oz. Crème de Cacao (White)

1 tbsp. Lemon Juice

1 dash Grenadine

Shake with ice and strain into chilled cocktail glass.

L.A. SUNRISE

1 oz. Vodka

½ oz. Crème de Banana

2 oz. Orange Juice

2 oz. Pineapple Juice

¼ oz. Rum

Pour first four ingredients into ice-filled hurricane or parfait glass. Float rum on top. Garnish with a lime wheel and a maraschino cherry.

LEMON CRUSH

2 oz. Citrus-flavored Vodka

1 oz. Limoncello Crema

1 oz. Triple Sec

2 oz. Lemon Juice

Shake with ice and strain into chilled, sugar-rimmed cocktail glass.

LE PARADINI

1½ oz. Vodka

½ oz. Raspberry-flavored Liqueur

1½ oz. Grand Marnier

1½ oz. Champagne, chilled

Shake first three ingredients with ice and strain into chilled cocktail glass. Top with Champagne.

VODKA

▽ LIMONCELLO MANZANILLA MARMALADE SOUR

1½ oz. Citrus Vodka

¾ oz. Limoncello

¾ oz. Manzanilla Sherry

¾ oz. Lemon Juice

1 barspoon Grapefruit Marmalade

Shake with ice and double-strain into chilled cocktail glass. Garnish with an orange twist.

▽ L'ITALIENNE

2 oz. Vodka

¼ oz. Lillet Blonde

¼ oz. Ramazzotti Amaro

1 dash Orange Bitters

Stir and strain into cocktail glass.

▢ LONG ISLAND ICED TEA

¾ oz. Vodka

¾ oz. Tequila

¾ oz. Gin

¾ oz. Light Rum

¾ oz. Triple Sec

½ oz. Superfine Sugar (or Simple Syrup)

½ oz. Lemon Juice

Cola

Combine first seven ingredients and pour into ice-filled highball glass. Add cola for color. Garnish with a wedge of lime.

▢ THE LOOP

2 oz. Effen Black Cherry Vodka

½ oz. Crème de Cacao (White)

½ oz. Chili Syrup*

Shake ingredients and serve straight up in an old-fashioned glass with grated dark chocolate.

* Chili Syrup: Add 2 tbsps. red pepper flakes to 1 pint of water; bring to boil. Simmer for 10 minutes. Stir in 2 cups of sugar. Transfer to sterile container and refrigerate.

▽ LYCHEE JUICY

1½ oz. Vodka

½ oz. Lychee Liqueur

1 oz. Orange Juice

1 oz. Pineapple Juice

2 dashes Angostura Bitters

Shake with ice and strain into chilled cocktail glass. Garnish with a pineapple leaf–stuffed lychee nut.

▢ MADRAS

1½ oz. Vodka

4 oz. Cranberry Juice

1 oz. Orange Juice

Pour into highball glass over ice. Garnish with a wedge of lime.

MARACUYA MOSQUITO

4 Basil Leaves
1½ oz. Vodka
½ oz. Green Chartreuse
½ oz. Lime Juice
½ oz. Simple Syrup
1 oz. Passion Fruit Juice

Muddle basil in mixing glass. Add rest of the ingredients. Shake with ice and double strain into Collins glass filled with crushed ice. Garnish with a basil leaf.

MISS JONES

1½ oz. Vanilla Vodka
1 oz. Lemon Juice
½ oz. Butterscotch Schnapps
½ oz. Limoncello

Shake with ice and strain into chilled cocktail glass. Garnish with a whole star anise pod.

MR. 404

1½ oz. Vodka
¾ oz. Elderflower Liqueur
¾ oz. Lemon Juice
½ oz. Simple Syrup
½ oz. Aperol

Shake with ice and strain into chilled cocktail glass. Garnish with an orange twist.

MOCHA EXPRESS

2 oz. Vodka
¾ oz. Irish Cream Liqueur
¾ oz. Kahlua
1 oz. Espresso Coffee

Shake with ice and strain into chilled cocktail glass.

MOSCOW MULE

1½ oz. Vodka
½ oz. Lime Juice
Ginger Beer

Pour vodka and lime juice into Irish coffee glass. Add ice cubes and fill with ginger beer. Drop lime wedge in mug for garnish.

NAKED PRETZEL

¾ oz. Vodka
1 oz. Melon Liqueur
½ oz. Crème de Cassis
2 oz. Pineapple Juice

Stir and pour into ice-filled old-fashioned glass.

NIJINSKI BLINI

1 oz. Vodka
2 oz. Pureed Peaches
½ oz. Lemon Juice
1 splash Peach Schnapps
1 splash Champagne, chilled

Pour into chilled champagne flute and stir gently.

NINOTCHKA COCKTAIL

1½ oz. Vodka
½ oz. Crème de Cacao (White)
1 tbsp. Lemon Juice

Shake with ice and strain into chilled cocktail glass.

VODKA

ORANG-A-TANG

1 oz. Vodka
½ oz. Triple Sec
1 splash Grenadine
6 oz. Orange Juice
1 splash Superfine Sugar
  (or Simple Syrup)
1 splash Lemon Juice
1 oz. 151-proof Rum

Lightly blend all ingredients except rum. Strain into large snifter half-filled with ice. Float rum on top. Garnish with tropical fruits.

PAVLOVA SUPREME

2 oz. Vodka, chilled
½ oz. Crème de Cassis

Mix in red-wine glass filled with crushed ice.

PEACH ICED TEA

1½ oz. Peach-flavored Vodka
½ oz. Orange Curaçao
2 oz. Iced Tea
¾ oz. Lemon Juice
½ oz. Honey Syrup

Shake with ice and strain into ice-filled Collins glass. Garnish with a slice of peach and a lemon wheel.

PETIT ZINC

1 oz. Vodka
½ oz. Triple Sec
½ oz. Sweet Vermouth
½ oz. Orange Juice
  (preferably Seville; otherwise, add ¼ oz. Lemon Juice)

Shake with ice and strain into chilled cocktail glass. Garnish with a wedge of orange.

PICKLED MARTINI

2 oz. Vodka
¼ oz. Dry Vermouth
¾ oz. Sweet Pickle Brine

Stir with ice and strain into chilled cocktail glass. Garnish with a pickle.

PINK LEMONADE

1½ oz. Citrus-flavored Vodka
1 splash Triple Sec
1 splash Lime Juice
1 splash Superfine Sugar
  (or Simple Syrup)
1 splash Lemon Juice
2 oz. Cranberry Juice

Shake and pour into ice-filled Collins glass. Garnish with a lemon wheel.

PINK PUSSYCAT

1½ oz. Vodka
Pineapple or Grapefruit Juice
1 dash Grenadine

Pour vodka into ice-filled highball glass. Fill with juice. Add grenadine for color and stir.

▽ POLYNESIAN COCKTAIL

1½ oz. Vodka
¾ oz. Cherry-flavored Brandy
1 oz. Lime Juice

Shake with ice and strain into chilled sugar-rimmed cocktail glass.

▯ PRETTY IN PINK

2 oz. Vodka
¾ oz. Crème de Noyaux
¾ oz. Lemon Juice
Club Soda

Shake first three ingredients and strain into ice-filled Collins glass. Top with club soda.

▽ PRIORITY COCKTAIL

2 oz. Vodka
½ oz. Calvados
½ oz. Coffee Liqueur

Stir with ice and strain into chilled cocktail glass. Garnish with a lemon twist.

▽ PURPLE MASK

1 oz. Vodka
1 oz. Grape Juice
½ oz. Crème de Cacao (White)

Shake with ice and strain into chilled cocktail glass.

▯ PURPLE PASSION

1½ oz. Vodka
3 oz. Grapefruit Juice
3 oz. Grape Juice
Sugar

Chill, stir, add sugar as needed, and serve in Collins glass.

▯ PURPLE PASSION TEA

¼ oz. Vodka
¼ oz. Rum
¼ oz. Gin
½ oz. Black Raspberry Liqueur
2 oz. Superfine Sugar (or Simple Syrup)
2 oz. Lemon Juice
3 oz. Lemon-lime Soda

Pour into ice-filled highball glass and stir. Garnish with a twist of lemon peel.

▽ PURPLE RUBY

1½ oz. Vodka
1½ oz. Pomegranate Juice
½ oz. Grapefruit Juice
¼ oz. Lime Juice
¼ oz. Honey Syrup

Shake with ice and strain into chilled cocktail glass. Garnish with a grapefruit twist.

▽ RED APPLE

1 oz. 100-proof Vodka
1 oz. Apple Juice
1 tbsp. Lemon Juice
1 tsp. Grenadine

Shake with ice and strain into chilled cocktail glass.

VODKA

♈ REDHEAD MARTINI

4 Whole Strawberries

¾ oz. Lemon Juice

¾ oz. Superfine Sugar
(or Simple Syrup)

1½ oz. Citrus-flavored Vodka

1 splash Moscato d'Asti (or
Sweet Sparkling Wine)

Muddle strawberries in mixing glass with lemon juice and sugar/syrup. Cover with ice, add vodka, and shake well. Strain into chilled cocktail glass. Splash with sparkling wine. Garnish with a strawberry.

♈ ROBIN'S NEST

1 oz. Vodka

1 oz. Cranberry Juice

½ oz. Crème de Cacao
(White)

Shake with ice and strain into chilled cocktail glass.

♈ ROUXBY RED

1½ oz. Grapefruit-flavored
Vodka

¼ oz. Lemon Juice

¾ oz. Grapefruit Juice

½ oz. Campari

½ oz. Simple Syrup

Shake with ice and strain into salt-rimmed cocktail glass.

♈ RUBY RED

2 oz. Grapefruit-flavored
Vodka

1½ oz. Triple Sec

1 splash Orange Juice

1½ oz. Grapefruit Juice

Shake with ice and strain into chilled cocktail glass. Garnish with a tangerine wedge.

♈ RUSSIAN BEAR COCKTAIL

1 oz. Vodka

½ oz. Crème de Cacao
(White)

1 tbsp. Light Cream

Stir with ice and strain into chilled cocktail glass.

♈ RUSSIAN COCKTAIL

¾ oz. Crème de Cacao
(White)

¾ oz. Gin

¾ oz. Vodka

Shake with ice and strain into chilled cocktail glass.

♈ SAM-TINI

1¼ oz. Vodka

1 splash Sambuca

1 dash Blue Curaçao

Stir with ice and strain into chilled cocktail glass. Garnish with a twist of orange.

☐ SCREWDRIVER

1½ oz. Vodka

5 oz. Orange Juice

Pour into ice-filled highball glass. Stir well.

☐ SEABREEZE

1½ oz. Vodka

4 oz. Cranberry Juice

1 oz. Grapefruit Juice

Pour into ice-filled highball glass. Garnish with a wedge of lime.

☐ SHALOM

1½ oz. 100-proof Vodka

1 oz. Madeira

1 tbsp. Orange Juice

Shake with ice and strain into ice-filled old-fashioned glass. Add an orange slice.

☐ SIBERIAN SLEIGHRIDE

1¼ oz. Vodka

¾ oz. Crème de Cacao (White)

½ oz. Crème de Menthe (White)

3 oz. Light Cream

Shake with ice and strain into chilled snifter. Sprinkle with chocolate shavings.

☐ SINO-SOVIET SPLIT

2 oz. Vodka

1 oz. Amaretto

Milk or Light Cream

Combine first two ingredients in ice-filled old-fashioned glass. Fill with milk or cream.

☐ SONIC BLASTER

½ oz. Vodka

½ oz. Light Rum

½ oz. Banana Liqueur

1 oz. Pineapple Juice

1 oz. Orange Juice

1 oz. Cranberry Juice

Shake and pour into ice-filled Collins glass. Garnish with orange and lime slices.

☐ SOVIET

1½ oz. Vodka

½ oz. Amontillado Sherry

½ oz. Dry Vermouth

Shake with ice and strain into ice-filled old-fashioned glass. Add a twist of lemon peel.

☐ SPUTNIK

1¼ oz. Vodka

1¼ oz. Peach Schnapps

3 oz. Orange Juice

3 oz. Light Cream

Shake with ice until frothy, and pour into red-wine glass. Garnish with a slice of fresh peach.

☐ STOCKHOLM 75

¾ oz. Citrus-flavored Vodka

¾ oz. Superfine Sugar (or Simple Syrup)

¾ oz. Lemon Juice

5 oz. Champagne, chilled

Shake vodka, sugar/syrup, and juice with ice. Strain into chilled, oversized, sugar-rimmed cocktail glass. Fill with Champagne.

VODKA

Y STUPID CUPID

2 oz. Citrus-flavored Vodka

½ oz. Sloe Gin

1 splash Superfine Sugar (or Simple Syrup)

1 splash Lemon Juice

Stir with ice and strain into chilled cocktail glass. Garnish with a maraschino cherry.

Y THE SUMMER OF LOVE

2 oz. Orange-flavored Vodka

2 drops Rose Water

1 oz. Lillet Blanc

¼ oz. Chambord

Shake with ice and strain into chilled cocktail glass. Garnish with a lemon twist.

Y SURF RIDER

3 oz. Vodka

1 oz. Sweet Vermouth

½ cup Orange Juice

1 oz. Lemon Juice

½ tsp. Grenadine

Shake with ice and strain into chilled cocktail glass. Garnish with an orange slice and a maraschino cherry.

Y SWEET MARIA

1 tbsp. Light Cream

½ oz. Amaretto

1 oz. Vodka

Shake with ice and strain into chilled cocktail glass.

Y SWISS MARTINI

3 oz. Vodka

¾ oz. Cherry-flavored Brandy

Stir with ice in mixing glass and strain into chilled cocktail glass. Garnish with a twist of lemon peel or an olive.

Y TABBY CAT

2 oz. Dubonnet Rouge

1 oz. Orange-flavored Vodka

2 dashes Orange Bitters

Stir with ice and strain into chilled cocktail glass. Garnish with a lemon twist.

Y TIGER TANAKA

3 Cilantro Leaves

¼-inch piece Peeled Ginger Root

2 oz. Citrus Vodka

½ oz. Limoncello

¾ oz. Pineapple Juice

Muddle the ginger and cilantro in mixing glass. Add rest of ingredients. Shake and double-strain into chilled cocktail glass.

Y THE TITIAN

1 oz. Orange-flavored Vodka

½ oz. Grand Marnier

1 oz. Passion Fruit Juice

½ oz. Lime Juice

½ oz. Pomegranate Syrup

Shake with ice and strain into chilled cocktail glass. Garnish with a fresh raspberry.

TOASTED DROP

1½ oz. Citrus Vodka
¾ oz. Limoncello
¼ oz. Amaretto
1 oz. Lemon Juice
1 Egg White

Shake without ice. Then shake with ice and strain into cinnamon-sugar-rimmed cocktail glass. Garnish with a lemon twist.

TOP BANANA

1 oz. Vodka
1 oz. Crème de Banana
2 oz. Orange Juice

Shake with ice and strain into ice-filled old-fashioned glass.

TRIDENT

1 oz. Aquavit (or Vodka)
½ oz. Cynar
1 oz. Dry Sherry
2 dashes Peach Bitters

Stir and strain into cocktail glass. Garnish with a lemon twist.

TROPICAL ICED TEA

½ oz. Vodka
½ oz. Rum
½ oz. Gin
½ oz. Triple Sec
½ oz. Superfine Sugar (or Simple Syrup)
½ oz. Lemon Juice
1 oz. Pineapple Juice
1 oz. Cranberry Juice
½ oz. Grenadine

Combine in mixing glass and strain into ice-filled Collins glass. Garnish with seasonal fruits.

TWISTER

2 oz. Vodka
⅓ oz. Lime Juice
Lemon Soda

Pour vodka and lime juice into Collins glass. Add several ice cubes and drop a lime twist into glass. Fill with lemon soda and stir.

VELVET HAMMER

1½ oz. Vodka
1 tbsp. Crème de Cacao
1 tbsp. Light Cream

Shake with ice and strain into chilled cocktail glass.

VODKA

☐ VELVET PEACH HAMMER

1¾ oz. Vodka

¾ oz. Peach Schnapps

1 splash Superfine Sugar (or Simple Syrup)

1 splash Lemon Juice

Pour vodka and schnapps into ice-filled old-fashioned glass. Stir and top with sugar/syrup and lemon juice. Garnish with a slice of fresh peach.

☐ VICTORY COLLINS

1½ oz. Vodka

3 oz. Unsweetened Grape Juice

3 oz. Lemon Juice

1 tsp. Superfine Sugar (or Simple Syrup)

Shake with ice and strain into ice-filled Collins glass. Add a slice of orange.

☐ VODKA AND APPLE JUICE

2 oz. Vodka

Apple Juice

Pour vodka into ice-filled highball glass. Fill with apple juice and stir.

☐ VODKA AND TONIC

2 oz. Vodka

Tonic Water

Pour vodka into highball glass over ice. Add tonic and stir. Garnish with a lemon wedge.

☐ VODKA COLLINS

1 oz. Lemon Juice

1 tsp. Superfine Sugar (or Simple Syrup)

2 oz. Vodka

Club Soda

Shake lemon juice, sugar/syrup, and vodka with ice and strain into chilled Collins glass. Add several ice cubes, fill with club soda, and stir. Garnish with slices of lemon and orange and a maraschino cherry. Serve with a straw.

☐ VODKA COOLER

½ tsp. Superfine Sugar (or Simple Syrup)

2 oz. Club Soda

2 oz. Vodka

Club Soda or Ginger Ale

In Collins glass, stir sugar/syrup with club soda. Fill glass with ice and add vodka. Fill with club soda or ginger ale and stir again. Insert a spiral of orange or lemon peel and dangle end over rim of glass.

☐ VODKA DAISY

1 oz. Lemon Juice

½ tsp. Superfine Sugar (or Simple Syrup)

1 tsp. Grenadine

2 oz. Vodka

Shake with ice and strain into chilled beer mug or metal cup. Add ice cubes and garnish with fruits.

VODKA GIMLET

1 oz. Lime Juice

1 tsp. Superfine Sugar
(or Simple Syrup)

1½ oz. Vodka

Shake with ice and strain
into chilled cocktail glass.

VODKA GRASSHOPPER

¾ oz. Vodka

¾ oz. Crème de Menthe
(Green)

¾ oz. Crème de Cacao
(White)

Shake with ice and strain
into chilled cocktail glass.

VODKA ON THE ROCKS

2 oz. Vodka

Put two or three ice cubes in
old-fashioned glass and add
vodka. Serve with a twist of
lemon peel.

VODKA SALTY DOG

1½ oz. Vodka

5 oz. Grapefruit Juice

¼ tsp. Salt

Pour into ice-filled highball
glass. Stir well.

VODKA "7"

2 oz. Vodka

½ oz. Lime Juice

Lemon-lime Soda

Pour vodka and lime juice
into ice-filled Collins glass.
Drop a twist of lime in glass,
fill with lemon-lime soda,
and stir.

VODKA SLING

1 tsp. Superfine Sugar
(or Simple Syrup)

1 tsp. Water

1 oz. Lemon Juice

2 oz. Vodka

Dissolve sugar/syrup in
water and lemon juice. Add
vodka. Pour into ice-filled
old-fashioned glass and stir.
Add a twist of orange peel.

VODKA SOUR

1 oz. Lemon Juice

½ tsp. Superfine Sugar
(or Simple Syrup)

2 oz. Vodka

Shake with ice and strain
into chilled sour glass. Garnish with a half-slice of
lemon and a maraschino
cherry.

VODKA STINGER

1 oz. Vodka

1 oz. Crème de Menthe
(White)

Shake with ice and strain
into chilled cocktail glass.

WARSAW COCKTAIL

1½ oz. Vodka

½ oz. Blackberry-flavored
Brandy

½ oz. Dry Vermouth

1 tsp. Lemon Juice

Shake with ice and strain
into chilled cocktail glass.

VODKA

Y WEST SIDE

1½ oz. Lemon Vodka
1 oz. Lemon Juice
½ oz. Simple Syrup
6 Mint Leaves
Club Soda

Shake first four ingredients
with ice and double-strain
into chilled cocktail glass.
Top with a splash of club
soda.

▯ WHITE RUSSIAN

1 oz. Coffee Liqueur
2 oz. Vodka
Milk or Cream

Pour coffee liqueur and
vodka into ice-filled old-
fashioned glass and fill with
milk or cream.

Bend Your Spoon

This trick will improve your stirring skills: Put a
slight bend in the long handle of a stainless steel
barspoon. Now slide the back of the bowl down
the inside of the mixing glass to the bottom. The
top end of the spoon should be directly over the
center of the mixing glass. The bend will allow the
spoon to rotate over the center of the glass with
almost no circular movement of the hand. The
back of the spoon will rotate around the inside
of the mixing glass—pushing the ice ahead so
that liquid and cubes rotate gracefully as a unit
in a clockwise direction. Graceful stirring will not
only insure a heavy, silky texture, but is essential in
achieving the style and ceremony with which these
drinks should be prepared.

—DALE DEGROFF (a.k.a. King Cocktail),
author of *The Craft of the Cocktail*

WHISKEY IS AN UMBRELLA TERM for four distinct spirits—Irish, Scotch, bourbon, and rye—distilled from a fermented mash of grain and aged in oak barrels. In Ireland and the United States, it's spelled with an "e"; in Scotland and Canada it's spelled without one.

Irish whiskey comprises corn-based grain whiskey, barley, and barley malt. In Scotch whisky production, a peat-fueled fire is used to flavor the final product. American whiskey falls into two categories: straight whiskey, which is made from at least 51 percent of a grain, and blended whiskey, a combination of at least two 100-proof straight whiskies blended with neutral spirits, grain spirits, or light whiskies. Straight whiskey is made in three styles: bourbon, Tennessee, and rye. Bourbon can be made with one of two types of mash: sweet, which employs fresh yeast to start fermentation, or sour, which combines a new batch of sweet mash with residual mash from the previous fermentation. Within the bourbon category are two styles: wheat and rye (not to be confused with rye whiskey).

Tennessee whiskey is similar to bourbon, except that before the whiskey goes into charred barrels to mature, it is painstakingly filtered through ten feet of sugar maple charcoal.

Rye (a.k.a. straight rye), once the leading brown spirit before Prohibition, is making a comeback. Though wheat and barley are commonly used to make rye whiskey, by U.S. law it must be made with a minimum of 51 percent rye, whereas in Canada anything goes.

The following recipes list a specific whiskey if it's traditional or integral to the drink. Where simply "whiskey" is listed, feel free to experiment.

19TH CENTURY

1½ oz. Whiskey (Bourbon)
¾ oz. Lemon Juice
¾ oz. Crème de Cacao, (White)
¾ oz. Lillet Rouge

Shake with ice and strain into chilled cocktail glass.

ADDERLEY COCKTAIL

2 oz. Whiskey (Rye)
¾ oz. Maraschino Liqueur
¾ oz. Fresh Lemon Juice
2 dashes Orange Bitters

Shake and strain into cocktail glass. Garnish with flamed orange twist.

AFFINITY COCKTAIL

1 oz. Dry Vermouth
1 oz. Sweet Vermouth
1 oz. Whisky (Scotch)
3 dashes Orange Bitters

Stir with ice and strain into chilled cocktail glass.

ALGONQUIN

1½ oz. Whiskey (Rye)
1 oz. Dry Vermouth
1 oz. Pineapple Juice

Shake with ice and strain into chilled cocktail glass.

ALLEGHENY

1 oz. Whiskey (Bourbon)
1 oz. Dry Vermouth
1½ tsps. Blackberry-flavored Brandy
1½ tsps. Lemon Juice

Shake with ice and strain into chilled cocktail glass. Add a twist of lemon peel on top.

AMERICANA

¼ oz. Whiskey (Tennessee)
½ tsp. Superfine Sugar (or Simple Syrup)
1–2 dashes Bitters
Champagne, chilled

Combine first three ingredients in ice-filled Collins glass, stirring until sugar is dissolved. Fill with Champagne and add a slice of peach.

AMERICAN TRILOGY

1 cube Brown Sugar
1 oz. Whiskey (Straight Rye)
1 oz. Applejack

Muddle sugar cube in mixing glass. Add rest of ingredients. Stir with ice and strain into chilled old-fashioned glass. Garnish with an orange twist.

☍ ANGEL'S SHARE

1½ oz. Whiskey (Bourbon)
½ oz. Amaro
¼ oz. Crème de Cassis
1 dash Orange Bitters

Stir with ice and strain into chilled cocktail glass. Garnish with a lemon twist.

☍ AQUARIUS

1½ oz. Whisky (Scotch)
½ oz. Cherry-flavored Brandy
1 oz. Cranberry Juice

Shake with ice and strain into old-fashioned glass over ice.

☍ AUTUMN LEAVES

¾ oz. Whiskey (Straight Rye)
¾ oz. Apple Brandy
¾ oz. Sweet Vermouth
¼ oz. Strega
2 dashes Angostura Bitters

Stir with ice and strain into ice-filled old-fashioned glass. Garnish with an orange twist.

☍ AZTEC'S MARK

1½ oz. Whiskey (Bourbon)
½ oz. Crème de Cacao (White)
¼ oz. Bénédictine
2 dashes Tabasco Sauce

Stir with ice and strain into chilled cocktail glass. Garnish with an orange twist.

☍ BACK PORCH SWIZZLE

1½ oz. Whiskey (Bourbon)
½ oz. Dry Vermouth
1 oz. Pineapple Juice
1 oz. Ginger Beer
Green Chartreuse

Build first four ingredients in highball glass filled with crushed ice. Swizzle until glass frosts. Float Chartreuse on top, and garnish with a mint sprig.

☍ BASIN STREET

2 oz. Whiskey (Bourbon)
1 oz. Triple Sec
1 oz. Lemon Juice

Shake well with ice and strain into chilled cocktail glass.

☍ BEADLESTONE COCKTAIL

1½ oz. Dry Vermouth
1½ oz. Whisky (Scotch)

Stir with ice and strain into chilled cocktail glass.

☍ BEALS COCKTAIL

1½ oz. Whisky (Scotch)
½ oz. Dry Vermouth
½ oz. Sweet Vermouth

Stir with ice and strain into chilled cocktail glass.

WHISKIES

¥ BENSONHURST

2 oz. Whiskey (Straight Rye)
1 oz. Dry Vermouth
¼ oz. Maraschino Liqueur
Cynar

Stir first three ingredients with ice and strain into chilled, Cynar-rinsed cocktail glass.

¥ BLACK HAWK

1¼ oz. Whiskey (Bourbon)
1¼ oz. Sloe Gin

Stir with ice and strain into chilled cocktail glass. Garnish with a maraschino cherry.

¥ BLARNEY STONE COCKTAIL

2 oz. Whiskey (Irish)
½ tsp. Anisette
½ tsp. Triple Sec
¼ tsp. Maraschino Liqueur
1 dash Bitters

Shake with ice and strain into chilled cocktail glass. Garnish with a twist of orange peel and an olive.

¥ THE BLINKER

2 oz. Whisky (Rye; Canadian)
1½ oz. Grapefruit Juice
1 tsp. Raspberry Syrup

Shake and strain into cocktail glass. Garnish with grapefruit twist or speared raspberry.

¥ BLOOD-AND-SAND COCKTAIL

½ oz. Whisky (Scotch)
½ oz. Cherry-flavored Brandy
½ oz. Sweet Vermouth
1 tbsp. Orange Juice

Shake with ice and strain into chilled cocktail glass.

¥ BOBBY BURNS COCKTAIL

1½ oz. Sweet Vermouth
1½ oz. Whisky (Scotch)
1¼ tsps. Bénédictine

Stir with ice and strain into chilled cocktail glass. Garnish with a twist of lemon peel.

⬚ THE BONE

2 oz. Whiskey (Bourbon)
⅓ oz. Lime Juice
⅓ oz. Simple Syrup
3 dashes Tabasco Sauce

Shake with ice and strain into chilled shot glass.

⬚ BOURBON À LA CRÈME

2 oz. Whiskey (Bourbon)
1 oz. Crème de Cacao (Brown)
1–2 Vanilla Beans

Combine with ice in mixing glass and refrigerate for at least 1 hour. Shake well and serve straight up in an old-fashioned glass.

BOURBON COBBLER

2½ oz. Whiskey (Bourbon)
1 tbsp. Lemon Juice
2 tsps. Grapefruit Juice
1½ tsps. Almond Extract

Combine all ingredients in mixing glass, and then pour into ice-filled old-fashioned glass. Garnish with a peach slice.

BOURBON CRUSTA

2 oz. Whiskey (Bourbon)
½ oz. Triple Sec
½ oz. Maraschino Liqueur
½ oz. Lemon Juice
2 dashes Orange Bitters

Shake with ice and strain into chilled cocktail glass. Garnish with an orange peel.

BOURBON AND ELDER

3 oz. Whiskey (Bourbon)
1 tbsp. Elderflower Syrup
1 dash Angostura Bitters

Stir and strain into chilled old-fashioned glass. Garnish with lemon twist.

BOURBON HIGHBALL

2 oz. Whiskey (Bourbon)
Ginger Ale or Club Soda

Combine in ice-filled highball glass and stir. Garnish with a twist of lemon peel.

BOURBON ON THE ROCKS

2 oz. Whiskey (Bourbon)

Pour bourbon into old-fashioned glass half-filled with ice.

BOURBON RENEWAL

2 oz. Whiskey (Bourbon)
1 oz. Lemon Juice
½ oz. Crème de Cassis
½ oz. Simple Syrup
1 dash Angostura Bitters

Shake with ice and strain into ice-filled old-fashioned glass.

BOURBON AND WATER

2 oz. Whiskey (Bourbon)
4 oz. Water

Pour bourbon and water into old-fashioned glass. Add ice and stir. Garnish with a twist of lemon peel.

BRIGHTON PUNCH

¾ oz. Whiskey (Bourbon)
¾ oz. Brandy
¾ oz. Bénédictine
2 oz. Orange Juice
1 oz. Lemon Juice
Club Soda

Shake first five ingredients with ice and pour into ice-filled Collins glass. Fill with club soda and stir gently. Garnish with orange and lemon slices and serve with a straw.

WHISKIES

Y BROOKLYN

1½ oz. Whiskey (Rye or Bourbon)

½ oz. Sweet Vermouth

1 dash Amer Picon

1 dash Maraschino Liqueur

Stir with ice and strain into chilled cocktail glass.

BUDDY'S FAVORITE

1½ oz. Whiskey (Bourbon)

6 oz. Water, cold

Pour ingredients into highball glass. Stir and serve without ice.

Y BULL AND BEAR

1½ oz. Whiskey (Bourbon)

¾ oz. Orange Curaçao

1 tbsp. Grenadine

1 oz. Lemon Juice

Shake with ice and strain into chilled cocktail glass. Garnish with a maraschino cherry and an orange slice.

CABLEGRAM

1 oz. Lemon Juice

1 tsp. Superfine Sugar (or Simple Syrup)

2 oz. Whiskey

Ginger Ale

Stir first three ingredients with ice cubes in highball glass and fill with ginger ale.

CALIFORNIA LEMONADE

2 oz. Lemon Juice

1 oz. Lime Juice

1 tbsp. Superfine Sugar (or Simple Syrup)

2 oz. Whiskey

¼ tsp. Grenadine

Club Soda

Shake first five ingredients with ice and strain into chilled Collins glass over shaved ice. Fill with club soda and garnish with slices of orange and lemon, and a maraschino cherry. Serve with straws.

You're in Charge

Ignore absolutes, as well as recipes that say this is the "only" way to make this drink. The best way is the way that works best for you. This also means that just because somebody passes on a tip, rule, or recipe to you, doesn't mean you should assume it is really the right way to do it. As the bartender, you should be the one to decide what really works.

—ROBERT HESS (a.k.a. DrinkBoy),
Mixology Research Engineer

Y CAMERON'S KICK COCKTAIL

¾ oz. Whisky (Scotch)
¾ oz. Whiskey (Irish)
½ oz. Lemon Juice
2 dashes Orange Bitters

Shake with ice and strain into chilled cocktail glass.

☐ CANADIAN BREEZE

1½ oz. Whisky (Canadian)
1 tsp. Pineapple Juice
1 tbsp. Lemon Juice
½ tsp. Maraschino Liqueur

Shake with ice and strain into ice-filled old-fashioned glass. Garnish with a pineapple wedge or spear and a maraschino cherry.

☐ CANADIAN CHERRY

1½ oz. Whisky (Canadian)
½ oz. Maraschino Liqueur
1½ tsps. Lemon Juice
1½ tsps. Orange Juice

Shake all ingredients and strain into ice-filled old-fashioned glass. Moisten glass rim with maraschino liqueur.

Y CANADIAN COCKTAIL

1½ oz. Whisky (Canadian)
1 dash Bitters
1½ tsps. Triple Sec
1 tsp. Superfine Sugar (or Simple Syrup)

Shake with ice and strain into chilled cocktail glass.

☐ CANADIAN PINEAPPLE

1½ oz. Whisky (Canadian)
1 tsp. Pineapple Juice
1 tbsp. Lemon Juice
½ tsp. Maraschino Liqueur

Shake with ice and strain into ice-filled old-fashioned glass. Add a stick of pineapple.

☐ CANAL STREET DAISY

¾ oz. Lemon Juice
1 oz. Orange Juice
1 oz. Whisky (Scotch)
Club Soda

Pour juices and Scotch into ice-filled Collins glass. Add club soda and an orange slice.

☐ CARRÉ REPRISE

1 oz. Whiskey (Straight Rye)
1 oz. Cognac
1 oz. Sweet Vermouth
½ oz. Elderflower Liqueur
1 dash Angostura Bitters
1 dash Peychaud's Bitters

Stir with ice and strain into chilled old-fashioned glass. Garnish with a lemon twist.

Y CHANCELLOR COCKTAIL

1½ oz. Whisky (Scotch)
½ oz. Dry Vermouth
½ oz. Port Wine
1 dash Peychaud's Bitters

Stir and strain into cocktail glass. Garnish with a twist of lemon.

WHISKIES

CHAPEL HILL

1½ oz. Whiskey (Bourbon)
½ oz. Triple Sec
1 tbsp. Lemon Juice

Shake with ice and strain into chilled cocktail glass. Add a twist of orange peel.

CHAPLIN

¾ oz. Whiskey (Bourbon)
¾ oz. Dry Sherry
¾ oz. Ramazzotti Amaro
⅛ oz. Triple Sec
2 dashes Orange Bitters

Stir with ice and strain into chilled cocktail glass. Garnish with a twist of lemon peel.

CHAS

1¼ oz. Whiskey (Bourbon)
⅛ oz. Amaretto
⅛ oz. Bénédictine
⅛ oz. Triple Sec
⅛ oz. Orange Curaçao

Stir with ice and strain into chilled cocktail glass. Garnish with an orange twist.

CHEF'S PAIN

2 oz. Whiskey (Bourbon)
¾ oz. Lime Juice
½ oz. Blackberry Liqueur
½ oz. B & B

Shake with ice and strain into chilled cocktail glass.

CHI-TOWN FLIP

2 oz. Whiskey (Bourbon)
¾ oz. Tawny Port
¾ oz. Lemon Juice
¾ oz. Licor 43
¼ oz. Simple Syrup
1 Whole Egg

Shake ingredients without ice. Then shake with ice and strain into Collins glass. Garnish with grated nutmeg and three drops angostura bitters.

COFFEE OLD-FASHIONED

1½ tsp. Instant Coffee
½ cup Water
2 tsps. Superfine Sugar (or Simple Syrup)
2 dashes Bitters
1 oz. Whiskey (Bourbon)
2 oz. Club Soda

Dissolve coffee in water; stir in sugar/syrup, bitters, and bourbon. Add club soda and pour into ice-filled old-fashioned glass. Garnish with an orange slice and a maraschino cherry.

COMMODORE COCKTAIL

2 oz. 1792 Ridgemont Reserve Bourbon Whiskey

¾ oz. Crème de Cacao (White)

½ oz. Lemon Juice

1 dash Grenadine

Shake with ice and strain into chilled champagne flute.

COWBOY COCKTAIL

1½ oz. Whiskey (Bourbon)

1 tbsp. Light Cream

Shake with ice and strain into chilled cocktail glass.

CREOLE LADY

1½ oz. Whiskey (Bourbon)

1½ oz. Madeira

1 tsp. Grenadine

Stir with ice and strain into chilled cocktail glass. Serve with one green and one red maraschino cherry.

DAISY DUELLER

1½ oz. Whiskey (Tennessee)

1½ tsps. Lemon Juice

1½ tsps. Superfine Sugar (or Simple Syrup)

Several drops Triple Sec

Club Soda

Shake first four ingredients with ice. Strain into chilled highball glass. Add ice and fill with soda. Garnish with fruit slices.

THE DEBONAIR

2½ oz. Whisky (Single Malt Scotch)

1 oz. Ginger Liqueur

Stir and strain into chilled cocktail glass. Garnish with a lemon twist.

DE LA LOUISIANE

¾ oz. Whiskey (Rye)

¾ oz. Sweet Vermouth

¾ oz. Bénédictine

3 dashes Pastis (or Pernod or other Absinthe substitute)

3 dashes Peychaud's Bitters

Stir with ice and strain into chilled cocktail glass. Garnish with a maraschino cherry.

THE DELMARVA COCKTAIL

2 oz. Whiskey (Rye)

½ oz. Dry Vermouth

½ oz. Crème de Menthe (White)

½ oz. Lemon Juice

Shake and strain into chilled cocktail glass. Garnish with a mint leaf.

DERBY

2 oz. Whiskey (Bourbon)

¼ oz. Bénédictine

1 dash Angostura Bitters

Stir with ice and strain into chilled cocktail glass. Garnish with a lemon peel.

WHISKIES

DESHLER

1½ oz. Whiskey (Rye)
½ oz. Dubonnet
¼ oz. Triple Sec
2 dashes Angostura Bitters

Stir and strain into champagne flute. Garnish with a lemon twist.

DINAH COCKTAIL

¾ oz. Lemon Juice
½ tsp. Superfine Sugar (or Simple Syrup)
1½ oz. Whiskey (Bourbon)

Shake well with ice and strain into chilled cocktail glass. Garnish with a mint leaf.

DIRTY HARRY

2 oz. Whiskey (Straight Rye)
½ oz. Sweet Vermouth
¼ oz. Maraschino Liqueur
1 splash Absinthe

Stir first three ingredients with ice and strain into chilled, absinthe-rinsed cocktail glass. Garnish with a cherry.

DIXIE JULEP

1 tsp. Superfine Sugar (or Simple Syrup)
2½ oz. Whiskey (Bourbon)

Combine sugar/syrup and bourbon in Collins glass. Fill with crushed ice and stir gently until glass is frosted. Garnish with sprigs of mint. Serve with straws.

DIXIE WHISKEY COCKTAIL

½ tsp. Superfine Sugar (or Simple Syrup)
1 dash Bitters
¼ tsp. Triple Sec
½ tsp. Crème de Menthe (White)
2 oz. Whiskey (Bourbon)

Shake with ice and strain into chilled cocktail glass.

DOLCE VITA

2 oz. Whiskey (Bourbon)
½ oz. Sweet Vermouth
½ oz. Hazelnut Liqueur

Stir and strain into cocktail glass rimmed with powdered dried fruit.

DOUBLE STANDARD SOUR

1 oz. Lemon Juice (or ½ oz. Lime Juice)
½ tsp. Superfine Sugar (or Simple Syrup)
¾ oz. Whiskey
¾ oz. Gin
½ tsp. Grenadine

Shake with ice and strain into chilled sour glass. Garnish with a half-slice of lemon and a maraschino cherry.

DUBLINER

2 oz. Whiskey (Irish)
½ oz. Sweet Vermouth
½ oz. Grand Marnier
2 dashes Orange Bitters

Stir and strain into champagne flute. Garnish with a flamed orange twist.

THE DUBOUDREAU COCKTAIL

2 oz. Whiskey (Straight Rye)
¾ oz. Dubonnet
¼ oz. Fernet Branca
¼ oz. Elderflower Liqueur

Stir with ice and strain into chilled cocktail glass. Garnish with a lemon twist.

DUFFTOWN FLIP

2 oz. Whisky (Single Malt Scotch)
½ oz. Port
½ oz. Demerara Syrup
½ oz. Almond Milk
1 Whole Egg

Shake without ice. Then shake with ice and strain into snifter. Garnish with grated nutmeg.

EASTER ELCHIES

2 oz. Whisky (Single Malt Scotch)
½ oz. Cherry Heering
½ oz. Punt y Mes
1 dash Orange Bitters

Stir with ice and strain into chilled cocktail glass. Garnish with a brandied cherry.

EASTERN SOUR

2 oz. Whiskey (Bourbon)
1½ oz. Orange Juice
1 oz. Lime Juice
¼ oz. Orgeat Syrup (Almond Syrup)
¼ oz. Superfine Sugar (or Simple Syrup)

Shake with ice and strain into ice-filled highball glass. Garnish with orange slices or spent shell of lime.

EASTERNER

2 oz. Whiskey (Straight Rye)
1 oz. Grapefruit Juice
½ oz. Maple Syrup

Shake with ice and strain into chilled cocktail glass. Garnish with a grapefruit twist.

EMPEROR NORTON'S MISTRESS

4 Medium Strawberries
1½ oz. Whiskey (Bourbon)
½ oz. Vanilla Liqueur
¼ oz. Triple Sec

Muddle 3 strawberries in mixing glass. Add rest of ingredients. Shake with ice and strain into ice-filled old-fashioned glass. Garnish with a slice of strawberry.

WHISKIES

∇ EVERYBODY'S IRISH COCKTAIL

1 tsp. Crème de Menthe (Green)

1 tsp. Chartreuse (Green)

2 oz. Whiskey (Irish)

Stir with ice and strain into chilled cocktail glass. Garnish with a green olive.

∇ FANCY-FREE COCKTAIL

2 oz. Whiskey (Bourbon)

½ oz. Maraschino Liqueur

1 dash Angostura Bitters

1 dash Orange Bitters

Stir with ice and strain into chilled cocktail glass.

∇ FANCY WHISKEY

2 oz. Whiskey (Bourbon or Rye)

1 dash Bitters

¼ tsp. Triple Sec

¼ tsp. Superfine Sugar (or Simple Syrup)

Shake with ice and strain into chilled cocktail glass. Add a twist of lemon peel.

∇ THE FINAL WARD

1 oz. Whiskey (Straight Rye)

1 oz. Maraschino Liqueur

1 oz. Green Chartreuse

1 oz. Lemon Juice

Shake with ice and strain into chilled cocktail glass.

∇ FLYING SCOTCHMAN

1 oz. Sweet Vermouth

1 oz. Whisky (Scotch)

1 dash Bitters

¼ tsp. Superfine Sugar (or Simple Syrup)

Stir with ice and strain into chilled cocktail glass.

∇ FOX RIVER COCKTAIL

1 tbsp. Crème de Cacao (Brown)

2 oz. Whiskey (Bourbon or Rye)

4 dashes Bitters

Stir with ice and strain into chilled cocktail glass.

∇ FRANCIS THE MULE

2 oz. Whiskey (Bourbon)

¼ oz. Orgeat Syrup

½ oz. Lemon Juice

½ oz. Coffee Liqueur

2 dashes Orange Bitters

Shake with ice and strain into chilled cocktail glass. Garnish with a lemon twist.

∇ FRATELLI COCKTAIL

2 oz. Whiskey (Straight Rye)

½ oz. Sweet Vermouth

½ oz. Yellow Chartreuse

¼ oz. Fernet Branca

Stir with ice and strain into chilled cocktail glass.

FRISCO SOUR

¾ oz. Lemon Juice

½ oz. Lime Juice

½ oz. Bénédictine

2 oz. Whiskey (Bourbon or Rye)

Shake with ice and strain into chilled sour glass. Garnish with slices of lemon and lime.

GENTLEMAN'S COCKTAIL

1½ oz. Whiskey (Bourbon)

½ oz. Brandy

½ oz. Crème de Menthe

Club Soda

Pour bourbon, brandy, and crème de menthe into ice-filled highball glass. Add club soda and garnish with a twist of lemon peel.

GILCHRIST

1¼ oz. Whisky (Blended Scotch)

¾ oz. Pear Brandy

¾ oz. Grapefruit Juice

½ oz. Amaro

2 dashes Grapefruit Bitters

Shake with ice and strain into chilled cocktail glass. Garnish with a lemon twist.

GODFATHER

1½ oz. Whisky (Scotch)

¾ oz. Amaretto

Combine in ice-filled old-fashioned glass.

GOLDRUSH

2 oz. Whiskey (Bourbon)

¾ oz. Lemon Juice

1 oz. Honey Syrup

Shake and strain into ice-filled old-fashioned glass.

GRANDFATHER

1 oz. Whiskey (Bourbon)

1 oz. Applejack

1 oz. Sweet Vermouth

1 dash Angostura Bitters

1 dash Peychaud's Bitters

Stir with ice and strain into chilled cocktail glass. Garnish with a cherry.

GREENPOINT

2 oz. Whiskey (Straight Rye)

½ oz. Yellow Chartreuse

½ oz. Sweet Vermouth

1 dash Angostura Bitters

1 dash Orange Bitters

Stir with ice and strain into chilled cocktail glass. Garnish with a lemon twist.

GROUNDS FOR DIVORCE

1½ oz. Whiskey (Straight Rye)

¾ oz. Kirschwasser

¼ oz. Cynar

½ oz. Amaro

Stir and strain into chilled cocktail glass. Garnish with an orange twist.

WHISKIES

▽ HARVEST MOON

1½ oz. Whiskey (Straight Rye)

1 oz. Lillet Blanc

½ oz. Apple Brandy

¼ oz. Green Chartreuse

2 dashes Angostura Bitters

Stir with ice and strain into chilled cocktail glass. Garnish with an orange twist.

▽ HEATHER BLUSH

1 oz. Whisky (Scotch)

1 oz. Strawberry Liqueur

3 oz. Sparkling Wine, chilled

Pour Scotch and liqueur into champagne flute. Top with sparkling wine. Garnish with a strawberry.

▽ HEAVENLY DRAM

2 oz. Whisky (Single Malt Scotch)

½ oz. Pedro Ximenez Sherry

¾ oz. Lemon Juice

¼ oz. Honey Syrup

Shake with ice and strain into chilled cocktail glass. Garnish with a lemon twist.

▯ HEBRIDES

1½ oz. Whisky (Single Malt Scotch)

½ oz. Maraschino Liqueur

½ oz. Triple Sec

2 oz. Apple Juice

½ oz. Lemon Juice

1 dash Angostura Bitters

Build in ice-filled Collins glass.

▽ HIGH COTTON

2 oz. Whiskey (Straight Rye)

½ oz. Pimm's #1 Cup

½ oz. Dubonnet Rouge

2 dashes Peach Bitters

Stir and strain into chilled cocktail glass. Garnish with a lemon twist and a mint leaf.

▯ HIGHLAND COOLER

½ tsp. Superfine Sugar (or Simple Syrup)

2 oz. Club Soda

2 oz. Whisky (Scotch)

Club Soda or Ginger Ale

Combine sugar/syrup and soda in Collins glass; stir. Add ice cubes and Scotch. Fill with soda and stir again. Insert a spiral of orange or lemon peel (or both) and dangle end over rim of glass.

▽ HIGHLAND FLING COCKTAIL

¾ oz. Sweet Vermouth

1½ oz. Whisky (Scotch)

2 dashes Orange Bitters

Stir with ice and strain into chilled cocktail glass. Garnish with an olive.

▽ HOLE-IN-ONE

1¾ oz. Whisky (Scotch)

¾ oz. Vermouth

¼ tsp. Lemon Juice

1 dash Orange Bitters

Shake with ice and strain into chilled cocktail glass.

Y HOOT MON COCKTAIL

¾ oz. Sweet Vermouth
1½ oz. Whisky (Scotch)
1 tsp. Bénédictine

Stir with ice and strain into chilled cocktail glass. Twist a lemon peel and drop into glass.

HORSE'S NECK (WITH A KICK)

2 oz. Whiskey (Bourbon)
Ginger Ale

Peel rind of whole lemon in spiral fashion and put in Collins glass with one end hanging over the rim. Fill glass with ice cubes. Add whiskey. Fill with ginger ale and stir well.

HOTEL D'ALSACE

1 sprig Rosemary
2 oz. Whiskey (Irish)
⅓ oz. Bénédictine
⅓ oz. Triple Sec

Muddle nettles from half-sprig of rosemary. Add rest of ingredients. Stir with ice and strain into ice-filled old-fashioned glass. Garnish with a half-sprig of rosemary.

HOT TODDY

12 oz. Water, boiling
½ oz. Honey
2 oz. Whiskey (Bourbon)

Preheat an Irish coffee glass with half the boiling water; then discard. Pour honey and bourbon into glass and top with remaining water. Garnish with a large, clove-studded lemon twist.

I.A.P.

2 oz. Whiskey (Tennessee)
¼ oz. Fernet Branca
3 oz. Cola

Build in ice-filled Collins glass.

IMPERIAL FIZZ

1 oz. Lemon Juice
½ oz. Light Rum
1½ oz. Whiskey (Bourbon or Rye)
1 tsp. Superfine Sugar (or Simple Syrup)
Club Soda

Shake first four ingredients with ice and strain into highball glass. Add two ice cubes. Fill with club soda and stir.

INCIDER COCKTAIL

1½ oz. Whiskey
Apple Cider

Mix whiskey with a generous helping of apple cider in old-fashioned glass. Top with ice and stir. Garnish with a slice of apple.

IRISH RICKEY

½ oz. Lime Juice
1½ oz. Whiskey (Irish)
Club Soda

Pour lime juice and whiskey into ice-filled highball glass. Fill with club soda and stir. Garnish with a wedge of lime.

IRISH SHILLELAGH

1 oz. Lemon Juice
1 tsp. Superfine Sugar (or Simple Syrup)
1½ oz. Whiskey (Irish)
1 tbsp. Sloe Gin
1 tbsp. Light Rum

Shake with ice and strain into Irish coffee glass. Garnish with fresh raspberries, strawberries, a maraschino cherry, and two peach slices.

IRISH WHISKEY

½ tsp. Triple Sec
½ tsp. Anisette
¼ tsp. Maraschino Liqueur
1 dash Bitters
2 oz. Whiskey (Irish)

Stir with ice and strain into chilled cocktail glass. Garnish with an olive.

IRISH WHISKEY HIGHBALL

2 oz. Whiskey (Irish)
Ginger Ale or Club Soda

Pour whiskey into ice-filled highball glass. Fill with ginger ale or club soda. Garnish with a twist of lemon peel, if desired, and stir.

JITTERBUG SOUR

2 oz. Whiskey (Rye)
½ oz. Bénédictine
½ oz. Honey Syrup
¾ oz. Lemon Juice
1 Egg White
1 dash Angostura Bitters

Shake first five ingredients and strain into cocktail glass. Add dash of angostura and a lemon twist.

JOCOSE JULEP

2½ oz. Whiskey (Bourbon)
½ oz. Crème de Menthe (Green)
1 oz. Lime Juice
1 tsp. Sugar
5 Mint Leaves, chopped
Club Soda

Combine all ingredients except club soda in blender without ice until smooth. Pour into ice-filled Collins glass. Fill with club soda and stir. Garnish with a sprig of mint.

JOHN COLLINS

1 oz. Lemon Juice

1 tsp. Superfine Sugar
(or Simple Syrup)

2 oz. Whiskey (Bourbon)

Club Soda

Shake first three ingredients with ice and strain into Collins glass. Add several cubes of ice, fill with club soda, and stir. Garnish with slices of orange and lemon, and a maraschino cherry. Serve with straws.

KEEGAN

1 oz. Whiskey (Bourbon)

¾ oz. Aperol

½ oz. Yellow Chartreuse

¾ oz. Lime Juice

Shake with ice and strain into chilled cocktail glass.

KENTUCKY BLIZZARD

1½ oz. Whiskey (Bourbon)

1½ oz. Cranberry Juice

½ oz. Lime Juice

½ oz. Grenadine

1 tsp. Sugar

Shake all ingredients with ice. Strain into chilled cocktail glass or over fresh ice in old-fashioned glass. Garnish with a half-slice of orange.

KENTUCKY COCKTAIL

¼ oz. Pineapple Juice

1½ oz. 1792 Ridgemont Reserve Bourbon Whiskey

Shake with ice and strain into chilled cocktail glass.

KENTUCKY COLONEL COCKTAIL

½ oz. Bénédictine

1½ oz. Whiskey (Bourbon)

Stir with ice and strain into chilled cocktail glass. Add a twist of lemon peel.

THE KENTUCKY LONGSHOT

2 oz. Whiskey (Bourbon)

½ oz. Ginger Liqueur

½ oz. Peach-flavored Brandy

1 dash Angostura Bitters

1 dash Peychaud's Bitters

Stir and strain into chilled cocktail glass. Garnish with candied ginger—if using long strips hang over the lip of the glass; smaller pieces can be dropped into the drink.

KING COLE COCKTAIL

1 slice Orange

1 slice Pineapple

½ tsp. Superfine Sugar
(or Simple Syrup)

2 oz. Whiskey

Muddle first three ingredients well in old-fashioned glass. Add whiskey and 2 ice cubes and stir.

KISS ON THE LIPS

2 oz. Whiskey (Bourbon)

6 oz. Apricot Nectar

Pour into ice-filled Collins glass and stir. Serve with a straw.

WHISKIES

KLONDIKE COOLER

½ tsp. Superfine Sugar
(or Simple Syrup)
2 oz. Club Soda
2 oz. Whiskey (Bourbon)
Club Soda or Ginger Ale

Mix sugar/syrup and club soda in Collins glass. Fill glass with ice and add whiskey. Fill with club soda or ginger ale and stir again. Insert a spiral of orange or lemon peel (or both) and dangle end over rim of glass.

LADIES' COCKTAIL

1¾ oz. Whiskey (Bourbon)
½ tsp. Anisette
2 dashes Bitters

Stir with ice and strain into chilled cocktail glass. Serve with a pineapple stick on top.

LA TAVOLA ROTONDA

2 oz. Whiskey (Bourbon)
1 oz. Pineapple Juice
½ oz. Campari
½ oz. Amaro
½ oz. Maraschino Liqueur
2 dashes Peychaud's Bitters

Shake with ice and strain into chilled cocktail glass. Garnish with a cherry.

LAWHILL COCKTAIL

¾ oz. Dry Vermouth
1½ oz. Whiskey (Rye)
¼ tsp. Anisette
¼ tsp. Maraschino Liqueur
1 dash Bitters

Stir with ice and strain into chilled cocktail glass.

LIBERAL

1½ oz. Whiskey (Rye)
½ oz. Sweet Vermouth
¼ oz. Amer Picon
1 dash Orange Bitters

Stir with ice and strain into chilled cocktail glass. Garnish with an orange twist.

LIMESTONE COCKTAIL

1½ oz. Whiskey (Bourbon)
1 oz. Lemon Juice
1 tsp. Superfine Sugar
(or Simple Syrup)
Club Soda

Stir first three ingredients in ice-filled highball glass. Fill with club soda; stir again.

LINSTEAD COCKTAIL

1 oz. Whiskey (Bourbon)
1 oz. Pineapple Juice
½ tsp. Superfine Sugar
(or Simple Syrup)
¼ tsp. Anisette
¼ tsp. Lemon Juice

Shake with ice and strain into chilled cocktail glass.

🍸 LOCH LOMOND

1 oz. Whisky (Scotch)
½ oz. Peach Schnapps
1 oz. Blue Curaçao
3 oz. Grapefruit Juice
½ oz. Lemon Juice

Shake all ingredients with ice and strain into ice-filled parfait or hurricane glass. Garnish with a slice of star fruit.

🥃 LOUISVILLE COOLER

1½ oz. 1792 Ridgemont Reserve Bourbon Whiskey
1 oz. Orange Juice
1 tbsp. Lime Juice
1 tsp. Superfine Sugar (or Simple Syrup)

Shake all ingredients with ice. Strain into old-fashioned glass over fresh ice. Garnish with a half-slice of orange.

🍸 LOUISVILLE LADY

1 oz. Whiskey (Bourbon)
¾ oz. Crème de Cacao (White)
¾ oz. Cream

Shake with ice and strain into chilled cocktail glass.

🥃 MAGNOLIA MAIDEN

1¼ oz. Whiskey (Bourbon)
1¼ oz. Mandarine Napoléon
1 splash Superfine Sugar (or Simple Syrup)
1 splash Club Soda

Shake bourbon, Mandarine Napoléon, and sugar/syrup with ice. Strain into ice-filled old-fashioned glass. Top with club soda.

🥃 MAMIE GILROY

½ oz. Lime Juice
2 oz. Whisky (Scotch)
Ginger Ale

Combine in ice-filled Collins glass and stir.

🍸 MANHASSET

1½ oz. Whiskey (Bourbon)
1½ tsp. Dry Vermouth
1½ tsp. Sweet Vermouth
1 tbsp. Lemon Juice

Shake with ice and strain into chilled cocktail glass.

Quality, Not Quantity

There is no substitute for quality. Just as you can't build a Ferrari out of Ford parts, you only get out of a cocktail what you put into it.

—TONY ABOU GANIM (a.k.a. The Modern Mixologist), host of the Fine Living Network's *Raising the Bar: America's Best Bar Chefs*

WHISKIES

MANHATTAN

2 oz. Whiskey (Rye or Bourbon)

½ oz. Sweet Vermouth

1 dash Angostura Bitters

Stir with ice and strain into chilled cocktail glass. Garnish with a maraschino cherry.

MANHATTAN (DRY)

2 oz. Whiskey (Rye or Bourbon)

½ oz. Dry Vermouth

1 dash Angostura Bitters

Stir with ice and strain into chilled cocktail glass. Garnish with an olive.

McCOY

1½ oz. Whiskey (Irish)

½ oz. Dry Sherry

¼ oz. Tuaca

2 dashes Peach Bitters

Stir and strain into champagne flute; garnish with an orange twist.

MIAMI BEACH COCKTAIL

¾ oz. Whisky (Scotch)

¾ oz. Dry Vermouth

¾ oz. Grapefruit Juice

Shake with ice and strain into chilled cocktail glass.

MINT JULEP

4 sprigs Mint

1 tsp. Superfine Sugar (or Simple Syrup)

2 tsps. Water

2½ oz. Whiskey (Bourbon)

In silver julep cup, silver mug, or Collins glass, muddle mint leaves, sugar/syrup, and water. Fill glass or mug with shaved or crushed ice and add bourbon. Top with more ice and garnish with a mint sprig and straws.

MINT JULEP (SOUTHERN STYLE)

1 tsp. Superfine Sugar (or Simple Syrup)

2 tsps. Water

2½ oz. Whiskey (Bourbon)

In silver mug or Collins glass, dissolve sugar/syrup with water. Fill with finely shaved ice and add bourbon. Stir until glass is heavily frosted, adding more ice if necessary. (Do not hold glass with hand while stirring.) Garnish with 5–6 sprigs of fresh mint so that the tops are about 2 inches above rim of glass. Use short straws so that it will be necessary to bury nose in mint, which is intended for scent rather than taste.

MODERN COCKTAIL

1½ oz. Whisky (Scotch)
½ tsp. Lemon Juice
¼ tsp. Anisette
½ tsp. Jamaican Rum
1 dash Orange Bitters

Shake with ice and strain into chilled cocktail glass. Garnish with a maraschino cherry.

MONTANA STUMP PULLER

2 oz. Whisky (Canadian)
1 oz. Crème de Menthe (White)

Stir with ice and strain into shot glass.

MONTE CARLO

2 oz. Whiskey (Rye)
½ oz. Bénédictine
2 dashes Angostura Bitters

Stir with ice and strain into chilled cocktail glass.

MOTO GUZZI

1 oz. Whiskey (Bourbon)
1 oz. Punt y Mes

Stir with ice and strain into chilled old-fashioned glass.

NARRAGANSETT

1½ oz. Whiskey (Bourbon)
1 oz. Sweet Vermouth
1 dash Anisette

Stir in ice-filled old-fashioned glass. Garnish with a twist of lemon peel.

NEVINS

1½ oz. Whiskey (Bourbon)
1½ tsps. Apricot-flavored Brandy
1 tbsp. Grapefruit Juice
1½ tsps. Lemon Juice
1 dash Bitters

Shake with ice and strain into chilled cocktail glass.

NEW YORK COCKTAIL (AKA NEW YORKER)

1 oz. Lime Juice (or 2 oz. Lemon Juice)
1 tsp. Superfine Sugar (or Simple Syrup)
1½ oz. Whiskey (Rye)
½ tsp. Grenadine

Shake with ice and strain into chilled cocktail glass. Garnish with a twist of lemon peel.

NEW YORK FLIP

2 oz. Whiskey (Rye)
¾ oz. Port
¾ oz. Demerara Syrup
1 oz. Heavy Cream
1 Whole Egg

Shake and strain into champagne flute. Garnish with fresh-grated nutmeg on top.

NEW YORK SOUR

1 oz. Lemon Juice

1 tsp. Superfine Sugar
(or Simple Syrup)

2 oz. Whiskey (Rye or
Bourbon)

Red Wine

Shake first three ingredients with ice and strain into chilled sour glass, leaving about ½ inch of space. Float red wine on top. Garnish with a half-slice of lemon and a maraschino cherry.

NUTCRACKER

2 oz. Whiskey (Bourbon)

½ oz. Frangelico

½ oz. Amaretto

½ oz. Orgeat Syrup

¾ oz. Lemon Juice

1 Egg White

Shake without ice. Then shake with ice and strain into ice-filled old-fashioned glass. Garnish with grated nutmeg.

OLD BAY RIDGE

1 oz. Whiskey (Straight Rye)

1 oz. Aquavit

½ oz. Demerara Syrup

2 dashes Angostura Bitters

Stir with ice and strain into chilled old-fashioned glass. Garnish with a lemon twist.

OLD-FASHIONED COCKTAIL

1 cube Sugar

1 dash Bitters

1 tsp. Water

2 oz. Whiskey (Rye or
Bourbon)

In old-fashioned glass, muddle sugar cube, bitters, and water. Add whiskey and stir. Add a twist of lemon peel and ice cubes. Garnish with a slice of orange and a maraschino cherry. Serve with a swizzle stick.

OLD PAL COCKTAIL

½ oz. Grenadine

½ oz. Sweet Vermouth

1¼ oz. Whiskey (Rye)

Stir with ice and strain into chilled cocktail glass.

OPENING COCKTAIL

½ oz. Grenadine

½ oz. Sweet Vermouth

1½ oz. Whiskey (Rye)

Stir with ice and strain into chilled cocktail glass.

ORIENTAL COCKTAIL

1 oz. Whiskey (Rye)

½ oz. Sweet Vermouth

½ oz. Triple Sec

½ oz. Lime Juice

Shake with ice and strain into chilled cocktail glass.

PADDY COCKTAIL

1½ oz. Whiskey (Irish)
1½ oz. Sweet Vermouth
1 dash Bitters

Stir with ice and strain into chilled cocktail glass.

PALMER COCKTAIL

2 oz. Whiskey (Rye)
1 dash Bitters
½ tsp. Lemon Juice

Stir with ice and strain into chilled cocktail glass.

PENDENNIS TODDY

1 cube Sugar
1 tsp. Water
2 oz. Whiskey (Bourbon)

Muddle cube of sugar with water in sour glass. Fill with ice, add bourbon, and stir. Garnish with two slices of lemon.

PENICILLIN

1¾ oz. Whisky (Blended Scotch)
¾ oz. Lemon Juice
⅜ oz. Honey Syrup
⅜ oz. Ginger Liqueur
¼ oz. Whisky (Islay Single Malt Scotch)

Shake first four ingredients with ice and strain into ice-filled old-fashioned glass. Float Scotch on top and garnish with a lemon wheel.

PLUMMED AWAY

¾ oz. Whiskey (Irish)
¾ oz. Plum Wine
1½ oz. Apple Juice
½ oz. Lemon Juice
½ oz. Simple Syrup

Build in highball glass filled with ice. Stir, then garnish with a lemon twist.

PREAKNESS COCKTAIL

¾ oz. Sweet Vermouth
1½ oz. Whiskey (Rye)
1 dash Bitters
½ tsp. Bénédictine

Stir with ice and strain into chilled cocktail glass. Garnish with a twist of lemon peel.

QUEBEC

1½ oz. Whisky (Canadian)
½ oz. Dry Vermouth
1½ tsps. Amer Picon (or Bitters)
1½ tsps. Maraschino Liqueur

Shake with ice and strain into chilled, sugar-rimmed cocktail glass.

RED HOOK

2 oz. Whiskey (Rye)
¼ oz. Maraschino Liqueur
¼ oz. Punt e Mes

Stir with ice and strain into chilled cocktail glass. Garnish with a maraschino cherry.

WHISKIES

RED-HOT PASSION

½ oz. Whiskey (Bourbon)
½ oz. Amaretto
½ oz. Whiskey (Tennessee Sour Mash)
¼ oz. Sloe Gin
1 splash Triple Sec
1 splash Orange Juice
1 splash Pineapple Juice

Pour all ingredients over ice into parfait or hurricane glass and stir gently. Garnish with an orange slice.

RED RAIDER

1 oz. Whiskey (Bourbon)
½ oz. Triple Sec
1 oz. Lemon Juice
1 dash Grenadine

Shake with ice and strain into chilled cocktail glass.

REMEMBER THE MAINE

2 oz. Whiskey (Straight Rye)
¾ oz. Sweet Vermouth
½ oz. Cherry Heering
¼ oz. Pastis

Stir with ice and strain into chilled cocktail glass. Garnish with a lemon twist.

ROBERT BURNS

1½ oz. Whisky (Scotch)
½ oz. Sweet Vermouth
1 dash Orange Bitters
1 dash Pernod (or Absinthe substitute)

Stir with ice and strain into chilled cocktail glass.

ROB ROY

¾ oz. Sweet Vermouth
1½ oz. Whisky (Scotch)

Stir with ice and strain into chilled cocktail glass.

RORY O'MORE

¾ oz. Sweet Vermouth
1½ oz. Whiskey (Irish)
1 dash Orange Bitters

Stir with ice and strain into chilled cocktail glass.

RUSTY NAIL

¾ oz. Whisky (Scotch)
¼ oz. Drambuie

Serve in old-fashioned glass with ice cubes. Float Drambuie on top.

RYE COCKTAIL

1 dash Bitters
1 tsp. Superfine Sugar (or Simple Syrup)
2 oz. Whiskey (Rye)

Shake with ice and strain into chilled cocktail glass. Garnish with a maraschino cherry.

RYE HIGHBALL

2 oz. Whiskey (Rye)
Ginger Ale or Club Soda

Pour whiskey into ice-filled highball glass. Fill with ginger ale or club soda and ice cubes. Garnish with a twist of lemon peel and stir.

SANTIAGO SCOTCH PLAID

1½ oz. Whisky (Scotch)
½ oz. Dry Vermouth
2 dashes Angostura Bitters

Stir with ice and strain into chilled cocktail glass. Garnish with a lemon twist.

SAZERAC

½ tsp. Pernod (or Absinthe substitute)
1 dash Peychaud's Bitters
1 cube Sugar (or ½ tsp. Simple Syrup)
2 oz. Whiskey (Rye)

Coat chilled old-fashioned glass with Pernod. Pour most of it out, then add bitters. Add sugar cube (or simple syrup) and muddle. Add whiskey. Garnish with a twist of lemon peel.

SCOFFLAW

1 oz. Whisky (Canadian)
1 oz. Dry Vermouth
¼ oz. Lemon Juice
1 dash Grenadine
1 dash Orange Bitters

Stir with ice and strain into chilled cocktail glass. Garnish with a lemon wedge.

SCOTCH BISHOP COCKTAIL

1 oz. Whisky (Scotch)
1 tbsp. Orange Juice
½ oz. Dry Vermouth
½ tsp. Triple Sec
¼ tsp. Superfine Sugar (or Simple Syrup)

Shake with ice and strain into chilled cocktail glass. Garnish with a twist of lemon peel.

SCOTCH BONNET

1¼ oz. Whisky (Single Malt Scotch)
¼ oz. Dry Vermouth
¼ oz. Aperol
2 dashes Tabasco Sauce

Stir with ice and strain into chilled cocktail glass. Garnish with a flamed orange twist.

SCOTCH BOUNTY

1 oz. Whisky (Scotch)
1 oz. Coconut-flavored Rum
1 oz. Crème de Cacao (White)
½ oz. Grenadine
4 oz. Orange Juice

Shake with ice and pour into hurricane or parfait glass. Garnish with a pineapple wedge and a maraschino cherry. Serve with a straw.

WHISKIES

SCOTCH COBBLER

2 oz. Whisky (Scotch)
4 dashes Curaçao
4 dashes Brandy

Combine in ice-filled old-fashioned glass. Garnish with a slice of orange and a mint sprig.

SCOTCH COOLER

2 oz. Whisky (Scotch)
3 dashes Crème de Menthe (White)
Club Soda, chilled

Pour Scotch and crème de menthe into ice-filled highball glass. Fill with club soda and stir.

SCOTCH HIGHBALL

2 oz. Whisky (Scotch)
Ginger Ale or Club Soda

Pour Scotch into ice-filled highball glass and fill with ginger ale or club soda. Add a twist of lemon peel and stir.

SCOTCH HOLIDAY SOUR

1½ oz. Whisky (Scotch)
1 oz. Cherry-flavored Brandy
½ oz. Sweet Vermouth
1 oz. Lemon Juice

Shake with ice and strain into ice-filled old-fashioned glass. Add a slice of lemon.

SCOTCH MIST

2 oz. Whisky (Scotch)

Pack old-fashioned glass with crushed ice. Pour in Scotch and add a twist of lemon peel. Serve with a short straw.

SCOTCH OLD-FASHIONED

1 cube Sugar
1 tsp. Water
1 dash Bitters
2 oz. Whisky (Scotch)

In old-fashioned glass, muddle sugar cube, water, and bitters. Add Scotch and stir. Add a twist of lemon peel and ice cubes. Garnish with slices of orange and lemon and a maraschino cherry.

SCOTCH RICKEY

½ oz. Lime Juice
1½ oz. Whisky (Scotch)
Club Soda

Pour lime juice and Scotch into ice-filled highball glass and fill with club soda. Add a twist of lime. Stir.

SCOTCH ON THE ROCKS

2 oz. Whisky (Scotch)

Pour Scotch into old-fashioned glass half-filled with ice.

SCOTCH ROYALE

1 cube Sugar
1½ oz. Whisky (Scotch)
1 dash Bitters
Champagne, chilled

Place sugar cube in champagne flute. Add Scotch and bitters, and fill with Champagne.

SCOTCH SOUR

1½ oz. Whisky (Scotch)
½ oz. Lime Juice
½ tsp. Superfine Sugar (or Simple Syrup)

Shake with ice and strain into chilled sour glass. Garnish with a half-slice of lemon and a maraschino cherry.

SCOTCH STINGER

½ oz. Crème de Menthe (White)
1½ oz. Whisky (Scotch)

Shake with ice and strain into chilled cocktail glass.

SCOTTISH GUARD

1½ oz. Whiskey (Bourbon)
½ oz. Lemon Juice
½ oz. Orange Juice
1 tsp. Grenadine

Shake with ice and strain into chilled cocktail glass.

SEABOARD

1 oz. Whiskey
1 oz. Gin
1 tbsp. Lemon Juice
1 tsp. Superfine Sugar (or Simple Syrup)

Shake with ice and strain into ice-filled old-fashioned glass. Garnish with mint leaves.

THE SEELBACH COCKTAIL

¾ oz. Whiskey (Bourbon)
½ oz. Triple Sec
7 dashes Angostura Bitters
7 dashes Peychaud's Bitters
4 oz. Champagne, chilled

Build, in the order given, in champagne flute. Garnish with a twist of orange peel.

SHAMROCK

1½ oz. Whiskey (Irish)
½ oz. Dry Vermouth
1 tsp. Crème de Menthe (Green)

Stir with ice and strain into chilled cocktail glass. Garnish with an olive.

THE SHOOT

1 oz. Whisky (Scotch)
1 oz. Dry Sherry
1 tsp. Orange Juice
1 tsp. Lemon Juice
½ tsp. Superfine Sugar (or Simple Syrup)

Shake with ice and strain into chilled cocktail glass.

WHISKIES

SHRUFFS END

1 oz. Whisky (Islay Single
   Malt Scotch)
1 oz. Apple Brandy
½ oz. Bénédictine
2 dashes Peychaud's Bitters

Stir with ice and strain into
chilled old-fashioned glass.

SILENT THIRD

1 oz. Triple Sec
2 oz. Whisky (Scotch)
1 oz. Lemon Juice

Shake with ice and strain
into chilled cocktail glass.

SILVER LINING

1½ oz. Whiskey (Straight
   Rye)
¾ oz. Lemon Juice
¾ oz. Licor 43
1 Egg White
Club Soda

Shake first four ingredients
without ice. Then shake with
ice and strain into ice-filled
Collins glass. Top with club
soda.

THE SLOPE

2 oz. Whiskey (Straight Rye)
¾ oz. Punt y Mes
½ oz. Apricot Liqueur
2 dashes Angostura Bitters

Stir with ice and strain into
chilled cocktail glass. Garnish with a cherry.

SOUTHERN BELLE

1¼ oz. Whiskey (Tennessee)
8 oz. Pineapple Juice
¼ oz. Triple Sec
2 oz. Orange Juice
1 splash Grenadine

Combine whiskey, Triple Sec,
and juices in ice-filled Collins
glass. Top with grenadine
and stir once.

SOUTHERN LADY

2 oz. Whiskey (Bourbon)
1 oz. Whiskey (Tennessee
   Sour Mash)
1 oz. Crème de Noyaux
3 oz. Pineapple Juice
2 oz. Lemon-lime Soda
1 oz. Lime Juice

Shake first four ingredi-
ents with ice and strain into
parfait or hurricane glass
half-filled with ice. Fill with
soda to within 1 inch of top
of glass and top with lime
juice. Garnish with a pineapple wheel and a mara-
schino cherry.

SOUTHERN PEACH

⅛ oz. Grenadine
1½ oz. Whiskey (Bourbon)
2 oz. Orange Juice
1 oz. Superfine Sugar
(or Simple Syrup)
1 oz. Lemon Juice
1 oz. Peach Schnapps

Fill parfait or hurricane glass with ice. Pour grenadine over ice; add bourbon. Shake remaining ingredients with ice and pour slowly into glass. Garnish with a peach slice.

STILETTO

1 oz. Lemon Juice
1½ tsps. Amaretto
1½ oz. Whiskey (Bourbon)

Pour into ice-filled old-fashioned glass and stir.

STONE FENCE

2 oz. Whisky (Scotch)
2 dashes Bitters
Club Soda or Cider

Pour Scotch and bitters into ice-filled highball glass. Fill with club soda or cider. Stir.

STRAIGHT RYE WITCH

2 oz. Whiskey (Straight Rye)
¼ oz. Strega
¼ oz. Palo Cortado Sherry
¼ oz. Simple Syrup
2 dashes Orange Bitters

Stir with ice and strain into chilled old-fashioned glass. Garnish with an orange twist.

SWISS FAMILY COCKTAIL

½ tsp. Anisette
2 dashes Bitters
¾ oz. Dry Vermouth
1½ oz. Whiskey

Stir with ice and strain into chilled cocktail glass.

T-BIRD

1⅛ oz. Whisky (Canadian)
¾ oz. Amaretto
2 oz. Pineapple Juice
1 oz. Orange Juice
2 dashes Grenadine

Shake with ice and strain into ice-filled highball glass. Garnish with an orange slice and a maraschino cherry. Serve with a straw.

T.N.T.

1½ oz. Whiskey (Rye or Bourbon)
1½ oz. Anisette

Shake with ice and strain into chilled cocktail glass.

THISTLE COCKTAIL

1½ oz. Sweet Vermouth
1½ oz. Whisky (Scotch)
2 dashes Bitters

Stir with ice and strain into chilled cocktail glass.

WHISKIES

THOROUGHBRED COOLER

1 oz. Whiskey (Bourbon)
½ oz. Superfine Sugar
(or Simple Syrup)
½ oz. Lemon Juice
1 oz. Orange Juice
Lemon-lime Soda
1 dash Grenadine

Pour first four ingredients over ice in highball glass. Fill with lemon-lime soda and stir. Add grenadine. Garnish with an orange wedge.

TIPPERARY COCKTAIL

¾ oz. Whiskey (Irish)
¾ oz. Chartreuse (Green)
¾ oz. Sweet Vermouth

Stir with ice and strain into chilled cocktail glass.

TOMBSTONE

2 oz. Whiskey (Straight Rye)
½ oz. Demerara Syrup
2 dashes Angostura Bitters

Shake with ice and strain into chilled cocktail glass. Garnish with a lemon twist.

TRILBY COCKTAIL

1½ oz. Whiskey (Bourbon)
¾ oz. Sweet Vermouth
2 dashes Orange Bitters

Stir with ice and strain into chilled cocktail glass.

TWIN HILLS

1½ oz. Whiskey
2 tsps. Bénédictine
1½ tsps. Lemon Juice
1½ tsps. Lime Juice
1 tsp. Sugar

Shake with ice and strain into sour glass. Garnish with a slice of lime and a slice of lemon.

VAGABOND

1½ oz. Whisky (Single Malt Scotch)
¾ oz. Punt y Mes
¾ oz. Sauternes

Stir with ice and strain into chilled cocktail glass. Garnish with an orange twist.

VERRAZANO

2 oz. Whiskey (Bourbon)
1 oz. Sweet Vermouth
¼ oz. Apricot Liqueur
1 splash Campari

Stir first three ingredients with ice and strain into chilled, Campari-rinsed cocktail glass. Garnish with an orange twist.

VIEUX CARRÉ

¾ oz. Whiskey (Rye)
¾ oz. Brandy
¾ oz. Sweet Vermouth
¼ oz. Bénédictine
1 dash Peychaud's Bitters
1 dash Angostura Bitters

Build, over ice, in old-fashioned glass.

WALTERS

1½ oz. Whisky (Scotch)
1 tbsp. Orange Juice
1 tbsp. Lemon Juice

Shake with ice and strain into chilled cocktail glass.

WARD EIGHT

¾ oz. Lemon Juice
1 tsp. Superfine Sugar (or Simple Syrup)
2 tsps. (scant) Grenadine
2 oz. Whiskey (Rye)

Shake with ice and strain into red-wine glass filled with ice. Garnish with slices of orange, lemon, and a maraschino cherry. Serve with straws.

WASHINGTON APPLE

2 oz. Black Velvet Reserve Canadian Whisky
2 oz. Sour Apple Schnapps
2 oz. Cranberry Juice

Pour into ice-filled highball glass and stir.

WEESKI

2 oz. Whiskey (Irish)
1 oz. Lillet Blanc
¼ oz. Triple Sec
2 dashes Orange Bitters

Stir with ice and strain into chilled cocktail glass. Garnish with an orange twist.

WHISKEY COBBLER

1 tsp. Superfine Sugar (or Simple Syrup)
2 oz. Club Soda
2 oz. Whiskey

Dissolve sugar/syrup in club soda in red-wine glass. Fill with shaved ice and add whiskey. Stir and garnish with seasonal fruit. Serve with a straw.

WHISKEY COCKTAIL

1 dash Bitters
1 tsp. Superfine Sugar (or Simple Syrup)
2 oz. Whiskey

Stir with ice and strain into chilled cocktail glass. Garnish with a maraschino cherry.

WHISKEY COLLINS

1 oz. Lemon Juice
1 tsp. Superfine Sugar (or Simple Syrup)
2 oz. Whiskey
Club Soda

Shake lemon juice, sugar/syrup, and whiskey with ice and strain into chilled Collins glass. Add several ice cubes, fill with club soda, and stir. Garnish with slices of lemon and orange and a maraschino cherry. Serve with a straw.

WHISKIES

WHISKEY DAISY

1 oz. Lemon Juice
½ tsp. Superfine Sugar
  (or Simple Syrup)
1 tsp. Grenadine
2 oz. Whiskey

Shake with ice and strain into chilled beer mug or metal cup. Add 1 ice cube and garnish with fruit.

WHISKEY FIX

1 oz. Lemon Juice
1 tsp. Superfine Sugar
  (or Simple Syrup)
2½ oz. Whiskey

Shake juice and sugar/syrup with ice and strain into chilled highball glass. Fill glass with ice and whiskey. Stir. Garnish with a slice of lemon. Serve with straws.

WHISKEY HIGHBALL

2 oz. Whiskey
Ginger Ale or Club Soda

Pour whiskey into ice-filled highball glass. Fill with ginger ale or club soda. Garnish with a twist of lemon peel and stir.

WHISKEY ORANGE

2 oz. Orange Juice
1 tsp. Superfine Sugar
  (or Simple Syrup)
½ tsp. Anisette
1½ oz. Whiskey

Shake with ice and strain into ice-filled highball glass. Garnish with slices of orange and lemon.

WHISKEY RICKEY

½ oz. Lime Juice
1½ oz. Whiskey
Club Soda

Pour lime juice and whiskey into highball glass over ice cubes and fill with club soda. Stir. Drop lime rind into glass.

WHISKEY SANGAREE

½ tsp. Superfine Sugar
  (or Simple Syrup)
1 tsp. Water
2 oz. Whiskey
1 splash Club Soda
1 tbsp. Port

Dissolve sugar/syrup in water in old-fashioned glass. Add whiskey, ice cubes, and club soda. Stir and then float port on top. Garnish with fresh-grated nutmeg on top.

WHISKEY SLING

1 tsp. Superfine Sugar
  (or Simple Syrup)
1 tsp. Water
1 oz. Lemon Juice
2 oz. Whiskey

In old-fashioned glass dissolve sugar/syrup in water and lemon juice. Add ice cubes and whiskey. Stir. Garnish with a twist of lemon peel.

WHISKEY SMASH

1 cube Sugar

1 oz. Club Soda

4 sprigs Mint

2 oz. Whiskey (Bourbon)

Muddle sugar with club soda and mint in old-fashioned glass. Add whiskey and then ice cubes. Stir. Garnish with a slice of orange, a maraschino cherry, and a twist of lemon peel.

WHISKEY SOUR

1 oz. Lemon Juice

½ tsp. Superfine Sugar (or Simple Syrup)

2 oz. Whiskey

Shake with ice and strain into chilled sour glass. Garnish with a half-slice of lemon and a maraschino cherry.

WHISKEY SQUIRT

1½ oz. Whiskey

1 tbsp. Superfine Sugar (or Simple Syrup)

1 tbsp. Grenadine

Club Soda

Shake first three ingredients with ice and strain into chilled highball glass. Fill with club soda and ice cubes. Garnish with cubes of pineapple and strawberries.

WHISKEY SWIZZLE

1 oz. Lime Juice

1 tsp. Superfine Sugar (or Simple Syrup)

2 oz. Club Soda

2 dashes Bitters

2 oz. Whiskey

Put lime juice, sugar/syrup, and club soda into Collins glass. Fill glass with ice and stir. Add bitters and whiskey. Fill with club soda and serve with a swizzle stick.

WHISPERS-OF-THE-FROST COCKTAIL

¾ oz. Whiskey (Bourbon)

¾ oz. Cream Sherry

¾ oz. Port

1 tsp. Superfine Sugar (or Simple Syrup)

Stir with ice and strain into chilled cocktail glass. Garnish with slices of lemon and orange.

WHITE PLUSH

2 oz. Whiskey

1 cup Milk

1 tsp. Superfine Sugar (or Simple Syrup)

Shake with ice and strain into chilled Collins glass.

☿ WHOA, NELLIE!

1½ oz. Whiskey (Straight Rye)

¾ oz. Dark Rum

½ oz. Lemon Juice

½ oz. Grapefruit Juice

½ oz. Simple Syrup

Shake with ice and strain into chilled cocktail glass. Garnish with a grapefruit twist.

☿ WOODWARD COCKTAIL

1½ oz. Whisky (Scotch)

½ oz. Dry Vermouth

1 tbsp. Grapefruit Juice

Shake with ice and strain into chilled cocktail glass.

☿ WOOLWORTH

2 oz. Whisky (Blended Scotch)

1 oz. Palo Cortado Sherry

½ oz. Bénédictine

2 dashes Orange Bitters

Stir with ice and strain into chilled cocktail glass.

CORDIALS AND LIQUEURS

CORDIALS AND LIQUEURS have been around since the Middle Ages, when they were concocted in European monasteries primarily for medicinal purposes. The historical distinction between cordials (fruit based) and liqueurs (herb based) doesn't really exist anymore, as the terms are often grouped together—though the word *liqueur* is typically used for both. In Europe, liqueurs and cordials have long been savored as after-dinner drinks, while Americans have tended to enjoy them mixed with other ingredients.

Liqueurs by today's definition are flavored spirits with between 2.5 percent and 40 percent sweetener, which can come from just about anything, including fruits, herbs, roots, spices, and nuts. The alcohol base used to make liqueurs is produced from grain, grapes, other fruits, or vegetables, and must be flavored in one of four ways: distillation, infusion, maceration, or percolation.

Liqueurs, however, should never be confused with fruit brandies, which are distilled from a mash of the fruit itself. Be aware that some producers mislabel their liqueurs as brandies, such as "blackberry brandy," when they are technically cordials (or liqueurs). Artificial colors are permitted in liqueurs, and some lesser brands use artificial flavors.

The best liqueurs come from all over the globe, and many have closely guarded secret recipes and processes, as well as their own proprietary brand names. Some of the most popular include amaretto (almond flavored, made from apricot pits); crème de cacao (cacao and vanilla beans); crème de cassis (black currants); curaçao (made from dried orange peel); sambuca (licorice-flavored, made from the elderberry bush's white flowers); sloe gin (sloe berries, from the blackthorn bush); and Triple Sec (orange-flavored form of curaçao).

ABSINTHE SPECIAL COCKTAIL

1½ oz. Anisette

1 oz. Water

¼ tsp. Superfine Sugar (or Simple Syrup)

1 dash Orange Bitters

Shake with ice and strain into chilled cocktail glass.

AMARETTO AND CREAM

1½ oz. Amaretto

1½ oz. Light Cream

Shake with ice and strain into chilled cocktail glass.

AMARETTO MIST

1½ oz. Amaretto

Serve in old-fashioned glass over crushed ice. Garnish with a twist of lemon or a wedge of lime.

AMARETTO ROSE

1½ oz. Amaretto

½ oz. Lemon Juice

1 tsp. Superfine Sugar (or Simple Syrup)

Club Soda

Pour first three ingredients into ice-filled Collins glass and fill with club soda. Stir and serve.

AMARETTO SOUR

1½ oz. Amaretto

¾ oz. Lemon Juice

Shake with ice and strain into chilled sour glass. Garnish with a slice of orange.

AMARETTO STINGER

1½ oz. Amaretto

¾ oz. Crème de Menthe (White)

Shake with ice and strain into chilled cocktail glass.

AMBER AMOUR

1½ oz. Amaretto

¼ oz. Superfine Sugar (or Simple Syrup)

¼ oz. Lemon Juice

Club Soda

Pour amaretto, sugar/syrup, and lemon juice into ice-filled Collins glass. Top with club soda and stir. Garnish with a maraschino cherry.

AMORE-ADE

1¼ oz. Amaretto

¾ oz. Triple Sec

3 oz. Club Soda

Combine all ingredients in oversized red-wine glass. Add ice and garnish with a lemon wedge.

☐ APPLE PIE

3 oz. Apple Schnapps

1 splash Cinnamon Schnapps

Pour into ice-filled old-fashioned glass and garnish with an apple slice and a sprinkle of cinnamon.

♟ ARISE MY LOVE

1 tsp. Crème de Menthe (Green)

Champagne, chilled

Put Crème de Menthe into champagne flute. Fill with Champagne.

☐ BANSHEE

1 oz. Crème de Banana

½ oz. Crème de Cacao (White)

½ oz. Light Cream

Shake with ice and strain into chilled cocktail glass.

☐ BLACKJACK

1 oz. Cherry-flavored Brandy

½ oz. Brandy

1 oz. Coffee

Shake with ice and strain into ice-filled old-fashioned glass.

☐ BLACKTHORN

1½ oz. Sloe Gin

1 oz. Sweet Vermouth

Stir with ice and strain into chilled cocktail glass. Garnish with a twist of lemon peel.

☐ BLANCHE

1 oz. Anisette

1 oz. Triple Sec

½ oz. Curaçao (White)

Shake with ice and strain into chilled cocktail glass.

☐ BOCCIE BALL

1½ oz. Amaretto

1½ oz. Orange Juice

2 oz. Club Soda

Serve in ice-filled highball glass.

☐ BOSTON ICED COFFEE

6 oz. Coffee (cooled)

1 oz. Crème de Menthe (White)

1 oz. Crème de Cacao (White)

1 oz. Brandy

Pour into ice-filled highball glass and stir. Garnish with a twist of lemon peel.

BURNING SUN

1½ oz. Strawberry Schnapps
4 oz. Pineapple Juice

Pour into ice-filled highball glass and stir. Garnish with a fresh strawberry.

BUSHWACKER

½ oz. Coffee Liqueur
½ oz. Amaretto
½ oz. Light Rum
½ oz. Irish Cream Liqueur
2 oz. Light Cream

Blend and pour into ice-filled old-fashioned glass.

CAFÉ CABANA

1 oz. Coffee Liqueur
3 oz. Club Soda

Pour into ice-filled Collins glass. Stir. Garnish with a lime wedge.

CHOCOLATE-COVERED STRAWBERRY

1 oz. Strawberry Schnapps
¼ oz. Crème de Cacao (White)
½ oz. Cream

Stir with ice and serve over ice in red-wine glass. Garnish with a fresh strawberry.

CRÈME DE MENTHE FRAPPÉ

2 oz. Crème de Menthe (Green)

Fill cocktail glass up to brim with shaved ice. Add Crème de Menthe. Serve with two short straws.

DEPTH CHARGE

Add a shot of any flavor of schnapps to a glass of beer.

DIANA COCKTAIL

Crème de Menthe (White)
Brandy

Fill cocktail glass with ice, then fill ¾ full with Crème de Menthe and float brandy on top.

DUCHESS

1½ oz. Anisette
½ oz. Dry Vermouth
½ oz. Sweet Vermouth

Shake with ice and strain into chilled cocktail glass.

FERRARI

1 oz. Amaretto
2 oz. Dry Vermouth

Mix in ice-filled old-fashioned glass. Garnish with a twist of lemon peel.

FRENCH CONNECTION

1½ oz. Cognac
¾ oz. Amaretto

Serve in ice-filled old-fashioned glass.

FRENCH FANTASY

1 oz. Black Raspberry Liqueur

1 oz. Mandarine Napoléon

2 oz. Cranberry Juice

2 oz. Orange Juice

Pour into ice-filled highball glass and stir. Garnish with an orange slice and a maraschino cherry.

FUZZY NAVEL

3 oz. 48-proof Peach Schnapps

3 oz. Orange Juice

Combine schnapps and orange juice and pour over ice in highball glass. Garnish with an orange slice.

GOLDEN CADILLAC

1 oz. Galliano

2 oz. Crème de Cacao (White)

1 oz. Light Cream

Combine with ½ cup of crushed ice in blender on low speed for 10 seconds. Strain into chilled champagne flute.

GOLDEN DREAM

1 tbsp. Orange Juice

½ oz. Triple Sec

1 oz. Galliano

1 tbsp. Light Cream

Shake with ice and strain into chilled cocktail glass.

GOOBER

1½ oz. Vodka

1½ oz. Black Raspberry Liqueur

1½ oz. Melon Liqueur

1 oz. Triple Sec

1 oz. Grenadine

3 oz. Pineapple Juice

4 oz. Orange Juice

Shake with ice and strain into ice-filled Collins glass. Garnish with an orange slice and a maraschino cherry. Serve with a straw.

GRASSHOPPER

¼ oz. Crème de Menthe (Green)

¼ oz. Crème de Cacao (White)

¼ oz. Light Cream

Shake with ice and strain into chilled cocktail glass.

HEAT WAVE

1¼ oz. Coconut-flavored Rum

½ oz. Peach Schnapps

3 oz. Pineapple Juice

3 oz. Orange Juice

½ oz. Grenadine

Pour first four ingredients into ice-filled hurricane or parfait glass. Top with grenadine. Garnish with a fresh peach slice.

ITALIAN SOMBRERO

1½ oz. Amaretto

3 oz. Light Cream

Put ingredients in blender or shake well. Serve over ice or straight up in champagne flute.

ITALIAN SURFER

1 oz. Amaretto

1 oz. Brandy

Pineapple Juice

Fill a Collins glass with ice. Add amaretto and brandy. Fill with pineapple juice. Garnish with a pineapple spear and a maraschino cherry.

JOHNNIE COCKTAIL

¾ oz. Triple Sec

1½ oz. Sloe Gin

1 tsp. Anisette

Shake with ice and strain into chilled cocktail glass.

LIMONCELLO SUNRISE

1 oz. Caravella Limoncello

3 oz. Orange Juice

1 dash Grenadine

Stir limoncello and orange juice with ice and strain into chilled old-fashioned glass. Top with a dash of grenadine.

LOVER'S KISS

½ oz. Amaretto

½ oz. Cherry-flavored Brandy

½ oz. Crème de Cacao (Brown)

1 oz. Cream

Shake with ice and strain into parfait glass. Top with whipped cream. Sprinkle with chocolate shavings and top with a maraschino cherry.

MARMALADE

1½ oz. Curaçao

Tonic Water

Pour Curaçao into ice-filled highball glass and fill with tonic water. Garnish with an orange slice.

McCLELLAND COCKTAIL

¾ oz. Triple Sec

1½ oz. Sloe Gin

1 dash Orange Bitters

Shake with ice and strain into chilled cocktail glass.

MELON COOLER

1 oz. Melon Liqueur

½ oz. Peach Schnapps

½ oz. Raspberry Schnapps

2 oz. Pineapple Juice

Shake with ice and pour into chilled margarita or cocktail glass. Garnish with a lime wheel and a maraschino cherry.

▢ MINT HIGHBALL

2 oz. Crème de Menthe (Green)

Ginger Ale or Club Soda

Pour crème de menthe into highball glass over ice cubes and fill with ginger ale or club soda. Stir. Garnish with a twist of lemon peel.

▢ MINT ON ROCKS

2 oz. Crème de Menthe (Green)

Pour over ice cubes in old-fashioned glass.

▽ MOULIN ROUGE

1½ oz. Sloe Gin

¾ oz. Sweet Vermouth

1 dash Bitters

Stir with ice and strain into chilled cocktail glass.

▽ PANAMA COCKTAIL

1 oz. Crème de Cacao (White)

1 oz. Light Cream

1 oz. Brandy

Shake with ice and strain into chilled cocktail glass.

▢ PEACH MELBA

1 oz. Peach Schnapps

½ oz. Black Raspberry Liqueur

3 oz. Cream

Shake with ice and pour into old-fashioned glass. Garnish with a peach slice. Serve with a short straw.

▢ PEPPERMINT ICEBERG

2 oz. Peppermint Schnapps

Pour into ice-filled old-fashioned glass. Stir and serve with a peppermint candy swizzle stick.

▽ PEPPERMINT STICK

1 oz. Peppermint Schnapps

1½ oz. Crème de Cacao (White)

1 oz. Light Cream

Shake with ice and strain into chilled champagne flute.

▢ PEPPERMINT TWIST

1½ oz. Peppermint Schnapps

½ oz. Crème de Cacao (White)

3 scoops Vanilla Ice Cream

Blend and pour into large parfait glass. Garnish with a mint sprig and a peppermint candy stick. Serve with a straw.

▽ PINK SQUIRREL

1 oz. Crème de Noyaux

1 tbsp. Crème de Cacao (White)

1 tbsp. Light Cream

Shake with ice and strain into chilled cocktail glass.

🍸 PORT AND STARBOARD

1 tbsp. Grenadine
½ oz. Crème de Menthe
(Green)

Pour carefully into pousse café glass, so that crème de menthe floats on grenadine.

🍸 POUSSE CAFÉ

EQUAL PARTS:

Grenadine
Chartreuse (Yellow)
Crème de Cassis
Crème de Menthe (White)
Chartreuse (Green)
Brandy

Pour carefully, in order given, into pousse café glass so that each ingredient floats on preceding one.

🍸 QUAALUDE

1 oz. Vodka
1 oz. Hazelnut Liqueur
1 oz. Coffee Liqueur
1 splash Milk

Pour into ice-filled old-fashioned glass.

🍸 RASPBERRY ROMANCE

¾ oz. Coffee Liqueur
¾ oz. Black Raspberry Liqueur
1¼ oz. Irish Cream Liqueur
Club Soda

Pour liqueurs into ice-filled parfait glass. Fill with club soda and stir.

🍸 RITZ FIZZ

Champagne, chilled
1 dash Lemon Juice
1 dash Blue Curaçao
1 dash Amaretto

Fill flute with Champagne. Add remaining ingredients and stir. Garnish with a twist of lemon peel.

🍸 ROAD RUNNER

1 oz. Vodka
½ oz. Amaretto
½ oz. Coconut Cream

Combine in blender with half-scoop of crushed ice for 15 seconds. Rim edge of chilled champagne flute with a slice of orange. Dip rim in a sugar and nutmeg mixture. Pour cocktail into the prepared glass. Garnish with fresh-grated nutmeg on top.

🍸 ROCKY MOUNTAIN COOLER

1½ oz. Peach Schnapps
4 oz. Pineapple Juice
2 oz. Lemon-lime Soda

Pour into ice-filled Collins glass and stir.

🍸 ST. PATRICK'S DAY

¼ oz. Crème de Menthe (Green)
¾ oz. Chartreuse (Green)
¾ oz. Irish Whiskey
1 dash Bitters

Stir with ice and strain into chilled cocktail glass.

SAMBUCA STRAIGHT

2 oz. Sambuca
3 Coffee Beans

Pour sambuca into snifter and float coffee beans on top.

SAN FRANCISCO COCKTAIL

¾ oz. Sloe Gin
¾ oz. Sweet Vermouth
¾ oz. Dry Vermouth
1 dash Bitters
1 dash Orange Bitters

Shake with ice and strain into chilled cocktail glass. Garnish with a maraschino cherry.

SANTINI'S POUSSE CAFÉ

½ oz. Brandy
1 tbsp. Maraschino Liqueur
½ oz. Triple Sec
½ oz. Rum

Pour in order given into pousse café glass.

SHEER ELEGANCE

1½ oz. Amaretto
1½ oz. Black Raspberry Liqueur
½ oz. Vodka

Shake with ice and strain into chilled cocktail glass.

SLOEBERRY COCKTAIL

1 dash Bitters
2 oz. Sloe Gin

Stir with ice and strain into chilled cocktail glass.

SLOE DRIVER

1½ oz. Sloe Gin
5 oz. Orange Juice

Pour ingredients into ice-filled highball glass and stir.

SLOE GIN COCKTAIL

2 oz. Sloe Gin
1 dash Orange Bitters
¼ oz. Dry Vermouth

Stir with ice and strain into chilled cocktail glass.

Three and Only Three

No more than three olives or onions in a Martini. Place extras on the side in a garnish dish. This is just common sense; the drink looks goofy chock full of olives or onions.

—DALE DEGROFF (a.k.a. King Cocktail), author of The Craft of the Cocktail

CORDIALS & LIQUEURS

SLOE GIN COLLINS
1 oz. Lemon Juice
2 oz. Sloe Gin
Club Soda

Shake lemon juice and sloe gin with ice and strain into chilled Collins glass. Add several ice cubes, fill with club soda, and stir. Garnish with slices of lemon and orange and a maraschino cherry. Serve with straws.

SLOE GIN FIZZ
1 oz. Lemon Juice
1 tsp. Superfine Sugar (or Simple Syrup)
2 oz. Sloe Gin
Club Soda

Shake lemon juice, sugar/syrup, and sloe gin with ice and strain into chilled highball glass with two ice cubes. Fill with club soda and stir. Garnish with a slice of lemon.

SLOE GIN RICKEY
½ oz. Lime Juice
2 oz. Sloe Gin
Club Soda

Pour into highball glass over ice cubes. Stir. Drop a lime rind into glass.

SLOE VERMOUTH
1 oz. Sloe Gin
1 oz. Dry Vermouth
1 tbsp. Lemon Juice

Shake with ice and strain into chilled cocktail glass.

SOMETHING DIFFERENT
1 oz. Peach Schnapps
1 oz. Amaretto
2 oz. Pineapple Juice
2 oz. Cranberry Juice

Shake with ice and pour into ice-filled highball glass.

STRAWBERRY FIELDS FOREVER
2 oz. Strawberry Schnapps
½ oz. Brandy
Club Soda

Pour schnapps and brandy into ice-filled highball glass. Fill with club soda. Garnish with a fresh strawberry.

STRAWBERRY SUNRISE
2 oz. Strawberry Schnapps
½ oz. Grenadine
Orange Juice

Pour schnapps and grenadine into ice-filled highball glass. Fill with orange juice. Garnish with a fresh strawberry.

SUN KISS

2 oz. Amaretto

4 oz. Orange Juice

Combine amaretto and orange juice in ice-filled Collins glass. Garnish with a lime wedge.

THUNDER CLOUD

½ oz. Crème de Noyaux

½ oz. Blue Curaçao

½ oz. Amaretto

¼ oz. Vodka

1 oz. Superfine Sugar (or Simple Syrup)

1 oz. Lemon Juice

1 oz. Lemon-lime Soda

Layer ingredients in ice-filled hurricane or parfait glass in order given. Whirl gently with a large straw.

TIKKI DREAM

¾ oz. Melon Liqueur

4¼ oz. Cranberry Juice

Pour into ice-filled, sugar-rimmed highball glass. Garnish with a wedge of watermelon.

TOASTED ALMOND

1½ oz. Coffee Liqueur

1 oz. Amaretto

1½ oz. Cream or Milk

Add all ingredients in ice-filled old-fashioned glass. Stir.

TROPICAL COCKTAIL

¾ oz. Crème de Cacao (White)

¾ oz. Maraschino Liqueur

¾ oz. Dry Vermouth

1 dash Bitters

Stir with ice and strain into chilled cocktail glass.

TWIN PEACH

2 oz. Peach Schnapps

Cranberry Juice

Pour schnapps into ice-filled highball glass, fill with cranberry juice, and stir. Garnish with an orange or peach slice.

WATERMELON

1 oz. Strawberry Liqueur

1 oz. Vodka

½ oz. Superfine Sugar (or Simple Syrup)

½ oz. Lemon Juice

1 oz. Orange Juice

Pour into ice-filled Collins glass. Garnish with an orange slice and serve with a straw.

Y YELLOW PARROT COCKTAIL

¾ oz. Anisette

¾ oz. Chartreuse (Yellow)

¾ oz. Apricot-flavored Brandy

Shake with ice and strain into chilled cocktail glass.

Y ZERO MIST

2 oz. Crème de Menthe

1 oz. Water

For each serving, chill liqueur and water in freezer compartment of refrigerator for 2 hours or longer (does not have to be frozen solid). Serve in cocktail glasses.

SHOOTERS

WHEN THIS BOOK DEBUTED 73 years ago, a "shot" was 2 ounces of straight whiskey knocked back in a single gulp—just like the scenes in those dusty old Westerns. Today, shots are called shooters, slammers, even tooters, usually preceded by fanciful names—B-52, Sex on the Beach, Kamikaze—and concocted with virtually any spirit and mixer handy in a well-stocked bar.

The universal appeal of shooters is partly attributable to the fact that many are fairly low in alcohol content. Frequently made with several juices, as well as lower-proof liqueurs, the small size of the shooter limits the amount of spirit contained in a single drink. Some, like the Rattlesnake, are skillfully layered works of art, similar to a Pousse Café. Others, like the Bloody Caesar, incorporate surprising ingredients such as clams or oysters.

The granddaddy of all shooters—a lick of salt, washed down with a shot of straight tequila, followed by a suck on a wedge of lime and the obligatory shudder—is not only still alive and kicking, it has inspired similar drinks like the Lemon Drop and the Cordless Screwdriver.

The common denominator for the drinks on the following pages is that they were created with a sense of humor and wit, which is how they should be enjoyed. Once you get the hang of making them, you can experiment with bumping up the recipes to make large batches for parties. You might also feel inspired to create your own, which is how every one of these recipes came to fruition. Imagination and creativity can create a great little drink.

♀ AFFAIR

1 oz. Strawberry Schnapps

1 oz. Cranberry Juice

1 oz. Orange Juice

Stir with ice and strain into chilled cordial glass.

▯ ALABAMA SLAMMER

1 oz. Amaretto

1 oz. Whiskey (Tennessee Sour Mash)

½ oz. Sloe Gin

1 splash Lemon Juice

Stir first three ingredients with ice and strain into chilled shot glass. Add lemon juice.

♀ ANGEL'S DELIGHT

1½ tsps. Grenadine

1½ tsps. Triple Sec

1½ tsps. Sloe Gin

1½ tsps. Light Cream

Into cordial glass pour carefully, in order given, so that each ingredient floats on preceding one without mixing.

♀ ANGEL'S KISS

¼ oz. Crème de Cacao (White)

¼ oz. Sloe Gin

¼ oz. Brandy

¼ oz. Light Cream

Into cordial glass pour carefully, in order given, so that each ingredient floats on preceding one without mixing.

♀ ANGEL'S TIP

¼ oz. Crème de Cacao (White)

¼ oz. Light Cream

Into cordial glass pour Crème de Cacao and then gently float cream on top. Garnish with a maraschino cherry on a cocktail pick across mouth of glass.

♀ ANGEL'S WING

½ oz. Crème de Cacao (White)

½ oz. Brandy

1 tbsp. Light Cream

Into cordial glass pour carefully, in order given, so that each ingredient floats on preceding one without mixing.

▯ B-52

½ oz. Coffee Liqueur

½ oz. Irish Cream Liqueur

½ oz. Mandarine Napoléon

Into shot glass pour carefully, in order given, so that each ingredient floats on preceding one without mixing.

▯ BANANA BOMBER

1 oz. 99 Bananas Flavored Schnapps

¾ oz. Triple Sec

1 splash Grenadine

Shake with ice and strain into chilled shot glass.

BANANA SLIP

1½ oz. Crème de Banana
1½ oz. Irish Cream Liqueur

Into cordial glass pour Crème de Banana and then gently float cream on top.

BETWEEN-THE-SHEETS

1 oz. Lemon Juice
½ oz. Brandy
½ oz. Triple Sec
½ oz. Light Rum

Shake with ice and strain into chilled shot glass.

BLOODY CAESAR SHOOTER

1 Littleneck Clam
1 oz. Vodka
2 drops Worcestershire Sauce
1½ oz. Tomato Juice
2 drops Tabasco Sauce
1 dash Horseradish Sauce
Celery Salt

Put clam in the bottom of a shot glass. Shake vodka, Worcestershire, tomato juice, Tabasco, and horseradish with ice, and strain into chilled shot glass. Sprinkle with celery salt and garnish with a lime wedge.

BLUE MARLIN

1 oz. Light Rum
½ oz. Blue Curaçao
1 oz. Lime Juice

Stir with ice and strain into chilled shot glass.

BONZAI PIPELINE

½ oz. Vodka
1 oz. Tropical Fruit Schnapps

Stir with ice and strain into chilled shot glass.

BUZZARD'S BREATH

½ oz. Amaretto
½ oz. Peppermint Schnapps
½ oz. Coffee Liqueur

Stir with ice and strain into chilled shot glass.

CAPRI

¾ oz. Crème de Cacao (White)
¾ oz. Crème de Banana
¾ oz. Light Cream

Shake with ice and strain into chilled cordial glass.

CARAMEL APPLE

1 oz. 99 Apples Flavored Schnapps
2 oz. Butterscotch Schnapps

Shake with ice and strain into chilled shot glass.

C.C. KAZI

1½ oz. Tequila
2 oz. Cranberry Juice
1 tsp. Lime Juice

Shake with ice and strain into chilled cordial glass.

CHARLIE CHAPLIN

1 oz. Sloe Gin

1 oz. Apricot-flavored Brandy

1 oz. Lemon Juice

Shake with ice and strain into chilled cordial glass.

CORDLESS SCREWDRIVER

1¾ oz. Vodka

Orange Wedge

Sugar

Chill vodka and strain into shot glass. Dip orange wedge in sugar. Shoot the vodka and immediately take a draw on the orange.

COSMOS

1½ oz. Vodka

½ oz. Lime Juice

Shake with ice and strain into chilled shot glass.

FIFTH AVENUE

½ oz. Crème de Cacao (Brown)

½ oz. Apricot-flavored Brandy

1 tbsp. Light Cream

Into cordial glass pour carefully, in order given, so that each ingredient floats on preceding one without mixing.

FLYING GRASSHOPPER

¾ oz. Crème de Menthe (Green)

¾ oz. Crème de Cacao (White)

¾ oz. Vodka

Stir with ice and strain into chilled cordial glass.

4TH OF JULY TOOTER

1 oz. Grenadine

1 oz. Vodka

1 oz. Blue Curaçao

Into cordial or shot glass pour carefully, in order given, so that each ingredient floats on preceding one without mixing.

FOXY LADY

1 oz. Amaretto

½ oz. Crème de Cacao (Brown)

1 oz. Heavy Cream

Shake with ice and strain into chilled cordial glass.

GALACTIC ALE

¾ oz. Vodka

¾ oz. Blue Curaçao

½ oz. Lime Juice

¼ oz. Black Raspberry Liqueur

Shake with ice and strain into chilled shot glass.

GREEN DEMON

½ oz. Vodka

½ oz. Rum

½ oz. Melon Liqueur

½ oz. Lemonade

Shake with ice and strain into chilled shot glass.

☐ INTERNATIONAL INCIDENT

¼ oz. Vodka
¼ oz. Coffee Liqueur
¼ oz. Amaretto
¼ oz. Hazelnut Liqueur
½ oz. Irish Cream Liqueur

Shake with ice and strain into chilled shot glass.

♢ IRISH CHARLIE

1 oz. Irish Cream Liqueur
1 oz. Crème de Menthe (White)

Stir with ice and strain into chilled cordial glass.

♢ IRISH FLAG

1 oz. Crème de Menthe (Green)
1 oz. Irish Cream Liqueur
1 oz. Mandarine Napoléon

Into cordial glass pour carefully, in order given, so that each ingredient floats on preceding one without mixing.

☐ JOHNNY ON THE BEACH

¾ oz. Vodka
½ oz. Melon Liqueur
½ oz. Black Raspberry Liqueur
¼ oz. Pineapple Juice
¼ oz. Orange Juice
¼ oz. Grapefruit Juice
¼ oz. Cranberry Juice

Stir with ice and strain into chilled shot glass.

☐ KAMIKAZE

½ oz. Lime Juice
½ oz. Triple Sec
½ oz. Vodka

Shake with ice and strain into chilled shot glass.

☐ LEMON DROP

1½ oz. Vodka
Lemon wedge
Sugar

Chill vodka and strain into chilled shot glass. Dip lemon wedge in sugar. Shoot the vodka and immediately take a draw on the lemon.

♢ MELON BALL

1 oz. Melon Liqueur
1 oz. Vodka
1 oz. Pineapple Juice

Shake with ice and strain into chilled cordial glass.

♢ MOCHA MINT

¾ oz. Coffee-flavored Brandy
¾ oz. Crème de Cacao (White)
¾ oz. Crème de Menthe (White)

Shake with ice and strain into chilled cordial glass.

MONKEY SHINE SHOOTER

½ oz. Bourbon Liqueur
½ oz. Crème de Banana
½ oz. Irish Cream Liqueur

Shake with ice and strain into chilled cordial glass.

NUTTY PROFESSOR

½ oz. Mandarine Napoléon
½ oz. Hazelnut Liqueur
½ oz. Irish Cream Liqueur

Stir and strain into shot glass.

OH MY GOSH

1 oz. Amaretto
1 oz. Peach Schnapps

Stir with ice and strain into chilled shot glass.

PARISIAN BLONDE

¾ oz. Light Rum
¾ oz. Triple Sec
¾ oz. Jamaican Rum

Shake with ice and strain into chilled cordial glass.

PEACH BUNNY

¾ oz. Peach-flavored Brandy
¾ oz. Crème de Cacao (White)
¾ oz. Light Cream

Shake with ice and strain into chilled cordial glass.

PEACH TART

1 oz. Peach Schnapps
½ oz. Lime Juice

Stir with ice and strain into chilled shot glass.

PEPPERMINT PATTIE

1 oz. Crème de Cacao (White)
1 oz. Crème de Menthe (White)

Shake with ice and strain into chilled cordial glass.

PIGSKIN SHOT

1 oz. Vodka
1 oz. Melon Liqueur
¼ oz. Superfine Sugar (or Simple Syrup)
¼ oz. Lemon Juice

Shake with ice and strain into chilled shot glass.

PINEAPPLE UPSIDE-DOWN CAKE

½ oz. Irish Cream Liqueur
½ oz. Vodka
½ oz. Butterscotch Schnapps
½ oz. Pineapple Juice

Stir and strain into shot glass.

PURPLE HOOTER

1½ oz. Citrus-flavored Vodka
½ oz. Triple Sec
¼ oz. Black Raspberry Liqueur

Shake with ice and strain into chilled shot glass.

♀ RATTLESNAKE

1 oz. Coffee Liqueur

1 oz. Crème de Cacao (White)

1 oz. Irish Cream Liqueur

Into cordial or shot glass pour carefully, in order given, so that each ingredient floats on preceding one without mixing.

▯ ROCKY MOUNTAIN

1 oz. Whiskey (Tennessee Sour Mash)

1 oz. Amaretto

½ oz. Lime Juice

Shake with ice and strain into chilled shot glass.

▯ SAMBUCA SLIDE

1 oz. Sambuca

½ oz. Vodka

½ oz. Light Cream

Stir with ice and strain into chilled shot glass.

♀ SCOOTER

1 oz. Amaretto

1 oz. Brandy

1 oz. Light Cream

Shake with cracked ice. Strain into chilled cordial glass.

♀ SEX ON THE BEACH

½ oz. Black Raspberry Liqueur

½ oz. Melon Liqueur

½ oz. Vodka

1 oz. Pineapple Juice

Cranberry Juice

Stir first four ingredients with ice and strain into chilled cordial or shot glass. Top with cranberry juice.

♀ SHAVETAIL

1½ oz. Peppermint Schnapps

1 oz. Pineapple Juice

1 oz. Light Cream

Shake with ice and strain into chilled cordial glass.

▯ SILVER SPIDER

½ oz. Vodka

½ oz. Rum

½ oz. Triple Sec

½ oz. Crème de Menthe (White)

Stir with ice and strain into chilled shot glass.

♀ SOUR APPLE

¼ oz. Vodka

¼ oz. Apple Liqueur

½ oz. Melon Liqueur

½ oz. Lemon-lime Soda

Shake and strain into cordial glass.

STALACTITE

1¼ oz. Sambuca
¼ oz. Irish Cream Liqueur
¼ oz. Black Raspberry
   Liqueur

Pour sambuca into cordial glass and then float Irish cream on top. Then carefully pour raspberry liqueur, drop by drop, as top layer. The raspberry liqueur will pull the Irish cream through the sambuca and settle on the bottom.

STARS AND STRIPES

⅓ oz. Grenadine
⅓ oz. Heavy Cream
⅓ oz. Blue Curaçao

Into cordial glass, pour carefully, in order given, so that each ingredient floats on preceding one without mixing.

TERMINATOR

½ oz. Coffee Liqueur
½ oz. Irish Cream Liqueur
½ oz. Sambuca
½ oz. Mandarine Napoléon
½ oz. Vodka

Into cordial glass pour carefully, in order given, so that each layer floats on preceding one without mixing.

TO THE MOON

½ oz. Coffee Liqueur
½ oz. Amaretto
½ oz. Irish Cream Liqueur
½ oz. 151-proof Rum

Stir with ice and strain into chilled shot glass.

TRAFFIC LIGHT

½ oz. Crème de Noyaux
½ oz. Galliano
½ oz. Melon Liqueur

Layer liqueurs in order given in cordial glass.

WOO WOO

½ oz. Peach Schnapps
½ oz. Vodka
1 oz. Cranberry Juice

Shake with ice and strain into chilled shot glass.

FROZEN DRINKS

FROZEN DRINKS ARE CERTAINLY PERFECT for summertime sipping, but they're also enjoyed year-round—much like ice cream. In fact, some are creamy concoctions made with ice cream. Others are tropical in nature, combining spirits or liqueurs with fruit juices, and blended with ice. Served in tall, generous glasses and garnished with an assortment of seasonal fruits, they're best sipped slowly—to prevent brain-freeze—through a straw.

Ice cream–based frozen drinks, often mixed with liqueurs such as crème de cacao, amaretto, or Irish cream and topped with whipped cream, also make delicious dessert substitutes. Just imagine sipping a strawberry shortcake or a raspberry cheesecake after a meal, and you sort of get the picture.

The most important ingredient to consider when planning to mix up frozen drinks is ice—and more than you think you could possibly need. Depending on the size and shape of the ice you use, it will melt differently when mixed with warm mixers and alcohol, and it will blend differently, too. And speaking of blending, having an electric blender to pulverize the ice will allow you to make professional-style smoothies at home. Otherwise, you'll need a hand-cranked crusher—or a mallet.

You'll find plenty of delicious recipes for every season in this section. Next time it's 90 degrees in the shade, you and your blender can quickly dispatch a Tidal Wave or a Maui Breeze to cool down. And when you have a hankering for a creamy treat any time of year, you'll find a recipe that will put you on cloud nine.

THE ALL-AMERICAN DAIQUIRI

BLUE LAYER

¾ oz. Light Rum or Vodka

¾ oz. Superfine Sugar (or Simple Syrup)

¾ oz. Lemon Juice

½ oz. Blueberry Flavoring

RED LAYER

¾ oz. Light Rum or Vodka

2 oz. Strawberry Daiquiri Mix

WHITE LAYER

Whipped Cream

For red and blue layers, combine ingredients in blender with 1 cup crushed ice and blend until very thick. Layer frozen colors—blue, red, and white—in parfait glass. Top with a maraschino cherry and an American flag frill pick.

APPLE COLADA

2 oz. Apple Schnapps

1 oz. Cream of Coconut

1 oz. Half-and-Half

Combine all ingredients with 1 cup crushed ice in blender until smooth. Pour into highball glass and serve with a straw. Garnish with an apple slice and a maraschino cherry.

APPLE GRANNY CRISP

1 oz. Apple Schnapps

½ oz. Brandy

½ oz. Irish Cream Liqueur

2 scoops Vanilla Ice Cream

Graham Cracker Crumbs

Combine all ingredients in blender until smooth. Pour into parfait glass and serve topped with whipped cream and cinnamon.

APPLE RIVER INNER TUBE

1 oz. Brandy

1 oz. Crème de Cacao (Brown)

1½ scoops Vanilla Ice Cream

Combine all ingredients with 1 cup crushed ice in blender until smooth. Pour into parfait glass. Garnish with half a spiced apple ring.

APRICOT CREAM SPRITZ

¾ cup Milk

½ cup Apricot Nectar

2 tbsps. Apricot-flavored Brandy

2 cups Sparkling Wine

Combine first three ingredients in blender with ¼ cup crushed ice until smooth. Pour equal amounts into 6 large red-wine glasses. Add about ⅓ cup sparkling wine to each glass. Stir gently. *Makes 6 servings.*

BANANA DAIQUIRI

1½ oz. Light Rum
1 tbsp. Triple Sec
1½ oz. Lime Juice
1 tsp. Sugar
1 Medium Banana, sliced

Combine all ingredients in blender with 1 cup crushed ice and blend until smooth. Pour into champagne flute. Garnish with a maraschino cherry.

BANANA DI AMORE

1 oz. Amaretto
1 oz. Crème de Banana
2 oz. Orange Juice
½ oz. Superfine Sugar (or Simple Syrup)
½ oz. Lemon Juice

Combine all ingredients with 1 cup crushed ice in blender until smooth. Serve in red-wine glass, garnished with orange and banana slices.

BANANA FOSTER

2 scoops Vanilla Ice Cream
1½ oz. Spiced Rum
½ oz. Banana Liqueur
1 Medium Banana, sliced

Combine all ingredients in blender until smooth. Pour into large brandy snifter and sprinkle with cinnamon.

BAY CITY BOMBER

½ oz. Vodka
½ oz. Rum
½ oz. Tequila
½ oz. Gin
½ oz. Triple Sec
1 oz. Orange Juice
1 oz. Pineapple Juice
1 oz. Cranberry Juice
½ oz. Superfine Sugar (or Simple Syrup)
½ oz. Lemon Juice
¼ oz. 151-proof Rum

Combine all ingredients except rum with 1 cup crushed ice in blender until smooth. Pour into parfait glass. Float rum on top. Garnish with a maraschino cherry and an orange slice.

BEACH BUM'S COOLER

1¼ oz. Irish Cream
¼ oz. Banana Liqueur
1½ oz. Piña Colada Mix
¾ oz. Light Rum
¼ Banana
2 scoops Vanilla Ice Cream
1 splash Cream

Combine all ingredients in blender until smooth. Pour into parfait glass and garnish with a pineapple slice and a paper umbrella.

FROZEN DRINKS

THE BIG CHILL

1½ oz. Dark Rum
1 oz. Pineapple Juice
1 oz. Orange Juice
1 oz. Cranberry Juice
1 oz. Cream of Coconut

Combine all ingredients in blender with 1 cup of crushed ice and blend until smooth. Pour into 12-oz. pilsner glass and garnish with a pineapple wedge and a maraschino cherry.

THE BLIZZARD

1 oz. Brandy
1 oz. Irish Cream Liqueur
1 oz. Coffee Liqueur
1 oz. Light Rum
2 scoops Vanilla Ice Cream
1 splash Light Cream

Combine all ingredients in blender until smooth. Pour into large snifter and garnish with fresh-grated nutmeg on top.

BLUE CLOUD COCKTAIL

1 oz. Amaretto
½ oz. Blue Curaçao
2 oz. Vanilla Ice Cream

Combine all ingredients in blender and blend until smooth. Pour into brandy snifter. Top with whipped cream and a maraschino cherry.

BLUE VELVET

1 oz. Black Raspberry Liqueur
1 oz. Melon Liqueur
4 oz. Vanilla Ice Cream
Blue Curaçao

Combine liqueurs and ice cream with 1 cup crushed ice in blender until smooth. Pour into parfait glass and top with whipped cream and drizzle with blue curaçao. Garnish with a maraschino cherry.

BLUSHIN' RUSSIAN

1 oz. Coffee Liqueur
¾ oz. Vodka
1 scoop Vanilla Ice Cream
4 Large Fresh Strawberries

Combine all ingredients in blender until smooth. Pour into parfait glass. Garnish with a chocolate-covered strawberry.

THE BRASS FIDDLE

2 oz. Peach Schnapps
¾ oz. Tennessee Whiskey
2 oz. Pineapple Juice
1 oz. Orange Juice
1 oz. Grenadine

Combine first four ingredients in blender with 1 cup ice and blend until smooth. Pour into parfait glass that has been swirled with grenadine. Garnish with a pineapple slice and a maraschino cherry.

Pretty in Pink

LEFT: Commodore Cocktail

ABOVE: Mint Julep

ABOVE: Limoncello Sunrise

RIGHT: Eastern Sour

LEFT: Coffee Nudge
ABOVE: Pimm's Cup

Champagne Punch

BUNKY PUNCH

1½ oz. Vodka

1 oz. Melon Liqueur

1 oz. Peach Schnapps

1½ oz. Cranberry Juice

2 oz. Orange Juice

½ oz. Grape Juice

Combine all ingredients with 1 cup crushed ice in blender until smooth. Pour into parfait glass and garnish with a slice of lime.

CANYON QUAKE

¾ oz. Irish Cream Liqueur

¾ oz. Brandy

1 oz. Amaretto

2 oz. Light Cream

Combine all ingredients with 1 cup crushed ice in blender until smooth. Pour into large snifter.

CAVANAUGH'S SPECIAL

1 oz. Coffee Liqueur

1 oz. Crème de Cacao (White)

1 oz. Amaretto

2 scoops Vanilla Ice Cream

In snifter, pour coffee liqueur and set aside. In blender, combine next three ingredients with 1 cup ice until smooth. Pour over coffee liqueur and top with whipped cream and chocolate sprinkles.

CHAMPAGNE CORNUCOPIA

1 oz. Cranberry Juice

2 scoops Rainbow Sherbet

1 oz. Vodka

¾ oz. Peach Schnapps

1 oz. Champagne

Pour cranberry juice into oversized red-wine glass. Combine sherbet, vodka, and schnapps in blender until smooth. Pour over cranberry juice to produce a swirl effect and layer Champagne on top. Garnish with an orange slice.

FROZEN DRINKS

CHERRY REPAIR KIT

½ oz. Half-and-Half

½ oz. Crème de Cacao (White)

½ oz. Amaretto

6 Maraschino Cherries

½ oz. Maraschino Liqueur

Combine all ingredients with 1 cup crushed ice in blender until smooth. Pour into parfait glass. Garnish with a maraschino cherry and serve with a straw.

CHI-CHI

1½ oz. Vodka

1 oz. Cream of Coconut

4 oz. Pineapple Juice

Combine all ingredients with 1 cup crushed ice in blender until smooth. Pour into red-wine glass. Garnish with a slice of pineapple and a maraschino cherry.

CHILLY IRISHMAN

3 oz. Cold Espresso
1 oz. Irish Whiskey
½ oz. Coffee Liqueur
½ oz. Irish Cream Liqueur
1 scoop Vanilla Ice Cream
1 dash Superfine Sugar (or Simple Syrup)

Combine all ingredients in blender with 4 cups of crushed ice and blend until smooth. Pour into parfait glass. Garnish with a 3- or 4-leaf clover.

CHOCO-BANANA SMASH

1¼ oz. Irish Cream Liqueur
¼ oz. Vanilla Extract
½ oz. Light Cream
½ scoop Vanilla Ice Cream
½ Medium Banana, sliced

Combine all ingredients with 1 cup crushed ice in blender until smooth. Pour into parfait glass. Garnish with a maraschino cherry and 1-inch banana slice on a cocktail pick. Top with whipped cream and chocolate sprinkles.

CHOCOLATE ALMOND CREAM

1 qt. Vanilla Ice Cream
½ cup Amaretto
½ cup Crème de Cacao (White)

Combine all ingredients in blender until smooth. Pour into parfait glasses. Garnish with shaved chocolate. *Makes 4 to 6 servings.*

CITRUS BANANA FLIP

1 Medium Banana, cut in pieces
10 oz. Club Soda
⅔ cup Orange Juice Concentrate
⅔ cup Milk
½ cup Dark Rum
½ cup Lime Juice
3 tbsps. Brown Sugar

Combine all ingredients with 1 cup crushed ice in blender until smooth. Pour into Collins glasses. *Makes 4 to 6 servings.*

CLOUD 9

8 oz. Vanilla Ice Cream
1 oz. Irish Cream Liqueur
½ oz. Black Raspberry Liqueur
1 oz. Amaretto

Combine all ingredients in blender and blend until smooth. Pour into parfait glass. Top with whipped cream and a chocolate–peanut butter cup, split in half.

COOL OPERATOR

1 oz. Melon Liqueur
½ oz. Lime Juice
½ oz. Vodka
½ oz. Light Rum
4 oz. Grapefruit Juice
2 oz. Orange Juice

Combine all ingredients with 1 cup crushed ice in blender until smooth. Pour into parfait glass. Garnish with a melon wedge and a maraschino cherry.

CRANBERRY COOLER

1½ oz. Bourbon
1½ oz. Cranberry Juice
½ oz. Lime Juice
1 tsp. Sugar

Combine all ingredients with 1 cup crushed ice in blender until smooth. Pour into parfait glass.

CREAMY GIN SOUR

½ cup Gin
½ cup Lime Juice
½ cup Lemon Juice
½ cup Heavy Cream
¼ cup Triple Sec
1 tbsp. Sugar
10 oz. Club Soda

Combine all ingredients with 1 cup crushed ice in blender until smooth. Pour into large red-wine glasses. *Makes 4 to 6 servings.*

DEATH BY CHOCOLATE

1 oz. Irish Cream Liqueur
½ oz. Crème de Cacao (Brown)
½ oz. Vodka
1 scoop Chocolate Ice Cream

Combine all ingredients in blender with 1 cup of crushed ice and blend until smooth. Pour into parfait glass. Garnish with whipped cream and chocolate curls. Serve with a straw.

DEVIL'S TAIL

1½ oz. Light Rum
1 oz. Vodka
1 tbsp. Lime Juice
1½ tsps. Grenadine
1½ tsps. Apricot-flavored Brandy

Combine all ingredients in blender with 1 cup of crushed ice and blend until smooth. Pour into champagne flute. Add a twist of lime peel.

FROZEN DRINKS

DI AMORE DREAM

1½ oz. Amaretto di Amore
¾ oz. Crème de Cacao (White)
2 oz. Orange Juice
2 scoops Vanilla Ice Cream

Combine all ingredients in blender until smooth. Pour into parfait glass. Garnish with an orange slice.

DREAMY MONKEY

1 oz. Vodka
½ oz. Crème de Banana
½ oz. Crème de Cacao (Brown)
1 Banana
2 scoops Vanilla Ice Cream
1 oz. Light Cream

Combine all ingredients in blender (use half of the banana) and blend until smooth. Pour into parfait glass. Top with whipped cream and garnish with remaining banana half.

FROSTY NOGGIN

1½ oz. Rum
¾ oz. Crème de Menthe (White)
3 oz. Prepared Dairy Eggnog
3 cups Vanilla Ice Cream

Combine all ingredients in blender and blend until smooth. Pour into parfait glass. Top with whipped cream. Garnish with a few drops of green crème de menthe and a cookie.

FROZEN BERKELEY

1½ oz. Light Rum
½ oz. Brandy
1 tbsp. Passion Fruit Syrup
1 tbsp. Lemon Juice

Combine all ingredients in blender with 1 cup of crushed ice and blend until smooth. Pour into champagne flute.

FROZEN CAPPUCCINO

½ oz. Irish Cream Liqueur
½ oz. Coffee Liqueur
½ oz. Hazelnut Liqueur
1 scoop Vanilla Ice Cream
1 dash Light Cream

Combine all ingredients in blender with 1 cup of crushed ice and blend until smooth. Pour into cinnamon-sugar-rimmed parfait glass. Garnish with a cinnamon stick and a straw.

FROZEN CITRON NEON

1½ oz. Citrus-flavored Vodka
1 oz. Melon Liqueur
½ oz. Blue Curaçao
½ oz. Lime Juice
½ oz. Superfine Sugar (or Simple Syrup)
½ oz. Lemon Juice

Combine all ingredients in blender with 1 cup of crushed ice and blend until smooth. Pour into parfait glass. Garnish with a lemon slice and a maraschino cherry.

FROZEN DAIQUIRI

1½ oz. Light Rum
1 tbsp. Triple Sec
1½ oz. Lime Juice
1 tsp. Sugar

Combine all ingredients in blender with 1 cup of crushed ice and blend until smooth. Pour into champagne flute. Top with a maraschino cherry.

FROZEN FUZZY

1 oz. Peach Schnapps
½ oz. Triple Sec
½ oz. Lime Juice
½ oz. Grenadine
1 splash Lemon-lime Soda

Combine all ingredients in blender with 1 cup of crushed ice and blend until smooth. Pour into champagne flute. Garnish with a lime wedge.

FROZEN MARGARITA

1½ oz. Tequila

½ oz. Triple Sec

1 oz. Lemon Juice or Lime Juice

Combine all ingredients in blender with 1 cup of crushed ice and blend until smooth. Pour into cocktail glass. Garnish with a slice of lemon or lime.

FROZEN MATADOR

1½ oz. Tequila

2 oz. Pineapple Juice

1 tbsp. Lime Juice

Combine all ingredients in blender with 1 cup of crushed ice and blend until smooth. Pour into old-fashioned glass. Add a pineapple stick.

FROZEN MINT DAIQUIRI

2 oz. Light Rum

1 tbsp. Lime Juice

6 Mint Leaves

1 tsp. Sugar

Combine all ingredients in blender with 1 cup of crushed ice and blend until smooth. Pour into old-fashioned glass.

FROZEN PINEAPPLE DAIQUIRI

1½ oz. Light Rum

4 Pineapple Chunks

1 tbsp. Lime Juice

½ tsp. Sugar

Combine all ingredients in blender with 1 cup of crushed ice and blend until smooth. Pour into champagne flute.

FROZEN DRINKS

FRUITY SMASH

1 pint Vanilla Ice Cream

⅓ cup Cherry-flavored Brandy

⅓ cup Crème de Banana

Combine all ingredients in blender with 1 cup of crushed ice and blend until smooth. Pour into large cocktail glasses. Garnish with maraschino cherries. *Makes 4 to 6 servings.*

GAELIC COFFEE

¾ oz. Irish Whiskey

¾ oz. Irish Cream Liqueur

1½ oz. Crème de Cacao (Brown)

2 oz. Milk

1 tsp. Instant Coffee

Combine all ingredients in blender with 1 cup of crushed ice and blend until smooth. Pour into Irish coffee glass. Top with whipped cream and sprinkle with green crème de menthe for color.

GEORGIO

2 oz. Coffee Liqueur
2 oz. Irish Cream Liqueur
1 Banana, ripe
½ cup Light Cream

Combine all ingredients in blender with 1 cup of crushed ice and blend until smooth. Pour equal amounts into 2 parfait glasses. Top with whipped cream and a light dusting of cocoa. Garnish with a sprig of fresh mint. *Makes 2 servings.*

GULF STREAM

1 oz. Blue Curaçao
3 oz. Champagne
½ oz. Light Rum
½ oz. Brandy
6 oz. Lemonade
1 oz. Lime Juice

Combine all ingredients in blender with 1 cup of crushed ice and blend until smooth. Pour into sugar-rimmed parfait glass. Garnish with a whole strawberry.

HUMMER

1 oz. Coffee Liqueur
1 oz. Light Rum
2 large scoops Vanilla Ice Cream

Combine all ingredients in blender until smooth. Serve in highball glass.

ICED COFFEE À L'ORANGE

1 qt. Vanilla Ice Cream
4 tsps. Instant Coffee
1 cup Triple Sec

Combine all ingredients in blender until smooth. Pour into parfait glasses. Garnish with orange slices. *Makes 5 to 6 servings.*

ICY RUMMED CACAO

1 qt. Vanilla Ice Cream
½ cup Dark Rum
½ cup Crème de Cacao (Brown)

Combine all ingredients in blender until smooth. Pour into parfait glasses. Garnish with shaved chocolate. *Makes 4 to 6 servings.*

IRISH DREAM

½ oz. Hazelnut Liqueur
½ oz. Irish Cream Liqueur
¾ oz. Crème de Cacao (Brown)
4 oz. Vanilla Ice Cream

Combine all ingredients in blender with 1 cup of crushed ice and blend until smooth. Pour into frosted pilsner glass. Top with whipped cream and chocolate sprinkles.

ITALIAN DREAM

1½ oz. Irish Cream Liqueur
½ oz. Amaretto
2 oz. Light Cream

Combine all ingredients in blender with 1 cup of

crushed ice and blend until smooth. Pour into parfait glass.

JACK'S JAM

½ oz. Peach Schnapps
½ oz. Apple Schnapps
½ oz. Strawberry Liqueur
¼ oz. Banana Liqueur
2 oz. Lemon Juice
1 oz. Orange Juice
2 tbsps. Powdered Sugar

Combine all ingredients in blender with 1 cup of crushed ice and blend until smooth. Pour into parfait glass. Garnish with a sprig of fresh mint and a maraschino cherry.

JAMAICAN BANANA

½ oz. Light Rum
½ oz. Crème de Cacao (White)
½ oz. Crème de Banana
2 scoops Vanilla Ice Cream
1 oz. Half-and-Half
1 Whole Banana

Combine all ingredients in blender with 1 cup of

crushed ice and blend until smooth. Pour into large brandy snifter and garnish with 2 slices banana, a strawberry, and fresh-grated nutmeg.

KOKOMO JOE

1 oz. Light Rum
1 oz. Banana Liqueur
5 oz. Orange Juice
3 oz. Piña Colada Mix
½ Banana

Combine all ingredients in blender with 1 cup of crushed ice and blend until smooth. Pour into parfait glass. Garnish with a slice of orange.

LEBANESE SNOW

1½ oz. Strawberry Liqueur
1 oz. Crème de Banana
1 oz. Light Cream

Combine all ingredients in blender with 1 cup of crushed ice and blend until smooth. Pour into parfait glass. Garnish with a strawberry.

Move It

Be a roving bartender and keep a wary eye. Avoid long involved conversations with guests. Everyone likes a friendly bartender, but everyone loves a bartender who makes his rounds, increasing the customers' rounds.

—DALE DEGROFF (a.k.a. King Cocktail),
author of *The Craft of the Cocktail*

LICORICE MIST

1¼ oz. Sambuca
½ oz. Coconut Liqueur
2 oz. Light Cream

Combine all ingredients in blender with 1 cup of crushed ice and blend until smooth. Pour into parfait glass. Cut off ends of licorice stick and use it as a straw/garnish.

LONELY NIGHT

¾ oz. Coffee Liqueur
1¼ oz. Irish Cream Liqueur
1¼ oz. Hazelnut Liqueur
1 scoop Vanilla Ice Cream

Combine all ingredients in blender with 1 cup of crushed ice and blend until smooth. Pour into parfait glass. Top with whipped cream and shaved chocolate.

MARASCHINO CHERRY

1 oz. Rum
½ oz. Amaretto
½ oz. Peach Schnapps
1 oz. Cranberry Juice
1 oz. Pineapple Juice
1 dash Grenadine

Combine all ingredients in blender with 1 cup of crushed ice and blend until smooth. Pour into parfait glass. Garnish with whipped cream and a maraschino cherry.

MAUI BREEZE

½ oz. Amaretto
½ oz. Triple Sec
½ oz. Brandy
½ oz. Superfine Sugar (or Simple Syrup)
½ oz. Lemon Juice
2 oz. Orange Juice
2 oz. Guava Juice

Combine all ingredients in blender with 1 cup of crushed ice and blend until smooth. Pour into parfait glass. Garnish with a pineapple spear, a maraschino cherry, and an orchid.

MISSISSIPPI MUD

1½ oz. Whiskey (Tennessee Sour Mash)
1½ oz. Coffee Liqueur
2 scoops Vanilla Ice Cream

Combine all ingredients in blender until smooth. Spoon into cocktail glass and top with shaved chocolate.

MONT BLANC

1 oz. Black Raspberry Liqueur
1 oz. Vodka
1 oz. Light Cream
1 scoop Vanilla Ice Cream

Combine all ingredients in blender until smooth. Pour into oversized red-wine glass.

NUTTY COLADA

3 oz. Amaretto

3 tbsps. Coconut Milk

3 tbsps. Crushed Pineapple

Combine all ingredients in blender with 1 cup of crushed ice and blend until smooth. Pour into Collins glass and serve with a straw.

ORANGE BLOSSOM SPECIAL

1 oz. Peach Schnapps

2½ oz. Lemon-lime Soda

3 oz. Orange Sherbet

1½ oz. Vanilla Ice Cream

2½ oz. Light Cream

Combine all ingredients in blender with 1 cup of crushed ice and blend until smooth. Pour into parfait glass and garnish with a maraschino cherry and an orange slice.

ORANGE TREE

1½ oz. Amaretto

¾ oz. Crème de Noyaux

1½ oz. Orange Juice

¾ oz. Vanilla Ice Cream

Combine all ingredients in blender until smooth. Pour into parfait glass. Top with whipped cream and garnish with a thin slice of orange.

OVER THE RAINBOW

2 oz. Spiced Rum

1 oz. Orange Curaçao

2 scoops Rainbow Sherbet

4 slices Fresh Peach, peeled

2 Strawberries

Combine all ingredients in blender with 1 cup ice and blend until smooth. Pour into parfait glass. Garnish with a strawberry and a peach slice.

PEACH MELBA FREEZE

¾ oz. Peach Schnapps

¾ oz. Black Raspberry Liqueur

¾ oz. Hazelnut Liqueur

4 oz. Vanilla Ice Cream

¾ oz. Light Cream

1 oz. Melba Sauce or Raspberry Jam

Combine all ingredients in blender and blend until smooth. Pour into parfait glass. Garnish with a peach slice.

PEACHY AMARETTO

1 cup Vanilla Ice Cream

1 cup Peaches

1 cup Amaretto

Combine all ingredients in blender and blend until smooth. Pour into parfait glasses. *Makes 3 to 4 servings.*

FROZEN DRINKS

PEPPERMINT PENGUIN

½ oz. Crème de Menthe (Green)

½ oz. Chocolate Mint Liqueur

3 Chocolate Sandwich Cookies

3 oz. Light Cream

Combine all ingredients in blender with 1 cup of crushed ice and blend until smooth. Pour into hurricane or parfait glass. Top with whipped cream. Garnish with a cookie and a maraschino cherry.

PINEAPPLE BANANA REFRESHER

2 cups Pineapple Juice

1 cup Pineapple Sherbet

½ cup Crème de Banana

½ cup Dark Rum

Combine all ingredients in blender until smooth. Pour into highball glasses. Garnish with a pineapple wedge and a banana slice. *Makes 4 to 5 servings.*

PISTACHIO MINT ICE CREAM

1 oz. Hazelnut Liqueur

½ oz. Crème de Menthe (Green)

1 oz. Vodka

2 oz. Heavy Cream

Shake all ingredients with ice. Strain into cocktail glass and garnish with a mint leaf.

RASPBERRY CHEESECAKE

1 tbsp. Cream Cheese, softened

1 oz. Crème de Cacao (White)

1 oz. Black Raspberry Liqueur

2 scoops Vanilla Ice Cream

Combine all ingredients in blender with 1 cup of crushed ice and blend until smooth. Pour into parfait glass.

SMOOTH MOVE

1 oz. Rum

2 oz. Pineapple Juice

2 oz. Prune Juice

1 oz. Superfine Sugar (or Simple Syrup)

1 oz. Lemon Juice

Combine all ingredients in blender with 1 cup of crushed ice and blend until smooth. Pour into sugar-rimmed parfait glass. Garnish with a pineapple spear and a maraschino cherry.

SPARKLING STRAWBERRY MIMOSA

2 oz. Frozen Sliced Strawberries in Syrup, partially thawed

2 oz. Orange Juice

4 oz. Champagne, chilled

Combine all ingredients in blender until smooth. Pour into ice-filled parfait glass. Fill with Champagne and garnish with a whole strawberry and an orange slice.

STRAWBERRIES AND CREAM

1 oz. Strawberry Schnapps

1½ tbsps. Sugar

2 oz. Half-and-Half

2 Whole Strawberries

Place first three ingredients in blender with 2 cups crushed ice and blend until smooth. Add strawberries and blend for 10 seconds. Pour into parfait glass and serve with a straw. Garnish with a fresh strawberry.

STRAWBERRY ALEXANDRA

5 oz. Frozen Sliced Strawberries in Syrup, partially thawed

1 scoop Vanilla Ice Cream

1 oz. Crème de Cacao (White)

1 oz. Brandy

Combine all ingredients in blender and blend until smooth. Pour into white-wine glass. Top with sweetened whipped cream. Garnish with chocolate curls. Serve with a straw and a spoon.

STRAWBERRY BANANA SPRITZ

1 pint Vanilla Ice Cream

1 cup Strawberries, fresh or frozen

1 cup Crème de Banana

10 oz. Club Soda

Combine all ingredients in blender and blend until smooth. Pour into parfait glasses. Garnish with whole strawberries. *Makes 4 to 6 servings.*

STRAWBERRY DAWN

1 oz. Gin

1 oz. Cream of Coconut

4 Fresh Strawberries (or ⅓ cup Frozen Strawberries)

Combine all ingredients in blender with 1 cup of crushed ice and blend until smooth. Pour into cocktail glass. Garnish with a strawberry slice and a mint sprig.

STRAWBERRY SHORTCAKE

1 oz. Amaretto

¾ oz. Crème de Cacao (White)

3 oz. Strawberries in Syrup

5 oz. Vanilla Ice Cream

Combine all ingredients in blender until smooth. Pour into oversized red-wine glass. Top with whipped cream and garnish with a fresh strawberry.

SURF'S UP

½ oz. Crème de Banana

½ oz. Crème de Cacao (White)

5 oz. Pineapple Juice

1 oz. Light Cream

Shake all ingredients with ice. Pour into parfait glass. Garnish with an orange slice and a maraschino cherry.

FROZEN DRINKS

SWEET-TART

2 oz. Vodka
3 oz. Cranberry Juice
3 oz. Pineapple Juice
1 dash Lime Juice

Combine all ingredients in blender with 1 cup of crushed ice and blend until smooth. Pour into parfait glass. Garnish with a lime wheel.

TENNESSEE WALTZ

1¼ oz. Peach Schnapps
2 oz. Pineapple Juice
1 oz. Passion Fruit Juice
4 oz. Vanilla Ice Cream

Combine all ingredients in blender until smooth. Pour into parfait glass. Garnish with whipped cream and a strawberry.

TEQUILA FROST

1¼ oz. Tequila
1¼ oz. Pineapple Juice
1¼ oz. Grapefruit Juice
½ oz. Honey
½ oz. Grenadine
2 oz. Vanilla Ice Milk

Combine all ingredients in blender until smooth. Pour into parfait glass. Garnish with an orange slice and a maraschino cherry.

TIDAL WAVE

1¾ oz. Melon Liqueur
1 oz. Pineapple Juice
1 oz. Orange Juice
½ oz. Coconut Syrup
¾ oz. Superfine Sugar (or Simple Syrup)
¾ oz. Lemon Juice
½ oz. Light Rum

Combine all ingredients in blender with 1 cup of crushed ice and blend until smooth. Pour into parfait glass. Garnish with a lime wheel and a maraschino cherry.

TIDBIT

1 oz. Gin
1 scoop Vanilla Ice Cream
1 dash Dry Sherry

Blend ingredients in blender at low speed and pour into highball glass.

TROLLEY CAR

1¼ oz. Amaretto
2 oz. Fresh Strawberries
2 scoops Vanilla Ice Cream

Combine all ingredients in blender until smooth. Pour into parfait glass and garnish with a fresh strawberry.

HOT DRINKS

HOT TODDIES, simple mixtures of hot water, sugar or honey, and a single spirit—usually bourbon, but any whiskey, rum, brandy, or even gin could be used—are remembered by many as old-fashioned cold remedies, especially by people who remember the first edition of this book. While it was thought that the spirit made you feel better, it was really the heat combined with the spirit that did the trick. Indeed, toddies are one of those classic comforts that we are loath to abandon even today. That's probably because hot drinks are both comforting and stimulating. You don't need a fireplace to feel the warmth of the hot drinks found on the following pages—though if you have a fireplace, all the better—from the classic Irish Coffee to the ethereal Hot Buttered Rum.

Many hot drinks employ coffee as their base, laced with either whiskey, rum, brandy, or liqueurs, or a combination of several of these. However, virtually any heated beverage can make a great hot drink, and in this section you'll find recipes made with hot chocolate, tea, cider, steamed milk, and even orange juice.

Whichever you choose, remember that the best hot drinks are made with high-quality ingredients: piping hot, freshly brewed coffee or tea, old-fashioned hot chocolate made with real cocoa and milk instead of a mix, cream you've whipped yourself (really, it only takes a couple of minutes), and fresh spices.

Lastly, heed the temperature of these drinks, take your time with them, and prolong the pleasure they bring.

AMARETTO TEA

6 oz. Hot Tea
2 oz. Amaretto

Pour hot tea into parfait glass, putting a spoon in the glass to prevent cracking. Add amaretto, but do not stir. Top with whipped cream.

AMERICAN GROG

1 cube Sugar
¾ oz. Lemon Juice
1½ oz. Light Rum

Pour ingredients into hot Irish coffee glass and fill with hot water. Stir.

APRIHOT

3 oz. Apricot-flavored Brandy
3 oz. Boiling Water

Combine in Irish coffee glass with a dash of cinnamon, and garnish with an orange or lemon slice.

BLACK GOLD

¼ oz. Triple Sec
¼ oz. Amaretto
¼ oz. Irish Cream Liqueur
¼ oz. Hazelnut Liqueur
4 oz. Hot Coffee
1 dash Cinnamon Schnapps

Pour first four ingredients into Irish coffee glass. Add coffee and schnapps and stir. Top with whipped cream and shaved chocolate. Serve with a cinnamon stick as stirrer.

BLUE BLAZER

2½ oz. Blended Whiskey
2½ oz. Boiling Water
1 tsp. Sugar

Use two large, silver-plated mugs with handles. Put the whiskey into one mug and the boiling water into the other. Ignite the whiskey and, while it is flaming, mix both ingredients by pouring them four or five times from one mug to the other. If done well, this will have the appearance of a continuous stream of liquid fire. Sweeten with sugar and serve with a twist of lemon peel. Serve in Irish coffee glass.

BOSTON CARIBBEAN COFFEE

1 oz. Crème de Cacao (Brown)
1 oz. Dark Rum
Hot Coffee

Pour liqueur and rum into sugar-rimmed Irish coffee glass. Fill with freshly brewed coffee. Top with whipped cream and sprinkle with cinnamon. Garnish with a cinnamon stick as a stirrer.

BRANDY BLAZER

1 cube Sugar

1 piece Orange Peel

2 oz. Brandy

Combine all ingredients in old-fashioned glass. Light the liquid with a match, stir with a long spoon for a few seconds, and strain into hot Irish coffee glass.

CAFÉ L'ORANGE

½ oz. Cognac

½ oz. Triple Sec

1 oz. Mandarine Napoléon

4 oz. Hot Coffee

Pour cognac and liqueurs into Irish coffee glass. Add coffee. Top with whipped cream and garnish with finely chopped orange rind.

CAFFÈ DI AMARETTO

1 oz. Amaretto

1 cup Hot Coffee

Add amaretto to a cup of hot black coffee, then transfer to Irish coffee glass. Top with whipped cream.

CAPRICCIO

1 tbsp. Sugar

½ oz. Brandy

½ oz. Crème de Café

1 oz. Amaretto

Hot Coffee

Put sugar in bottom of Irish coffee glass rimmed with cinnamon-sugar. Add brandy and liqueurs. Fill ¾ full with coffee. Top with whipped cream, toasted almond slices, and a maraschino cherry.

CHOCOLATE COFFEE KISS

¾ oz. Coffee Liqueur

¾ oz. Irish Cream Liqueur

1 splash Crème de Cacao (Brown)

1 splash Mandarine Napoléon

1½ oz. Chocolate Syrup

Hot Coffee

Combine first five ingredients in Irish coffee glass, and then fill with coffee. Top with whipped cream and garnish with shaved chocolate and a maraschino cherry.

HOT DRINKS

COFFEE NUDGE (KIOKE COFFEE)

½ oz. Brandy

½ oz. Coffee Liqueur

½ oz. Crème de Cacao (Dark)

5 oz. Hot Coffee

In a pre-warmed Irish coffee glass, add the brandy, coffee liqueur, and crème de cacao. Pour in the coffee. Top with a dollop of whipped cream. Optional: Sprinkle grated chocolate as a garnish. Serve with cocktail straws.

DOUBLEMINT

1 oz. Spearmint Schnapps

Hot Coffee

1 dash Crème de Menthe (Green)

Pour schnapps into Irish coffee glass and then fill with coffee. Top with whipped cream. Add crème de menthe for color.

GIN TODDY (HOT)

1 cube Sugar

Boiling Water

2 oz. Gin

Put sugar into Irish coffee glass and fill ⅔ full with boiling water. Add gin. Stir and garnish with a slice of lemon. Garnish with fresh-grated nutmeg on top.

HANDICAPPER'S CHOICE

1 oz. Irish Whiskey

1 oz. Amaretto

5 oz. Hot Coffee

Pour whiskey and Amaretto into Irish coffee glass and fill with hot coffee. Top with whipped cream.

HOT BRANDY ALEXANDER

¾ oz. Brandy

¾ oz. Crème de Cacao (Brown)

4 oz. Steamed Milk

Pour ingredients into heated Irish coffee glass. Top with whipped cream and chocolate shavings.

HOT BRANDY TODDY

1 cube Sugar

Boiling Water

2 oz. Brandy

Put sugar into Irish coffee glass and fill ⅔ full with boiling water. Add brandy and stir. Garnish with a slice of lemon and fresh-grated nutmeg.

HOT BRICK TODDY

1 tsp. Butter
1 tsp. Powdered Sugar
3 pinches Cinnamon
1 oz. Whiskey
1 oz. Boiling Water

Put first three ingredients into Irish coffee glass. Dissolve thoroughly. Add whiskey, fill with boiling water, and stir.

HOT BUTTERED RUM

1 tsp. Brown Sugar
Boiling Water
1 tbsp. Butter
2 oz. Dark Rum

Put sugar into Irish coffee glass and fill ⅔ full with boiling water. Add butter and rum. Stir and garnish with fresh-grated nutmeg on top.

HOT BUTTERED WINE

½ cup Muscatel
¼ cup Water
1 tsp. Butter
2 tsps. Maple Syrup

Heat wine and water just to simmering—do not boil. Preheat Irish coffee glass with boiling water. Pour heated wine mixture into glass and add butter and maple syrup. Stir and garnish with fresh-grated nutmeg on top.

HOT CINNAMON ROLL

Hot Apple Cider
1½ oz. Cinnamon Schnapps

Pour hot cider into Irish coffee glass. Add schnapps. Top with whipped cream. Add a cinnamon stick as a stirrer.

HOT GOLD

6 oz. Very Warm Orange Juice
3 oz. Amaretto

Pour orange juice into red-wine glass or mug. Add amaretto and garnish with cinnamon stick as stirrer.

HOT KISS

½ oz. Crème de Menthe (White)
½ oz. Crème de Cacao (White)
1 oz. Irish Whiskey
6 oz. Hot Coffee

Pour liqueurs and whiskey into Irish coffee glass. Add coffee and stir. Top with whipped cream and garnish with a chocolate-covered mint.

HOT DRINKS

INDIAN SUMMER

2 oz. Apple Schnapps

Hot Apple Cider

Wet rim of sour glass and dip in cinnamon. Add schnapps and top off with cider. Garnish with a cinnamon stick, if desired.

IRISH COFFEE

1½ oz. Irish Whiskey

Hot Coffee

Sugar to taste

Into Irish coffee glass rimmed with sugar, pour Irish whiskey. Fill to within ½ inch of top with coffee. Add sugar, if desired. Cover surface to brim with whipped cream.

ITALIAN COFFEE

½ oz. Amaretto

Hot Coffee

1½ tbsps. Coffee Ice Cream

Pour amaretto into Irish coffee glass. Fill with hot coffee. Top with coffee ice cream and sprinkle with ground coriander.

JAMAICA COFFEE

1 oz. Coffee-flavored Brandy

¾ oz. Light Rum

Hot Coffee

Pour brandy and rum into Irish coffee glass. Fill with hot coffee. Sweeten to taste. Top with whipped cream and fresh-grated nutmeg.

MEXICAN COFFEE

1 oz. Coffee Liqueur

½ oz. Tequila

5 oz. Hot Coffee

Stir coffee liqueur and tequila in Irish coffee glass, add coffee, and top with whipped cream.

MEXITALY COFFEE

¾ oz. Coffee Liqueur

¾ oz. Amaretto

Hot Coffee

Dip rim of Irish coffee glass in maraschino cherry juice, then in cinnamon-sugar. Pour liqueurs into glass and add coffee. Top with whipped cream and shaved chocolate.

MULLED CLARET

1 cube Sugar

1 oz. Lemon Juice

1 dash Bitters

1 tsp. Mixed Cinnamon and Nutmeg

5 oz. Claret or Red Wine

Put all ingredients into a metal mug. Heat poker red-hot and hold in liquid until boiling and serve—or just warm on a stove and serve in Irish coffee glass.

RAZZMATAZZ

1 oz. Black Raspberry Liqueur

½ oz. Crème de Cassis

½ oz. Coffee Liqueur

Hot Coffee

Pour liqueurs into Irish coffee glass. Add coffee. Top with whipped cream and garnish with berries in season.

RUEDESHEIM KAFFE

3 cubes Sugar

1½ oz. Brandy

Hot Coffee

Place sugar cubes in Irish coffee glass. Add brandy and set aflame. Allow to burn for a good minute, and then fill with coffee. Top with whipped cream and sprinkle with grated chocolate.

RUM TODDY (HOT)

1 cube Sugar

Boiling Water

2 oz. Light or Dark Rum

Put sugar into Irish coffee glass and fill ⅔ full with boiling water. Add rum and stir. Garnish with a slice of lemon and fresh-grated nutmeg.

RUSSIAN COFFEE

½ oz. Coffee Liqueur

½ oz. Hazelnut Liqueur

¼ oz. Vodka

Hot Coffee

Pour liqueurs and vodka into Irish coffee glass. Add coffee. Top with whipped cream.

SNOW BUNNY

1½ oz. Triple Sec

Hot Chocolate

Pour Triple Sec into Irish coffee glass. Fill with hot chocolate. Garnish with a stick of cinnamon for flavoring and to use as a stirrer.

SPANISH COFFEE

1 oz. Spanish Brandy

Hot Coffee

Add coffee to brandy in Irish coffee glass and top with whipped cream.

HOT DRINKS

STEAMING PEACH

2 oz. Peach Schnapps
4 oz. Hot Water

Pour schnapps into snifter. Add hot water and stir. Float an orange slice as a garnish.

WHISKEY TODDY (HOT)

1 cube Sugar
Boiling Water
2 oz. Blended Whiskey

Put sugar into Irish coffee glass and fill ⅔ full with boiling water. Add whiskey and stir. Garnish with a slice of lemon and fresh-grated nutmeg.

EGGNOGS AND PUNCHES

EGGNOG FIRST BECAME POPULAR during colonial times. Rum was the favorite spirit of the early Americans; they mixed it with milk, eggs, and sugar. Over the years, whiskey and brandy have been used as substitutes for rum. Today, eggnog is enjoyed mostly as a holiday drink, which is a shame. This is probably the result of the proliferation of pasteurized prepared eggnogs, which are seldom as good as homemade (though easier to serve), coupled with concerns over salmonella poisoning associated with raw eggs.

Fortunately, there are solutions to the raw egg problem: One, use a prepared mix such as Mr. Boston EggNog. Two, use pasteurized eggs. Three, if using regular, unpasteurized eggs, cook the egg mixture very slowly to 160°F, at which point the mixture thickens enough to coat a spoon, and then refrigerate immediately. If a recipe calls for folding raw, beaten egg whites into the eggnog, you can use either the whites of prepasteurized eggs or prepackaged pasteurized egg whites. Hopefully, you'll feel inspired—and safe enough—to make your own homemade eggnog (see page 249) before transforming it.

Punches are ideal for serving a large number of guests. They are usually made with a single spirit, wine, Champagne, or even beer. Recipes for both cold and hot punches can be found in this section, as well as for several nonalcoholic punches.

While cold punches in smaller quantities can be mixed in and served from a pitcher, larger recipes are usually served in a punch bowl from which guests help themselves. Use a block of ice, not ice cubes, to keep punch chilled.

EGGNOGS

AMBASSADOR'S MORNING LIFT

32 oz. Eggnog

6 oz. Cognac

3 oz. Jamaican Rum

3 oz. Crème de Cacao (Brown)

Combine all ingredients in large punch bowl and serve in Irish coffee glasses. Sprinkle fresh-grated nutmeg on top of each serving. Brandy or bourbon may be substituted for cognac. *Makes 10 to 12 servings.*

BALTIMORE EGGNOG

32 oz. Eggnog

5 oz. Brandy

5 oz. Jamaican Rum

5 oz. Madeira Wine

Combine all ingredients in large punch bowl and serve in Irish coffee glasses. Sprinkle fresh-grated nutmeg on top of each serving. *Makes 10 to 12 servings.*

BRANDY EGGNOG

32 oz. Eggnog

12 oz. Brandy

Combine all ingredients in large punch bowl and serve in Irish coffee glasses. Sprinkle fresh-grated nutmeg on top of each serving. *Makes 10 to 12 servings.*

BREAKFAST EGGNOG

32 oz. Eggnog

10 oz. Apricot-flavored Brandy

2½ oz. Triple Sec

Combine all ingredients in large punch bowl and serve in Irish coffee glasses. Sprinkle fresh-grated nutmeg on top of each serving. *Makes 10 to 12 servings.*

CHRISTMAS YULE EGGNOG

32 oz. Eggnog

12 oz. Whiskey

1½ oz. Light Rum

Combine all ingredients in large punch bowl and serve in Irish coffee glasses. Sprinkle fresh-grated nutmeg on top of each serving. *Makes 10 to 12 servings.*

EGG CRUSHER

8 oz. Eggnog

1 oz. Light Rum

1 oz. Coffee Liqueur

Stir with ice and strain into oversized snifter. Garnish with fresh-grated nutmeg on top.

🍺 EGGNOG (HOMEMADE)

6 Eggs

1 cup Sugar

½ tsp. Salt

1 cup Golden Rum

1 pint Half-and-Half

1 pint Milk

In a large bowl, beat eggs until light and foamy. Add sugar and salt, beating until thick and lemon colored. Stir in rum, cream, and milk. Chill at least 3 hours. Serve in Irish coffee glasses. Garnish with a sprinkle of fresh-grated nutmeg on top. *Makes 10 to 12 servings.*

🍺 FROSTY NOG

½ cup Eggnog

2 tbsps. Sugar

Combine eggnog and sugar in blender. Slowly add up to 3 cups of ice, blending at medium speed, until smooth. Pour into parfait glass. Garnish with almond slivers and fresh-grated nutmeg.

🍺 IMPERIAL EGGNOG

32 oz. Eggnog

10 oz. Brandy

2 oz. Apricot-flavored Brandy

Combine all ingredients in large punch bowl and serve in Irish coffee glasses. Sprinkle fresh-grated nutmeg on top of each serving. *Makes 10 to 12 servings.*

🍺 MAPLE EGGNOG

32 oz. Eggnog

½ cup Maple Syrup

Combine all ingredients in large pitcher and chill. Stir before serving. Serve in Irish coffee glasses. Garnish with fresh-grated nutmeg on top, if desired. *Makes 8 servings.*

🍺 NASHVILLE EGGNOG

32 oz. Eggnog

6 oz. Whiskey (Bourbon)

3 oz. Brandy

3 oz. Jamaican Rum

Combine all ingredients in large punch bowl and serve in Irish coffee glasses. Sprinkle fresh-grated nutmeg on top of each serving. *Makes 10 to 12 servings.*

🍺 NOG DE CACAO

1½ oz. Crème de Cacao

1½ oz. Eggnog

Pour over ice in old-fashioned glass and stir.

🍺 PORT WINE EGGNOG

32 oz. Eggnog

18 oz. Port Wine

Combine all ingredients in large punch bowl and serve in Irish coffee glasses. Sprinkle fresh-grated nutmeg on top of each serving. *Makes 10 to 12 servings.*

EGGNOGS & PUNCHES

RUM EGGNOG

32 oz. Eggnog
12 oz. Light Rum

Combine all ingredients in large punch bowl and serve in Irish coffee glasses. Sprinkle fresh-grated nutmeg on top of each serving. *Makes 10 to 12 servings.*

RUSSIAN NOG

1 oz. Vodka
1 oz. Coffee Liqueur
1 oz. Eggnog

Pour over ice in old-fashioned glass and stir.

SHERRY EGGNOG

32 oz. Eggnog
18 oz. Cream Sherry

Combine all ingredients in large punch bowl and serve in Irish coffee glasses. Sprinkle fresh-grated nutmeg on top of each serving. *Makes 10 to 12 servings.*

WHISKEY EGGNOG

32 oz. Eggnog
12 oz. Blended Whiskey

Combine all ingredients in large punch bowl and serve in Irish coffee glasses. Sprinkle fresh-grated nutmeg on top of each serving. *Makes 10 to 12 servings.*

COLD PUNCHES

APRICOT ORANGE FIZZ

1½ cups Orange Juice
½ cup Light Rum
¼ cup Apricot-flavored Brandy
2 tbsps. Lime Juice
Club Soda

Combine first four ingredients in pitcher and stir. Pour into ice-filled Collins glasses about ⅔ full. Top with club soda. Stir and garnish with lime slices. *Makes 6 servings.*

BOMBAY PUNCH

3 cups Lemon Juice
Superfine Sugar (or Simple Syrup)
32 oz. Brandy
32 oz. Dry Sherry
½ cup Maraschino Liqueur
½ cup Triple Sec
4 bottles (750-ml) Champagne, chilled
64 oz. Club Soda, chilled

Add enough sugar/syrup to sweeten lemon juice. Pour over a large block of ice in punch bowl and stir. Then add remaining ingredients. Stir well and garnish with fruits in season. Serve in Irish coffee glasses. *Makes 60 servings.*

🍹 BOOM BOOM PUNCH

64 oz. Light Rum

32 oz. Orange Juice

1 bottle (750-ml) Sweet Vermouth

1 bottle (750-ml) Champagne, chilled

Pour all ingredients except Champagne into punch bowl over large block of ice. Stir. Top with Champagne. Garnish with sliced bananas. Serve in Irish coffee glasses. *Makes 36 servings.*

🍹 BRANDY PUNCH

3 cups Lemon Juice

2 cups Orange Juice

Superfine Sugar (or Simple Syrup)

1 cup Grenadine

32 oz. Club Soda

1 cup Triple Sec

1.75 liters Brandy

2 cups Tea (optional)

In pitcher add enough sugar/ syrup to sweeten lemon and orange juice and mix with grenadine and club soda. Pour over large block of ice in punch bowl and stir well. Then add Triple Sec, brandy, and tea, if desired. Stir well and garnish with fruits in season. Serve in Irish coffee glasses. *Makes 32 servings.*

🍹 BRUNCH PUNCH

3 qts. Tomato Juice, chilled

1 liter Light or Dark Rum

2½ tsps. Worcestershire Sauce

5 oz. Lemon or Lime Juice

Salt and Pepper as needed

Combine all ingredients in large container and stir. Pour over block of ice in punch bowl and garnish with thinly sliced lemons or limes. Serve in Irish coffee glasses. *Makes 40 servings.*

EGGNOGS & PUNCHES

Squeeze Fruit Warm

Never store lemons, limes, or oranges that are meant for juicing in the refrigerator because cold fruit is stingy with juice. If the fruit is cold, soak it in warm water for 15 or 20 minutes, then roll it under the palm of your hand to break the cells and release the juice. Follow these simple steps and you'll almost double the amount of juice from the same fruit.

—DALE DEGROFF (a.k.a. King Cocktail), author of *The Craft of the Cocktail*

CAPE CODDER PUNCH

3 bottles (32-oz.) Cranberry-apple Drink

3 cups Vodka

2 cups Orange Juice

⅔ cup Lemon Juice

½ cup Sugar

1 bottle (28-oz.) Mineral Water, chilled

Combine first five ingredients in punch bowl, stirring until sugar dissolves, and chill. Stir in mineral water just before serving. Serve in Irish coffee glasses. *Makes 40 servings.*

CARDINAL PUNCH

3 cups Lemon Juice

Superfine Sugar (or Simple Syrup)

16 oz. Brandy

16 oz. Light Rum

1 split Champagne, chilled

64 oz. Red Wine

32 oz. Club Soda

8 oz. Sweet Vermouth

16 oz. Strong Tea (optional)

Add enough sugar/syrup to sweeten lemon juice. Pour over large block of ice in punch bowl and stir well. Then add remaining ingredients. Stir well and garnish with fruits in season. Serve in Irish coffee glasses. *Makes 42 servings.*

CHAMPAGNE CUP

4 tsps. Superfine Sugar (or Simple Syrup)

6 oz. Club Soda

1 oz. Triple Sec

2 oz. Brandy

16 oz. Champagne, chilled

Fill large glass pitcher with cubes of ice and all ingredients except Champagne. Stir well, then add Champagne. Stir well and garnish with fruits in season and rind of cucumber inserted on each side of pitcher. Top with a small bunch of mint. Serve in red-wine glasses. *Makes 6 servings.*

CHAMPAGNE PUNCH

3 cups Lemon Juice

Superfine Sugar (or Simple Syrup)

1 cup Maraschino Liqueur

1 cup Triple Sec

16 oz. Brandy

2 bottles (750-ml) Champagne, chilled

16 oz. Club Soda

16 oz. Strong Tea (optional)

Add enough sugar/syrup to sweeten lemon juice. Pour over large block of ice in punch bowl and stir well. Then add remaining ingredients. Stir well and garnish with fruits in season. Serve in Irish coffee glasses. *Makes 32 servings.*

CHAMPAGNE SHERBET PUNCH

3 cups Pineapple Juice, chilled

¼ cup Lemon Juice

1 qt. Pineapple Sherbet

1 bottle (750-ml) Champagne, chilled

In punch bowl combine juices. Just before serving, scoop sherbet into punch bowl, then add Champagne. Stir gently. Serve in Irish coffee glasses. *Makes 20 servings.*

CIDER CUP

4 tsps. Superfine Sugar (or Simple Syrup)

6 oz. Club Soda

1 oz. Triple Sec

2 oz. Brandy

16 oz. Apple Cider

Fill large glass pitcher with ice. Stir in the ingredients and garnish with fruits in season and a rind of cucumber inserted on each side of pitcher. Top with a small bunch of mint. Serve in red-wine glasses. *Makes 6 servings.*

CITRUS-BEER PUNCH

6 Lemons

2 cups Sugar

2 cups Water

1 cup Grapefruit Juice, chilled

2 cans (12-oz.) Light Beer, chilled

Remove peel from lemons and set aside. Juice lemons (about 2 cups juice). In large saucepan, stir together sugar and water. Bring to a boil and add reserved lemon peel. Remove from heat. Cover and let stand 5 minutes. Remove and discard peel. Add lemon juice and grapefruit juice to sugar mixture. Transfer mixture to a 3-quart pitcher; cover and chill. Just before serving, add beer. Pour into Irish coffee glasses over ice and garnish with lemon slices. *Makes 8 servings.*

CLARET CUP

4 tsps. Superfine Sugar (or Simple Syrup)

6 oz. Club Soda

1 oz. Triple Sec

2 oz. Brandy

16 oz. Red Wine

Fill large glass pitcher with ice. Stir in the ingredients and garnish with fruits in season and a rind of cucumber inserted on each side of pitcher. Top with a small bunch of mint. Serve in red-wine glasses. *Makes 6 servings.*

EGGNOGS & PUNCHES

CLARET PUNCH

3 cups Lemon Juice
Superfine Sugar (or Simple Syrup)
1 cup Triple Sec
16 oz. Brandy
3 bottles (750-ml) Red Wine
32 oz. Club Soda
32 oz. Strong Tea (optional)

Add enough sugar/syrup to sweeten lemon juice. Pour over large block of ice in punch bowl and stir well. Then add remaining ingredients. Stir and garnish with fruits in season. Serve in Irish coffee glasses. *Makes 40 servings.*

EXTRA-KICK PUNCH

2 qts. Water
1 cup Brown Sugar
2 cups Dark Rum
1 cup Brandy
1 cup Lemon Juice
1 cup Pineapple Juice
¼ cup Peach Brandy

Combine water and brown sugar, stirring until sugar dissolves. Add remaining ingredients; chill. Pour over block of ice in punch bowl. Serve in Irish coffee glasses. *Makes 28 servings.*

FISH HOUSE PUNCH

3 cups Lemon Juice
Superfine Sugar (or Simple Syrup)
1½ liters Brandy
1 liter Peach-flavored Brandy
16 oz. Light Rum
32 oz. Club Soda
16 oz. Strong Tea (optional)

Add enough sugar/syrup to sweeten lemon juice. Pour over large block of ice in punch bowl and stir well. Then add remaining ingredients. Stir well and garnish with fruits in season. Serve in Irish coffee glasses. *Makes 40 servings.*

KENTUCKY PUNCH

12 oz. Frozen Orange Juice Concentrate, thawed and undiluted
12 oz. Frozen Lemonade Concentrate, thawed and undiluted
1 cup Lemon Juice
1 liter Whiskey (Bourbon)
1 bottle (2-liter) Lemon-lime Soda

Combine all ingredients except soda in large container and chill. Pour into punch bowl over large block of ice and stir in soda. *Makes 32 servings.*

LOVING CUP

4 tsps. Superfine Sugar (or Simple Syrup)
6 oz. Club Soda
1 oz. Triple Sec
2 oz. Brandy
16 oz. Red Wine

Fill large glass pitcher with ice and stir in the ingredients. Garnish with fruits in season and a rind of cucumber inserted on each side of the pitcher. Top with a small bunch of mint sprigs. Serve in Irish coffee glasses. *Makes 6 servings.*

MINT JULEP PUNCH

1 cup Mint Jelly

4 cups Water

3¼ cups Whiskey (Bourbon)

6 cups Pineapple Juice

½ cup Lime Juice

7 cups Lemon-lime Soda

Combine mint jelly and 2 cups of water in saucepan, stirring over low heat until jelly melts. Cool. Add bourbon, pineapple juice, remaining water, and lime juice; chill. To serve, pour mixture over a block of ice in punch bowl. Slowly pour in soda, stirring gently. Garnish with lime slices and fresh mint leaves, if desired. Serve in Irish coffee glasses. *Makes 44 servings.*

RHINE WINE CUP

4 tsps. Superfine Sugar (or Simple Syrup)

6 oz. Club Soda

1 oz. Triple Sec

2 oz. Brandy

16 oz. White Wine

Mix ingredients and pour into large glass pitcher over cubes of ice. Stir and garnish with fruits in season. Insert a rind of cucumber on each side of pitcher. Top with mint sprigs. Serve in red-wine glasses. *Makes 6 servings.*

SANGRIA

¼ cup Superfine Sugar (or Simple Syrup)

1 cup Water

1 Thinly Sliced Orange

1 Thinly Sliced Lime

1 bottle (750-ml) Red or Rosé Wine

6 oz. Sparkling Water

Assorted Seasonal Fruits (Bananas, Strawberries, etc.)

Dissolve sugar/syrup in water in large pitcher. Add fruit and wine and 12 or more ice cubes. Stir until cold. Add sparkling water. Serve in red-wine glasses, putting some fruit in each glass. *Makes 10 servings.*

TEQUILA PUNCH

1 liter Tequila, chilled

1 bottle (750-ml) Champagne, chilled

4 bottles (750-ml) White Wine

64 oz. Fresh Fruits (cubes or balls)

Put all ingredients in large punch bowl and sweeten as needed with simple syrup. Add ice cubes just before serving. Serve in Irish coffee glasses. *Makes 40 servings.*

EGGNOGS & PUNCHES

WEST INDIAN PUNCH

¾ cup Superfine Sugar (or Simple Syrup)

1 tsp. Grated Nutmeg

1 tsp. Cinnamon

½ tsp. Grated Cloves

6 oz. Club Soda

64 oz. Light Rum

1 bottle (750-ml) Crème de Banana

32 oz. Pineapple Juice

32 oz. Orange Juice

32 oz. Lemon Juice

Dissolve sugar/syrup and spices in club soda. Pour into large punch bowl over a block of ice and add rum, crème de banana, and juices. Stir and garnish with sliced bananas. Serve in Irish coffee glasses. *Makes 48 servings.*

WHISKEY SOUR PUNCH

3 cans (6-oz.) Frozen Lemonade Concentrate, thawed and undiluted

4 cups Whiskey (Bourbon)

3 cups Orange Juice

1 bottle (2-liter) chilled Club Soda

Combine all ingredients over block of ice in punch bowl. Stir gently. Garnish with orange slices. Serve in Irish coffee glasses. *Makes 32 servings.*

WHITE WINE CUP

4 tsps. Superfine Sugar (or Simple Syrup)

6 oz. Club Soda

1 tbsp. Triple Sec

1 tbsp. Curaçao

2 oz. Brandy

16 oz. White Wine

Put all ingredients in large glass pitcher with ice. Stir and garnish with fruits in season and a rind of cucumber inserted on each side of pitcher. Top with a small bunch of mint sprigs. Serve in white-wine glasses. *Makes 6 servings.*

HOT PUNCHES

HOT APPLE BRANDY

6 cups Apple Juice

1½ cups Apricot-flavored Brandy

3 Cinnamon Sticks

½ tsp. Ground Cloves

Simmer all ingredients over low heat for 30 minutes. Serve warm in brandy snifters. *Makes 6 to 8 servings.*

HOT BURGUNDY PUNCH

¼ cup Sugar

1½ cups Boiling Water

Peel of ½ Lemon

1 Cinnamon Stick

5 Cloves

½ tsp. Ground Allspice

1 cup Apple Juice

1 bottle (750-ml) Red Burgundy Wine (or Pinot Noir)

In large saucepan, dissolve sugar in boiling water. Add lemon peel, cinnamon, cloves, allspice, and apple juice. Cook over moderately high heat for 15 minutes. Strain into another saucepan and add wine. Simmer over low heat but do not boil. Serve hot in Irish coffee glasses with a sprinkle of fresh-grated nutmeg on top. *Makes 16 servings.*

HOT RUMMED CIDER

1½ qts. Apple Cider

6 tbsps. Brown Sugar

3 tbsps. Butter

1½ cups Light Rum

Bring cider and sugar to a boil in large saucepan. Reduce heat and add butter. When butter is melted, add rum. Serve in heat-proof punch bowl or pitcher and provide Irish coffee glasses. *Makes 6 to 8 servings.*

SMUGGLER'S BREW

1½ cups Dark Rum

1 qt. Tea

3 tbsps. Butter

½ cup Sugar

½ tsp. Nutmeg

½ cup Brandy

Heat all ingredients except brandy in large saucepan until boiling. Heat brandy in small saucepan until barely warm and add to rum mixture. Pour into heat-proof punch bowl to serve and provide Irish coffee glasses. *Makes 8 servings.*

WINTER CIDER

1 gal. Apple Cider

6 Cinnamon Sticks

1½ cups Rum

1 cup Peach-flavored Brandy

¾ cup Peach Schnapps

In large saucepan, bring cider and cinnamon to a full boil over medium heat. Reduce heat and add rum, brandy, and schnapps, stirring until heated through. Serve in Irish coffee glasses, garnished with a cinnamon stick and an apple slice. *Makes 18 to 20 servings.*

EGGNOGS & PUNCHES

NONALCOHOLIC PUNCHES

BANANA PUNCH

1½ qts. Water

3 cups Sugar

12 oz. Frozen Orange Juice Concentrate, thawed and undiluted

46 oz. Pineapple-Grapefruit Juice

4 Bananas, mashed

Club Soda

Mix water and sugar. Add juices and bananas. Pour into quart-size freezer containers and freeze overnight. About 1 hour before serving, remove from freezer and place mixture in punch bowl. Add 1 liter of club soda per 2 quarts of mix and stir gently. Serve in Irish coffee glasses. *Makes 40 servings.*

DOUBLE BERRY PUNCH

2 qts. Cranberry Juice

3 cups Raspberry-flavored Soda, chilled

1 qt. Raspberry Sherbet

Chill cranberry juice in punch bowl. Just before serving, slowly pour in soda and stir gently. Serve over small scoops of sherbet in Irish coffee glasses and garnish with raspberries. *Makes 25 to 30 servings.*

FUNSHINE FIZZ

2 cups Orange Juice

2 cups Pineapple Juice

1 pint Orange Sherbet

1 cup Club Soda

Combine first three ingredients in blender, blending until smooth. Pour mixture into pitcher and stir in club soda. Serve in Collins glasses. *Makes 6 to 8 servings.*

TROPICAL CREAM PUNCH

14 oz. Sweetened Condensed Milk

6 oz. Frozen Orange Juice Concentrate, thawed and undiluted

6 oz. Frozen Pineapple Juice Concentrate, thawed and undiluted

1 bottle (2-liter) chilled Club Soda

In punch bowl, combine sweetened condensed milk and juice concentrates; mix well. Add club soda and stir gently. Add block of ice and garnish with orange slices. Serve in Irish coffee glasses. *Makes 22 servings.*

WINE IN MIXED DRINKS

SOME COCKTAILS EMPLOY classic varietal wines like Chardonnay, Cabernet, or Merlot (we list a couple in this section). But wine is a broad term for several subcategories less familiar to classic wine drinkers until you say their names—many of which are proprietary. Do Fernet Branca, Dubonnet, and Lillet sound familiar? How about bitters or vermouth? All of these are examples of wines that are aromatized—the basic grape flavor is augmented with the addition of flavorings such as spices, herbs, flowers, nuts, honey, or even pine resin.

Proprietary aromatics are often sipped solo in Europe either before or after a meal, whereas in the United States they more often show up in cocktails. Anyone who drinks Martinis or Manhattans is familiar with vermouth, a wine infused with herbs, alcohol, sugar, caramel, and water. There are three types of vermouth: dry, sweet, and half-sweet.

Sparkling wine or Champagne is used in many cocktails, often splashed on top to add a touch of fizz. In the classic Champagne Cocktail, the bubbly is the main ingredient; unless specified, use a dry (brut) style of Champagne or a sparkling wine, such as Spanish cava or Italian prosecco.

Lastly, claret begs description, as its inclusion in recipes such as the Claret Cobbler harks back to the very first edition of this book. Claret was a British term used to describe what was originally a rosé wine from Bordeaux—*clairet* in French—but, by the advent of the cocktail, it had simply come to mean red Bordeaux wine. Therefore, feel free to use whatever red wine you like in recipes calling for claret.

1815

2 oz. Ramazzotti Amaro
½ oz. Lemon Juice
½ oz. Lime Juice
Ginger Ale

Shake first three ingredients with ice and strain into ice-filled Collins glass. Top with ginger ale and garnish with lemons and lime wedges.

AMERICANO

2 oz. Sweet Vermouth
2 oz. Campari
Club Soda

Pour vermouth and Campari into ice-filled highball glass. Fill with club soda and stir. Add a twist of lemon peel.

ANDALUSIA

1½ oz. Dry Sherry
½ oz. Brandy
½ oz. Light Rum

Stir well with ice and strain into chilled cocktail glass.

BISHOP

¾ oz. Lemon Juice
1 oz. Orange Juice
1 tsp. Superfine Sugar (or Simple Syrup)
Red Burgundy

Shake first three ingredients with ice and strain into chilled highball glass. Add two ice cubes, fill with Burgundy, and stir well. Garnish with seasonal fruits.

BRAZIL COCKTAIL

1½ oz. Dry Vermouth
1½ oz. Dry Sherry
1 dash Bitters
¼ tsp. Anisette

Stir with ice and strain into chilled cocktail glass.

BROKEN SPUR COCKTAIL

¾ oz. Sweet Vermouth
1½ oz. Port
¼ tsp. Triple Sec

Stir with ice and strain into chilled cocktail glass.

CHAMPAGNE COCKTAIL

1 cube Sugar
2 dashes Bitters
Champagne, chilled

Place sugar and bitters in champagne flute and fill with Champagne. Add a twist of lemon peel.

CHRYSANTHEMUM COCKTAIL

1½ oz. Dry Vermouth
¾ oz. Bénédictine
3 dashes Pastis (or Pernod or other Absinthe substitute)

Stir with ice and strain into chilled cocktail glass. Garnish with a twist of orange.

♈ CLARET COBBLER

1 tsp. Superfine Sugar (or Simple Syrup)

2 oz. Club Soda

3 oz. Claret or Red Wine

Dissolve sugar/syrup in club soda in red-wine glass. Add claret, then top with ice and stir. Garnish with fruits in season. Serve with straws.

DEATH IN THE AFTERNOON

1 oz. Pastis (or Pernod or other Absinthe substitute)

5 oz. Champagne, chilled

Pour pastis into champagne flute. Top with Champagne.

♈ DIPLOMAT

1½ oz. Dry Vermouth

½ oz. Sweet Vermouth

2 dashes Bitters

½ tsp. Maraschino Liqueur

Stir with ice and strain into chilled cocktail glass. Serve with a half-slice of lemon and a maraschino cherry.

♈ FALLING LEAVES

2 oz. Riesling (Alsatian)

1 oz. Pear Eau De Vie

½ oz. Honey Syrup*

½ oz. Orange Curaçao

1 dash Peychaud's Bitters

Shake all ingredients with ice and strain into chilled cocktail glass. Garnish with star anise.

* To make Honey Syrup: Mix equal parts of honey and warm water. Stir until dissolved, and then chill.

♈ KIR ROYALE

6 oz. Champagne, chilled

1 splash Crème de Cassis

Pour into large champagne flute or white-wine glass.

LEMONADE (CLARET)

2 tsps. Superfine Sugar (or Simple Syrup)

2 oz. Lemon Juice

2 oz. Claret or Red Wine

Dissolve sugar/syrup and lemon juice in Collins glass. Add ice and enough water to fill glass, leaving room to float wine. Garnish with slices of orange and lemon, and a maraschino cherry. Serve with straws.

LEMONADE (MODERN)

1 Lemon

2 tsps. Superfine Sugar (or Simple Syrup)

1½ oz. Dry Sherry

1 oz. Sloe Gin

Club Soda

Cut lemon into quarters and muddle well with sugar/syrup. Add sherry and sloe gin. Shake with ice and strain into chilled Collins glass. Fill glass with club soda.

WINE IN MIXED DRINKS

LONDON SPECIAL

1 cube Sugar
2 dashes Bitters
Champagne, chilled

Put a large twist of orange peel into champagne flute. Add sugar and bitters. Fill with Champagne and stir.

PIMM'S CUP

2 oz. Pimm's Number One
3 oz. Ginger Ale or Lemon-lime Soda

Pour Pimm's into Collins glass; fill with ice. Top with chilled ginger ale. Garnish with cucumber slices or a slice of lemon.

PORT WINE COCKTAIL

2½ oz. Port
½ tsp. Brandy

Stir with ice and strain into chilled cocktail glass.

PORT WINE SANGAREE

½ tsp. Superfine Sugar (or Simple Syrup)
1 tsp. Water
2 oz. Port
Club Soda
1 tbsp. Brandy

Dissolve sugar/syrup in water in highball glass. Add port and ice cubes. Fill with club soda to nearly top of glass and stir. Float brandy on top and sprinkle with fresh-grated nutmeg.

TRIDENT

1 oz. Dry Sherry
1 oz. Cynar
1 oz. Aquavit
2 dashes Peach Bitters

Stir with ice and strain into chilled cocktail glass. Garnish with a twist of lemon peel.

NONALCOHOLIC DRINKS

THERE'S A VERY GOOD CHANCE that, among your circle of friends and acquaintances, there are those who do not consume alcohol at all. While it's certainly important that you respect their personal choice not to drink, there's no reason why nondrinkers cannot raise their glasses in a toast with a libation that's prepared with the care and creativity with which all mixed drinks and cocktails are made.

Most everyone has heard of a Virgin Mary and Shirley Temple, and recipes for these old standards are included here. But there are also nonalcoholic versions of other popular cocktails, such as the Unfuzzy Navel and Punchless Piña Colada. From the frosty Summertime Barbarian to the refreshingly tangy Yellowjacket, you'll find quaffs to offer nondrinkers that are a giant step above plain old soft drinks.

Who knows? Perhaps you may even make one for yourself when you're the designated driver, or order one when you're at a business meal or important meeting. Feel free to be creative and experiment with omitting the alcohol in some of the standard cocktail recipes throughout this book, especially those made with a variety of fresh fruit juices. And, of course, don't forget that presentation is just as important with these drinks as with any other.

BEACH BLANKET BINGO

3 oz. Cranberry Juice

3 oz. Varietal Grape Juice (Chenin Blanc, etc.)

Club Soda

Pour juices into ice-filled highball glass. Top with club soda and stir. Garnish with a lime wedge.

BUBBLETART

3 oz. Cranberry Juice

1 oz. Lime Juice

3 oz. Mineral Water

Shake juices with ice and strain into chilled highball glass. Fill with mineral water. Garnish with a lime wheel.

BUBBLY ORANGEADE

4 tsps. Orange Juice Concentrate, thawed and undiluted

¾ cup Club Soda

Stir together in Collins glass and then add ice. Garnish with an orange slice.

COFFEE ALMOND FLOAT

¼ cup Instant Coffee

2 tbsps. Water

4 cups Milk

2 tbsps. Brown Sugar

¼ tsp. Almond Extract

Chocolate Ice Cream

Dissolve coffee in water in a pitcher. Add milk, brown sugar, and almond extract. Stir well and pour over ice cubes into parfait glasses. Top with a scoop of ice cream. *Makes 4 to 6 servings.*

COFFEE-COLA COOLER

2 cups Cold Coffee

1 tbsp. Maple Syrup

12 oz. Cola, chilled

Combine coffee and maple syrup. Slowly stir in cola. Serve in ice-filled Collins glasses. Garnish with lemon slices. *Makes 3 to 4 servings.*

CRANBERRY COOLER

2 oz. Cranberry Juice

½ tbsp. Lime Juice

Club Soda

Add juices to ice-filled Collins glass. Top with club soda and stir. Garnish with a twist of lime.

☐ CREAMY CREAMSICLE

8 oz. Orange Juice
2 scoops Vanilla Ice Cream

Combine ingredients in blender on low speed. Pour into highball glass and garnish with an orange slice.

☐ CROW'S NEST

4 oz. Orange Juice
1 oz. Cranberry Juice
½ tsp. Grenadine

Shake with ice and strain into ice-filled old-fashioned glass. Garnish with a lime slice.

☐ FLAMINGO

4 oz. Cranberry Juice
2 oz. Pineapple Juice
½ oz. Lemon Juice
2 oz. Club Soda

Shake juices with ice and strain into highball glass. Top with club soda and stir. Garnish with a lime wedge.

☐ FRUIT SMOOTHIE

8 oz. Orange Juice, chilled
1 Banana, peeled and sliced
½ cup Ripe Strawberries, Blueberries, or Raspberries

Combine all ingredients in blender on low speed. Pour into highball glass and garnish with assorted fruits.

☐ FUZZY LEMON FIZZ

6 oz. Peach Nectar
4 oz. Lemon-lime Soda

Pour ingredients into ice-filled highball glass. Garnish with a twist of lemon peel.

☐ GRAPEBERRY

3 oz. Cranberry Juice
3 oz. Grapefruit Juice

Combine juices in large ice-filled red-wine glass. Garnish with a wedge of lime and serve with a short straw.

☐ ICED MOCHA

2 cups Milk
⅓ cup Chocolate Syrup
1 tbsp. Instant Coffee

Combine ingredients and mix well. Pour into ice-filled Collins glasses. Top with whipped cream and chocolate shavings. *Makes 3 to 4 servings.*

☐ INNOCENT PASSION

4 oz. Passion Fruit Juice
1 dash Cranberry Juice
1 dash Lemon Juice
Club Soda

Combine juices in ice-filled highball glass. Top with club soda and stir. Add a maraschino cherry and a long straw.

NONALCOHOLIC DRINKS

LAVA FLOW

4 oz. Light Cream

½ oz. Coconut Cream

3 oz. Pineapple Juice

½ Banana

½ cup Strawberries, sliced

Combine all ingredients except strawberries in blender with 1 cup ice and blend until smooth. Put strawberries at the bottom of a parfait glass, then quickly pour in blended mixture for a starburst effect.

LEMONADE (CARBONATED)

2 tsps. Superfine Sugar (or Simple Syrup)

1 oz. Lemon Juice

Club Soda

Dissolve sugar/syrup and lemon juice in Collins glass. Add ice and enough club soda to fill glass, and then stir. Garnish with slices of orange and lemon, and a maraschino cherry. Serve with straws.

LEMONADE (FRUIT)

1 oz. Lemon Juice

2 tsps. Superfine Sugar (or Simple Syrup)

1 oz. Raspberry Syrup

Water

Combine first three ingredients in Collins glass. Add ice cubes and enough water to fill glass, and then stir. Garnish with slices of orange and lemon, and a maraschino cherry. Serve with straws.

LEMONADE (PLAIN)

2 tsps. Superfine Sugar (or Simple Syrup)

1 oz. Lemon Juice

Water

Stir sugar/syrup and lemon juice in Collins glass. Fill glass with ice. Fill with water and stir well. Garnish with slices of orange and lemon, and a maraschino cherry.

LEMON SQUASH

1 Lemon, peeled and quartered

2 tsps. Superfine Sugar (or Simple Syrup)

Club Soda

Muddle lemon and sugar/syrup well in Collins glass until juice is well extracted. Then fill glass with ice. Add club soda and stir. Garnish with fruits.

LIMEADE

3 oz. Lime Juice

3 tsps. Superfine Sugar (or Simple Syrup)

Water

Combine juice and sugar/syrup in Collins glass, then add ice and enough water to fill glass. Stir, and add a wedge of lime and a maraschino cherry. Serve with straws.

LIME COLA

½ oz. Lime Juice

Cola

Add juice to ice-filled Collins glass. Fill with cola. Stir and add a long twist of lime.

LIME COOLER

1 tbsp. Lime Juice

Tonic Water

Add lime juice to ice-filled Collins glass. Top with tonic water. Garnish with a lime wedge.

LITTLE ENGINEER

4 oz. Pineapple Juice

4 oz. Orange Juice

½ oz. Grenadine

Pour over ice in parfait glass. Garnish with a paper flag.

ORANGE AND TONIC

6 oz. Orange Juice

4 oz. Tonic Water

Pour ingredients over ice into highball glass. Garnish with a lime wedge.

ORANGEADE

6 oz. Orange Juice

1 tsp. Superfine Sugar (or Simple Syrup)

Mix in Collins glass. Add ice cubes and enough water to fill glass, and stir. Garnish with slices of orange and lemon, and two maraschino cherries. Serve with straws.

PASSION FRUIT SPRITZER

4 oz. Passion Fruit Juice

Club Soda

Pour juice into champagne flute and fill with club soda. Garnish with a lime wedge.

PEACH MELBA

8 oz. Peach Nectar

2 scoops Vanilla Ice Cream

½ Whole Sliced Peach

3 oz. Raspberries, ripe

Combine all ingredients in blender on low speed. Pour into highball glass and garnish with raspberries.

NONALCOHOLIC DRINKS

PUNCHLESS PIÑA COLADA

1 oz. Cream of Coconut
1 oz. Pineapple Juice
1 tsp. Lime Juice

Combine all ingredients in blender with 1 cup of crushed ice. Pour into Collins glass. Garnish with a slice of pineapple and a maraschino cherry.

RUMLESS RICKEY

1 oz. Lime Juice
1 dash Grenadine
1 dash Bitters
Club Soda

Add juice, grenadine, and bitters to ice-filled old-fashioned glass. Top with club soda. Stir. Garnish with a long twist of lime.

RUNNER'S MARK

4 oz. V-8 Vegetable Juice
2 drops Tabasco Sauce
2 drops Lemon Juice
1 dash Worcestershire Sauce

Combine all ingredients in ice-filled old-fashioned glass. Stir, and garnish with a celery stalk or scallion.

SHIRLEY TEMPLE

1 dash Grenadine
Ginger Ale

Add grenadine to ice-filled Collins glass; top with ginger ale. Garnish with an orange slice and a maraschino cherry.

STRAWBERRY WONDERLAND

1 oz. Coconut Cream
2 oz. Frozen Strawberries
3 oz. Pineapple Juice
½ oz. Superfine Sugar (or Simple Syrup)
½ oz. Lemon Juice

Combine all ingredients in blender with 1 cup ice and blend until smooth. Pour into snifter. Top with whipped cream and garnish with a strawberry.

SUMMERTIME BARBARIAN

½ cup Fresh Strawberries
½ cup Fresh Pineapple
½ cup Grapefruit Juice

Combine ingredients in blender with 1 cup ice and blend until smooth. Pour into Collins glasses. Garnish with kiwi fruit wheels. *Makes 2 servings.*

SUNSHINE SPLASH

3 oz. Pineapple Juice

3 oz. Orange Juice

½ oz. Superfine Sugar (or Simple Syrup)

½ oz. Lemon Juice

½ oz. Grenadine

2 oz. Lemon-lime Soda

Pour into ice-filled parfait glass and stir. Garnish with a pineapple slice.

TOMATO COOLER

8 oz. Tomato Juice

2 tbsps. Lemon or Lime Juice

Tonic Water

Combine juices in ice-filled highball glass and top with tonic water. Garnish with a wedge of lime, a sprig of dill, and a cucumber slice.

UNFUZZY NAVEL

3 oz. Peach Nectar

1 tbsp. Lemon Juice

3 oz. Orange Juice

1 dash Grenadine

Combine all ingredients in shaker with ice. Strain into chilled red-wine glass. Garnish with an orange slice.

VIRGIN MARY

4 oz. Tomato Juice

1 dash Lemon Juice

½ tsp. Worcestershire Sauce

2 drops Tabasco Sauce

Salt and Pepper as needed

Fill a large red-wine glass with ice. Add tomato juice, then remainder of ingredients. Stir and garnish with a wedge of lime.

WAVEBENDER

1 oz. Orange Juice

½ oz. Lemon Juice

1 tsp. Grenadine

5 oz. Ginger Ale

Shake juices and grenadine with ice and strain into ice-filled highball glass. Top with ginger ale and stir.

YELLOWJACKET

2 oz. Pineapple Juice

2 oz. Orange Juice

½ oz. Lemon Juice

Shake with ice and strain into ice-filled old-fashioned glass. Garish with a lemon slice.

RESOURCES

Drinks Databases

Ardent Spirits

www.ardentspirits.com

A website by Gary and Mardee Regan, perhaps the most prolific authors on the subject of cocktails and spirits today; they've written several must-have books, including *New Classic Cocktails*, *The Martini Companion*, and *The Joy of Mixology*.

B.A.R.

www.beveragealcoholresource.com

Comprehensive spirits and mixology training programs designed to provide a well-rounded education in mixology and spirits can be found here.

Cocktail.com

www.cocktail.com

Paul Harrington's site's mission is simple: to bring the drink aficionados and bartenders of the world the best cocktail recipes and advice.

CocktailDB

www.cocktaildb.com

CocktailDB is the brainchild of Martin Doudoroff and Ted Haigh (a.k.a. Dr. Cocktail), offering an extensive anthology of cocktails authenticated in print, coupled with a massive ingredients database.

Cocktail Spirit

www.smallscreennetwork.com

Home of the wildly popular educational podcast, "The Cocktail Spirit with Robert Hess."

DrinkBoy

www.drinkboy.com

Robert Hess's scholarly database incorporates history, tips, advice, and recipes—just like a proper barman.

Esquire Drinking Database

www.esquire.com/drinks/

A great collection of cocktail recipes and wisdom, including much imparted by resident spirits expert David Wondrich. Every week it showcases a new recipe worth checking out.

King Cocktail

www.kingcocktail.com

One of the most recognized bartenders in New York and author of *The Craft of the Cocktail,* Dale DeGroff shares insights and recipes, plus great tips and advice.

Miss Charming

www.miss-charming.com

Cheryl Charming, author of *Miss Charming's Book of Bar Amusements,* provides useful information and resources to both budding and experienced bartenders.

The Modern Mixologist

www.themodernmixologist.com

The cyberhome of one of the smoothest mixmasters on the planet, Tony Abou-Ganim, where you'll find tips and tricks of the trade. His video *Modern Mixology: Making Great Cocktails at Home* is worth seeking out.

Spirit Journal

www.spiritjournal.com

Writer Paul Pacult's newsletter rating spirits, wine, and beer.

Fruit, Mixers, Juices, and Garnishes

BITTERS

Angostura Bitters

www.angostura.com

Mixers, sauces, rums, events.

Fee Brothers Bitters

www.kalustyans.com

Source for orange bitters and other difficult-to-find ingredients.

Peychaud's Bitters

www.buffalotrace.com

Great source for hard-to-find tinctures like this New Orleans staple.

Regan's Orange Bitters

www.buffalotrace.com

Great source for Gary Regans's delicious necessity.

GARNISHES

Goya Pitted Manzanilla Olives

www.latinmerchant.com

All other olives for Martini making pale in comparison.

Luxardo Cherries

www.preissimports.com

Excellent source for cherries.

Les Parisiennes Cherries in Brandy

www.emarkys.com

Second only to real marasca cherries, these are perfect for Manhattans.

Sable and Rosenfeld Cocktail Onions

www.sableandrosenfeld.com

A Gibson isn't a Gibson without proper onions.

HERBS, SPICES, AND TEAS

Demerara Sugar

www.igourmet.com

There's sugar, and then there's Demerara sugar.

Lemon Salt/Citric Acid

www.kalustyans.com

If you've never heard of it, they have it.

Quinine and Cinchona Bark

www.rain-tree.com

The source for top tonics, etc.

Teas

www.inpusuitoftea.com

Excellent source for teas of every kind.

JUICES

Perfect Purée

www.perfectpuree.com

The Perfect Purée Company of Napa Valley produces a wonderful selection of fruit and vegetable purees, including a fabulous White Peach elixir that's perfect for Bellinis.

Trader Vic's

www.tradervics.com

From the originator of the Mai Tai cocktail comes a source for a wealth of mixers, batters, and syrups.

SODA

Malta India

www.sodapopstop.com

Cola replacements that will change your life.

Note: Where recipes call for club soda, you may prefer to substitute seltzer or soda water, which don't contain the additives typically found in club soda.

SYRUPS AND PRESERVES

Almond Syrup, Rose Syrup (Mymoune), and Orgeat (Alwadi/Kassatly)

www.kalustyans.com

If you've never heard of it, they have it.

Cane Syrup (Depaz)

www.igourmet.com

Mojitos will never be the same once you've mixed them with Depaz.

Chai Apple Preserves (Robert Rothschild)

www.cookscorner.net

Great gourmet goodies here.

Elderflower and Raspberry Syrup (D'Arbo)

www.farawayfoods.com

Excellent source for exotic syrups.

Orange Flower Water (A. Monteux)

www.kalustyans.com

If you've never heard of it, they have it.

Sonoma Syrup Co.

www.sonomasyrup.com

Great fruit and spice syrups for every cocktail.

Three-Citrus Marmalade

www.stonewallkitchen.com

Source for delicious fruit compotes.

Bar Supplies

Bar Equipment World

www.barequipmentworld.com

The name says it all.

A Best Kitchen

www.akitchen.com

Great prices on all sorts of barware.

Big Tray

www.bigtray.com

A great resource for all kinds of bar supplies, from equipment to accessories.

Co-Rect Products

www.co-rectproducts.com

Bar and restaurant supplies specifically for the trade.

General Bar Supplies

www.webtender.barstore.com

Excellent source for consumers and enthusiasts alike.

Glassware

www.amazon.com **and** www.crateandbarrel.com

If there's a glass size to be found, you'll find it here.

Muddlers

www.mistermojito.com and www.themodernmixologist.com

Must-have muddlers for Mojitos.

Speed Pourers

www.evo-lution.org

Great source for every size bottle imaginable.

Sur la Table

www.surlatable.com

Excellent source for kitchen equipment and superior ice trays.

INDEX